Usury, Interest and the Reformation

By the same author

The Common Fields of England
Trade and Banking in Early Modern England
Textile Manufactures in Early Modern England
The Farmers of Old England
Agrarian Problems in the Sixteenth Century and After
The Agricultural Revolution

Usury, Interest and the Reformation

ERIC KERRIDGE

Ashgate

Published by
Ashgate Publishing Limited
Gower House
Croft Road
Aldershot
Hants GU11 3HR
England

Ashgate Publishing Company
131 Main Street
Burlington VT 05401–5600 USA

Ashgate website: http://www.ashgate.com

British Library Cataloguing in Publication Data

Kerridge, Eric.
  Usury, Interest and the Reformation.
  (St Andrews Studies in Reformation History)
  1. Usury—England—History—16th century. 2. Usury—
  England—History—16th century—Sources. 3. Usury—
  Religious aspects—Christianity.
  I. Title.
  332.8'3'0942'09031

Library of Congress Cataloging-in-Publication Data

Kerridge, Eric.
  Usury, interest and the Reformation/Eric Kerridge.
      p.   cm. (St Andrews Studies in Reformation History)
  Includes bibliographical references and indexes.
  ISBN 0–7546–0688–0 (alk. paper)
  1. Usury—Religious aspects—Christianity. 2. Reformation.
  I. Title. II. Series.
  BR115.I68 K47   2002
  241'.644—dc21

                                                    2001053769

ISBN 0 7546 0688 0

This book is printed on acid-free paper

Typeset in Sabon by J. L. & G. A. Wheatley Design, Aldershot and printed in
Great Britain by MPG Books Ltd., Bodmin, Cornwall.

Contents

St Andrews Studies in Reformation History

Music as Propaganda in the German Reformation
Rebecca Wagner Oettinger

John Foxe and his World
edited by Christopher Highley and John N. King

Confessional Identity in East-Central Europe
edited by Maria Crăciun, Ovidiu Ghitta and Graeme Murdock

The Bible in the Renaissance:
Essays on Biblical Commentary and Translation
in the Fifteenth and Sixteenth Centuries
edited by Richard Griffiths

Obedient Heretics: Mennonite Identities in Lutheran Hamburg
and Altona during the Confessional Age
Michael D. Driedger

The Construction of Martyrdom in the
English Catholic Community, 1535–1603
Anne Dillon

Baptism and Spiritual Kinship in Early Modern England
Will Coster

To Violet

Preface

I am grateful to the ever helpful staffs of the Public Record Office, of the many local record offices and archives listed below in the Summary of Select Manuscript Sources, of the British, Bodleian, Bristol University, Huntington, Liverpool University and Shakespeare's Birthplace libraries, of the Institute of Historical Research, of the Borthwick Institute of Historical Research and, above all, of St Deiniol's Library. My thanks are also due to my family, colleagues and friends, who have helped in various ways, and to Mr M. K. Tutton, who enabled me to go on living a scholar's life.

All errors and omissions are attributable to me alone.

Acknowledgement

The author wishes to thank the Bodleian Library, University of Oxford, for kind permission to reproduce part of Chapter 9 of 'A Treatise of Usury', MS. Rawl. D. 677 (Doc. 35).

Abbreviations

Acc.	Accession
Add.	Additional
BL	British Library
Ch.	Charter
D.L.	Duchy of Lancaster
EETS	Early English Text Society
Harl.	Harleian
Lans.	Lansdowne
PRO	Public Record Office
R.	Roll
RO	Record Office

'Usury and trewe interest be thinges as contrary as falshod is to truth.'

(Public Record Office, State Papers Domestic, Elizabeth, 75/54)

Introduction

Shylock is the only usurer most people could name, and he a fictitious character in Shakespeare's *Merchant of Venice*. Shylock hated others who lent money gratis, but himself lent it gratis to Bassanio. Yet when Shylock lent on usury, Antonio called this gain 'interest', thus in some way confounding the one with the other. The perplexed playgoer or reader might then turn to a commonly-used, standard dictionary. This defines a Shylock as a ruthless creditor or a very grasping person, usury as taking (now only iniquitous or illegal) interest on a loan, and a usurer as a moneylender (now for excessive interest). A zealous enquirer might then resort to the biggest of all English dictionaries. Alas, this would bring hardly more enlightenment, for here a Shylock is defined as an extortionate usurer and usury as the fact or practice of lending money at interest or, in later use, as receiving excessive or illegal rates of interest. Small wonder generations of students have been left mystified, for these definitions are incomplete, misleading and incorrect, even self-contradictory, for in everyday English what is genuine interest cannot be usury, nor usury genuine interest. To make matters worse, most dictionaries turn a blind eye to the inconvenient fact that John Calvin and others favoured and used an entirely different set of words and terms in which to discuss the subject, and this new terminology has, more often than not, been jumbled together with the old, making confusion worse confounded. This confusion, spread by R. H. Tawney, has crept into countless history books and into most English translations of Martin Luther's works, baffling readers of history and theology alike and, worse, causing rank error in the works of a succession of often otherwise good authors. Such error, constantly repeated at every turn over scores and scores of years, cannot be overcome by uttering a casual sentence or two; it must be torn up by the roots, which can be accomplished only by a full exposition of Christian teachings on the matter.

The first part of the book introduces the subject, the second reproduces a selection of documentary sources. In the first part, the reader's attention is drawn (in brackets) to the individual document that has particular bearing on the matter under immediate consideration; but each document is also of more general relevance. Many documents and quotations appear in their original language, followed by my translations, so, if the reader wishes, he can skip the Latin or German and pass straight to the English.

PART ONE
The Argument

CHAPTER ONE

Usury and Interest

There is all the difference in the world between usury and interest. '*Id quod interest, omnino differt ab usuris*', said Philip Melanchthon – 'That which is interest differs totally from usuries'.[1] 'Usury and trewe interest', says an Elizabethan memorandum, 'be thinges as contrary as falshod is to truth'.[2]

Usury or fenory is the taking of payment over and above the amount lent merely and solely in return for a secured loan. In the words of Thomas Aquinas, '*Accipere pecuniam in pretium pro pecunia mutuata, quod est accipere usuram ... pretium usus, quod usura dicitur*' – 'To take money as the price of money lent, that is to take usury ... the price for use, that is called usury'.[3] What is now called fenory or usury was originally known to the English as 'wocar' or 'wocor', while 'wocorlice' meant usurious. Later, 'ocker' was used as both noun and verb, and the word for usurer was 'ockerer'. These words correspond to the German *Wucher* and *Wucherer*, and to similar ones in all the other Germanic languages. They were being dropped in polite society in southern England in the early sixteenth century and in the north in the early seventeenth, but have persisted in use (and misuse) among the lower orders, to the perplexity of some lexicographers, who follow Charles Dickens in confusing 'ocker' with 'ochre', despite the 'o' in ocker being short.

Interest is in compensation of a man's *verum interesse*, of his true interest in a business. As John Jewel explains, 'Here ... you may learn wherefore it is called interest, because he may say, *Interfuit mea habuisse*' ('To have had possession has been important to me').[4] As the Doctor explains in *A Discourse uppon Usurye*, '*Interest mea*, that is to saye, it behoveth me, or it belongeth to mee, or it is for mine avail, or it is reason, that I shall bee

---

1 P. Melanchthon, *Catechesis Puerilis*, in *Operum Reverendi Viri Philippi Melanchonis*, 4 pts (vols) Wittemberg, 1562–67, vol. i, fo. 19.

2 Public Record Office (hereafter PRO), State Papers Domestic, Elizabeth, 75/54.

3 T. Aquinas, *Summa Theologica*, II, ii, quaestio 78, in *Divi Thomae Aquinatis doctoris angelici*, in *Opera*, 28 vols, Venice, 1775–88, vol. xxii, pp. 322–3; and see St Bernardine, *In Apocalypsim beati Joannis Commentarii*, in *Opera*, 5 vols, Venice, 1745, vol. v, p. 93; H. Hostiensis (Bartholomaeis) *Summa Hostiensis*, Leiden, n.d., fos 443ᵛ seqq., 449; *idem*, *Sumnia Aurea*, Leiden, 1548, fos 250, 252.

4 J. Jewel, *The Works of John Jewel*, ed. J. Ayre, Parker Society, 4 vols, 1845–50, vol. ii, p. 858.

aunswered all losses and dammages'.[5] All entitlement to interest was for the sole end of avoiding loss to the lender.[6]

This being so, nothing in Christianity gave good ground for any objection to interest in the true sense. Christ seems to have condoned the taking of interest by showing no hint of disapproval when telling the parable of the talents, even though it was but a parable. Usury, in the ordinary English sense, is not even alluded to, for the talent would have been deposited with a banker, not lent to him. The man given a single talent, hid it.

> But his lord ... said unto him, Thou wicked and slothful servant, thou knewest that I reap where I sowed not, and gather where I did not scatter; thou oughtest therefore to have put my money to the bankers and at my coming I should have received back mine own with interest.

This is how St Matthew is translated in the 1930 Revised Version. The corresponding sentence in St Luke is, 'Wherefore gavest thou not my money into the bank, and I at my coming should have required it with interest'. That the Authorized Version of Matthew has 'exchangers' instead of 'bank', has no significance, for these were exchange-banks. That the Authorized Version, of both gospels, has 'usury' instead of 'interest', suggests that 'usury' is here being used in its academic, unfamiliar and widest possible sense, which included interest. Interestingly, Erasmus points to the Psalmist who, when faced with the question, 'Lord, who shall sojourn in thy tabernacle?', answers, amongst other things, 'He that putteth not out his money to usury'. Erasmus then goes on:

> *Sed hic occurrit scrupulus, quum in Evangelio damnatur servus qui pecuniam sibi creditam non dederat ad usuram, qui convenit ut hic laudetur, qui non dederit ad usuram. Nihil ista pugnant: Dominus amat usuram, quae ipsi lucrum adfert: odit usuram, quam servus sibi vindicat.*

> But at this point a doubt creeps in, when in the Gospel the servant who gave not to usury the money provided to him, when it was meetest he be praised for that he gave it not to usury. No contradiction here: the Lord loves usury that yields Him profit, hates usury that a servant takes to his own self.

We are expected to use the talents God has given us in His service, not our own.[7] Or, translated into everyday terms, Gurney, the banker, was right

---

[5] T. Wilson, *A Discourse uppon Usurye by way of dialogue and oracions, for the better varietye and more delite of all those that shall reade thys treatise*, ed. R. H. Tawney, 1925, p. 319.

[6] J. A. Schumpeter, *History of Economic Analysis*, 1954, p. 104; St Bernardine, *Quadragesimale Evangelio Aeterno: Caritaris et ... de Usura*, sermo XLII ad init.; art. i, ad init., in *Opera*, vol. ii, pp. 248–9.

[7] Matthew xxv. 24–7; Luke xix. 20–24; Psalm xv. 1, 5; D. Erasmus, De *Puritate Tabernaculi sive Ecclesiae Christianae*, in *Opera Omnia*, 10 vols, Leiden, 1706, vol. v, col. 306, at F. For wider meaning sometimes attached to usury, see inf. at Chapter 2, nn. 16, 18, 20, 22–8.

when he wrote in 1822, 'By the Psalmist, all usury seems unlawful; by the parable of the talents, interest allowable'.[8] This has been the Christian standpoint from the earliest times. Christianity allowed interest under the extrinsic titles of *periculum sortis*, *poena conventionalis*, *lucrum cessans* and *damnum emergens*.

One might only take what interest one was entitled to, and entitlement could not be claimed simply as interest, but solely under one of the extrinsic titles, of which one always, and two usually, depended on *titulus morae*, on tardy or defaulted repayment of a loan.

Of the four titles to interest, *poena conventionalis* was the commonest in England. It bore some superficial resemblance to usury. A contract for a loan stipulated a penalty to be paid in event of repayment of the principal being delayed beyond a specified, agreed date, in England commonly three or six months hence, sometimes twelve. This penalty was usually a percentage of the sum borrowed and was the compensation earned by the creditor for his forbearance in not having the debtor's bond or obligation forfeited or taking legal proceedings to recover the principal. To avoid the taint of usury, the rate of interest had to be moderate and reasonable, conforming to the range of normal market rates and to any statutory limit. The borrower was not obliged to pay anything for the use of the money loaned, only to repay it at the agreed time and place. The Shuttleworths of Gawthorpe Hall, for example, made many loans and took some loans on these terms, so whether or not they received or paid interest depended upon whether or not payment was made at the due date. In default, interest was owed to the lender for his forbearance from demanding a lump sum by way of penalty.[9] The whole transaction was thus analogous to one with a modern credit card, where the debtor owes interest only if he

---

8 W. H. Bidwell, *Annals of an East Anglian Bank*, Norwich, 1900, p. 159.

9 B. W. Dempsey, *Interest and Usury*, 1948, pp. 174–5; J. Harland, *The House and Farm Accounts of the Shuttleworths of Gawthorpe Hall*, Chetham Society, 1856–58, xxv, xli, xliii, xlvi, pp. 61–3, 65, 71, 104, 113, 183, 186, 195, 204, 206, 210, 215–16, 218, 225–6, 230–31, 233, 236–7, 240, 242, 246, 248–9, 257, especially 183, 186, 246, 249; M. Beloff, 'Humphrey Shalcrosse and the Great Civil War', *English Historical Review*, 1939, 54, 686, 688; Hostiensis, *Summa Hostiensis*, fo. 448ᵛ; St Antonine, *Summa Major*, 4 vols (pts), Venice, 1503, pt 2, bk 1, cap. vii, #19 (fo. 27); Aquinas, *Summa Theologica*, II, ii, quaestio 78, art. ii, in *Opera*, vol. xxii, p. 324; St Bernardine, *Quadragesimale Evangelio Aeterno Charitatis ... et de Usura*, sermo XLII, art. iii, cap. i, in *Opera*, vol. ii, p. 253; John Duns Scotus, *Quaestiones in Quartum Librum Sententiarum*, distinctio XV, quaestio ii, in *Opera Omnia*, 26 vols, Paris, 1891–95, vol. xviii, p. 293; Richard Middleton (Ricardus de Media Villa) *Sententiarum Questiones Persubtilissime*, 4 bks, Venice, 1507–09, liber IV, *Sententiarum Resolute Questiones*, dist. xv, art. v, questio v (fo. 75); T. Lodge, 'An Alarum against Usurers, containing tryed experiences against worldly abuses' (1584), in T. Lodge, *A Defence of Poesie, Music and Stage Plays*, Shakespeare Society, 1853, pp. 46, 65; Anon. *The Death of Usury, or the disgrace of usurers*, Cambridge, 1594, p. 25; T. P. McLaughlin, 'The teaching of the canonists on usury', *Medieval Studies*, 1939, 1, pp. 83–5, 91, 95 seqq., 145–7.

fails to repay on time. The most famous example of apparent *poena conventionalis* occurs in Shakespeare's *Merchant of Venice*. Had Antonio repaid the principal within the agreed three months, he would then have owed nothing. But as Shylock had stipulated a grossly excessive penalty, the whole transaction was usurious and he was not entitled to any interest.[10] In less dramatic forms, the earning of interest by forbearance in not enforcing the penalty was favoured by early modern English lenders. They made short loans and then readily showed forbearance, on payment of interest and a reasonable sum of 'continuance money' for the prolonging of the loan. Complications could arise from the practice of passing bonds from hand to hand like currency, but few English lenders seem to have schemed to gain by the forfeiture of bonds; the usual practice was to refuse loans to those reported upon unfavourably by the scriveners or brokers who compiled credit ratings. Unfortunately, as Bacon discovered, it was not unknown for the raters to 'value unsound men to serve their own ends'. Then, again, both the loan itself, and forbearance for the non-repayment of it, could be used as a cloak for usury, for the lender who schemed or hoped to get a penalty was thereby a secret usurer. Moreover, usurers often disguised their usury *quasi ex mora*, as though it were due on account of delayed repayment. No wonder even the most righteous bankers lived in some fear of accusations of usury when making loans.[11]

How forbearance might operate in practice may be seen in this example. On 30 June 1606 the Earl of Pembroke writes 'To my most assured frend Sir Michael Hicks knight' as follows:

> Good Sir Michael Hicks, I must give you many thanks for the forbearing the money I owe you; and must entreate you to lend me the six hundred pound you promised. You shall have what security you will desire; and uppon any reasonable notice that you have occation to use it, you shall receave the whole summe. You shall doe me in this a very extraordinarie kindnes and bind me to remaine ever, Your most assured frend – Pembroke.

Hicks lent him the £600 on security of Knighton manor. On the 14 January following, Pembroke requested further forbearance, and the same again on 3 June and 14 November 1607, 9 May and 6 November 1609, 9 November 1610, 8 November 1611 and 27 April 1612. By May 1609

---

[10] *Merchant of Venice*, I, iii; III, ii, iii; IV, i.

[11] E. Kerridge, *Trade and Banking in Early Modern England*, Manchester, 1988, p. 67; Wilson, op. cit., p. 250; F. T. Melton, *Sir Robert Clayton and the Origins of English Deposit Banking 1658–1685*, Cambridge, 1986, pp. 153–5; BL, Egerton MS 2983 (Heath and Verney Papers vi) fos 31ᵛ–2; Bodleian Library, Western Manuscripts, Rawl. MS. D. 911, fo. 196; Hostiensis, *Summa Aurea*, fo. 251; Middleton, op. cit., lib. IV, dist. xv, art. v, qu. v (fo. 75); Huntington Library, Hastings MSS, HAF box 6, folder 3, Th. Harvey's accounts to Earl of Huntingdon, 1605–13; PRO, State Papers Domestic, Elizabeth 99/26; Supplementary vol. 87, fo. 7; Early Chancery Proceedings 64/291.

the debt was already £1,600 and still rising. It seems the Earl of Montgomery took over this burden, for in 1613 he is found entreating Lady Hicks 'to forbeare to arrest his mene, and he would paye the mony'. She apparently agreed to this.[12]

There were two other ways of earning interest by *titulus morae*. Here the date and place of repayment were contracted, but not the penalty for non-payment, in event of which the lender who had not taken a bond or who forbore from having a bond forfeited, was entitled to reasonable interest to compensate him for the delay. If the lender could prove he had suffered loss through the lack of his principal, he could claim compensatory interest under title of *damnum emergens* (emergent loss or damages) or of *lucrum cessans* (cessant gain).[13]

Damnum emergens, interesse damni emergentis, damnum occurrentis, or emergent loss, was the title by which interest was claimed for losses to the lender arising from the loan itself, these losses being over and above any legitimate and deductible expenses for transaction costs like having to travel and fetch back the money or goods to be lent, scrivener's fees, accounting costs, insurance premiums or broker's commission, which last became regulated by statute in England. Emergent loss could be incurred in various ways. The lender's house might suddenly be damaged and then suffer further damage because he had lent the money needed for repairs and could not get repayment on the date it was due. Or the debtor's default might even drive the creditor to the extremity of having to take up money at usury. *Interesse damni emergentis* might then rightfully be claimed. It could likewise be claimed from the borrower by the guarantor of his loan when the borrower defaulted, leaving the guarantor to pay both principal and interest. Emergent loss incurred before the due day could also be claimed and, if justified, could be stipulated in the initial contract. But any emergent loss claimed had to be a loss in something other than moneylending, and any claim or stipulation for emergent loss had to be capable of proof and subject to impartial assessment, so that interest could be fairly calculated.[14]

---

12 BL, Lansdowne MSS 89, no. 87, fos 169, 170ᵛ; 90, no. 1, fos 2, 3ᵛ; no. 21, fo. 42; no. 34, fo. 67; 91, no. 16, fos 45, 46ᵛ; no. 26, fos 63, 64ᵛ; 92, no. 35, fos 64, 65ᵛ; no. 70, fos 143, 144ᵛ; no. 93, fos 163, 164ᵛ; 93, no. 2, fos 4, 5ᵛ.

13 Wilson, op. cit., pp. 235, 246–7, 253, 315; Dempsey, op. cit., pp. 171, 174–5.

14 Dempsey, pp. 171, 173; Wilson, op. cit., pp. 235, 316, 319; Hostiensis, *Summa Hostiensis*, fos 448–9; Middleton, op. cit., lib. IV, dist. xv, art. v, qu. v (fo. 75); Aquinas, *Questiones Disputatae de Malo*, qu. 13, De Avaritia, art. IV, resp., para. 14, in *Opera*, vol. xv, p. 212; Bernardine, *Quadragesimale de Evangelio Aeterno*, sermo XLI, art. I, ad init., cap. ii, iii; sermo XLII, art. I, ad init., cap. i, ii, iii, in *Opera*, vol. ii, pp. 237–9, 249–51; T. Pie, *Usuries Spright Coniured or a Scholasticall Determination of Usury*, 1604, pp. [7, 8]; for brokers' commission, see Stats 13 Eliz. c. 8; 21 Jas c. 17; 12 Chas 2 c. 13; 13 Anne c. 15; C. H. Firth and R. S. Rait, *Acts and Ordinances of the Interregnum*, 3 vols, 1911, vol. ii,

The counterpart of *damnum emergens* was *lucrum cessans, interesse lucri cessantis*, or cessant gain. This title arose when a lender, because he had not been repaid on time, missed an opportunity to profit elsewhere. And, like emergent loss, it could be contracted for at the outset, before any delay or due date. In addition, cessant gain could, rarely and exceptionally, be claimed for an opportunity lost before the due date and caused merely by the act of lending, provided a contract to this effect had been signed and the lender, when making the loan, had been motivated solely by piety or charity and by the borrower's necessity. Most Christian divines allowed such a claim, but very charily, and all were wary of its abuse. They insisted that all claims for cessant gain be substantiated by clear evidence and subjected to close scrutiny and careful assessment, and were especially strict when it was claimed before the due day, and merely from finding the money that was to be lent. Furthermore, always and in all cases this cessant gain, like emergent loss, had to be in industry, agriculture, landownership or trade, or in the purchase of some means of production or of rents or annuities, or in a part of a ship, a share in a partnership, company or bank – in short, in almost anything other than moneylending. Fittingly, under this title, as under emergent loss, interest was payable immediately from the time of the loss or the lost opportunity.[15] Cessant gain was often also held payable from the outset of a forced loan and, with equal justice, a sovereign who took such a loan and failed to repay by the promised date, fell liable for interest *titulo morae*.[16]

Periculum sortis was a much availed of title to interest. Here the lender or investor shared the risks of the business with the borrower or partner. But the lender was not entitled to interest on account of any loss or risk of loss. Whether the business made a profit or a loss was neither here nor there. The person typically earning this kind of interest was a sleeping partner or anyone else who put into a venture money or goods that he stood to lose should things go wrong. Any gain, no matter how great, was

---

p. 549; P. Melanchthon, *Philosophiae Moralis Epitomes*, in *Opera quae supersunt Omnia*, Halle and Brunswick, 28 vols, 1834–60, vol. xvi, col. 140.

[15] Melanchthon, *Philosophiae Moralis Epitomes*, cols 137–40; Dempsey, op. cit., pp. 166, 171–4, 178; Pie, op. cit., p. [8]; J. Kirshner in Intro. to R. De Roover, *Business, Banking and Economic Thought in Late Medieval and Early Modern Europe: Selected Studies of Raymond de Roover*, ed. J. Kirshner, Chicago and London, 1974, pp. 30–31; Bernardine, *Quadragesimale de Evangelio Aeterno*, sermo XLI, art. I, cap. ii, iii; sermo XLII, ad init., art. II, ad init., cap. i, ii, in *Opera*, vol. ii, pp. 238–9, 249, 251–2; cf. S. D'Ewes, *Autobiography and Correspondence of Sir Simonds D'Ewes during the reigns of James I and Charles I*, ed. J. O. Halliwell, 2 vols, 1845, vol. i, pp. 43, 322.

[16] Bernardine, *Quadragesimale de Evangelio Aeterno*, sermo XLI, art. I, ad init., cap. i, ii, iii, in *Opera*, vol. ii, pp. 237–9; H. Ellis, *Original Letters Illustrative of English History*, 2nd series, 4 vols, 1827, vol. ii, pp. 317–18. Cf. J. T. Noonan, *The Scholastic Analysis of Usury*, Cambridge, MA, 1957, p. 128; N. Jones, *God and the Moneylenders: Usury and Law in Early Modern England*, Oxford, 1989, pp. 52–3.

then lawful interest, not usury.[17] Roger Fenton gives a good example of this entitlement:

> A man unskilfull in trading hath a stock of money, which he delivereth to a merchant or tradesman to imploy; receiveth part of gaine, and beareth part of hazard proportionably. This is no usurie, but partnership. No usury, because his money is not lent by mutuation, so long as he reserveth a propertie in it himselfe, *in contractu societatis cessat obiectum usurae*.[18]

Periculum sortis also applied where the lender risked total loss of an entirely unsecured loan. The clearest example of this was in bottomry (*foenus nauticum*), where the shipowner or master paid anything between 30 and 50 per cent, but the lender lost all his principal and any hope of interest if the ship and its cargo were lost.[19] Under the title of *periculum sortis*, the greater the risk of ultimate default on the principal, the higher the justifiable rate of interest. Since the risk could be infinite, no theoretical limit could be put on the rate of interest, and up to 300 per cent or so might rightly be charged.[20] As Lord Bramwell put it, 'Suppose you were asked to lend a mutton chop to a ravenous dog, upon what terms would you lend it?'[21] Nevertheless, unduly high, harsh and unconscionable rates

---

[17] Kirshner in Intro. to De Roover, *Business, Banking, and Economic Thought*, pp. 31–2; Pie, op. cit., p. 14; Hostiensis, *Summa Aurea,* fos 250ᵛ, 252; *idem, Summa Hostiensis,* fo. 447; Middleton, op. cit., lib. IV, dist. xv, art. v, qu. v (fo. 75); J. Blaxton, *The English Usurer, or Usury condemned,* 1634, pp. 7, 8; Wilson, op. cit., pp. 254, 262–4; Bernardine, *Quadragesimale de Evangelio Aeterno,* sermo XXXIX, art. I, ad init., cap. i, ii, in *Opera,* vol. ii, pp. 225–6; R. Fenton, *A Treatise of Usurie,* 1611, pp. 24, 71. I have found no instance in England of a partner insuring against loss by triple contract (*contractus trimus*), for which see A. W. B. Simpson, *A History of the Common Law of Contract: The Rise of the Action of Assumpsit,* Oxford, 1975, p. 512.

[18] Fenton, op. cit., p. 19.

[19] Ibid., p. 71; Hostiensis, *Summa Aurea,* fos 250ᵛ, 252; Middleton, op. cit., lib. IV, dist. art. v, qu. v (fo. 75); T. Siderfin, *Les Reports de divers Special Cases argue et adjudge en le Court del Bank le Roy, et auxi en le Comen Banc et l'Exchequer en les primier dix ans apres le Restauration del ... Roy Charles le II,* 2 pts, 1714 and var. edns, pt i, p. 27; G. Croke, *Reports ... of such selected Cases as were adjudged ... during the reign of King James the First,* 1791 and var. edns, 208–9; D. North, *Discourses upon Trade; principally directed to the cases of the interest, coynage, clipping, increase of money,* 1691, p. 7; G. Malynes, *Consuetudo, vel Lex Mercatoria or the Ancient Law-Merchant,* 1622, p. 171; Erasmus, *Collectanea Adagiorum Veterum,* chilias iv, centur. ix, Prov. xc, in *Opera Omnia,* vol. ii, col. 1157 (B); F. Braudel, *Civilization and Capitalism 15th–18th Century,* 3 vols, 1984, vol. ii, p. 365; vol. iii, p. 130.

[20] R. Sutton and N. P. Shannon, *Sutton and Shannon on Contracts,* ed. K. W. Wedderburn, 1956, pp. 216–17; D. E. C. Yale, *Lord Nottingham's Chancery Cases,* 2 vols, Selden Society, lxxiii, lxxix, 1957–61 (for 1954, 1961–62), vol. ii, pp. 694–5; G. Stone and D. Meston, *The Law Relating to Money-Lenders,* 1927, pp. 150 seqq.; cf. W. Petty, *The Economic Writings of Sir William Petty,* ed. C. H. Hull, 2 vols, Cambridge, 1899, vol. i, p. 48.

[21] Stone and Meston, op. cit., p. 157.

were disallowed by equity, in England in the Court of Chancery or of Requests.[22]

Contrary to some modern opinion, neither interest nor usury could arise directly from *cambium et recambium* (exchange and rechange) in genuine foreign exchanges, because no loan was involved. The merchant banker or other deliverer incorporated his intended profit in the rate of exchange, so causing a disparity in rates between one commercial and financial centre and another, as between London and Antwerp or Amsterdam. This meant that the London deliverer could expect, for example, to receive, for his £100 sterling, a little over £112 groat in Antwerp, and by then returning this money to London, end up with about £101 10s. sterling, so having earned 30s. for a month's usance. To and from more distant places, the usance was longer: for Hamburg, two months (double usance), for Italy, three months (treble usance). Thus, if he could keep his money continually in the exchanges, a man could earn about 9 per cent per annum. The risks were slight, and he nearly always gained, yet the extent of his gain (or loss) was by no means certain, for he could not certainly foretell how the exchanges were going to fluctuate in response to the vagaries of trade and of the terms of trade. Occasionally, a debasement of some currency or other untoward event might even cause him to lose. Playing the exchanges in this way was a modification of ordinary commercial practice. Instead of the taker drawing a bill on his overseas factor or correspondent, who would pay the deliverer's factor or agent, the taker, lacking a factor or correspondent of his own, drew a bill on the deliverer's factor payable to the selfsame factor. Then this factor drew a bill on the taker and so payable to the banker who had been the first deliverer. In exceptional circumstances, this arrangement might seem convenient, as when, say, a young merchant adventurer with no factor in Antwerp, needed to raise money to pay the clothiers, and expected to recoup himself and settle his debts from the proceeds of his sales. But dry or fictitious exchange, where no bills went out or came in, where the parties themselves were partly or wholly fictitious and where the so-called rates of exchange were fixed in advance, was purely and simply a camouflage for usury, as was the practice of making bills on Amsterdam or Antwerp payable two, three or four months after delivery.[23]

---

[22] J. Ritchie, *Reports of Cases decided by Francis Bacon in the High Court of Chancery (1617–1621)*, 1932, pp. 143–4.

[23] De Roover, *Business, Banking and Economic Thought*, pp. 183 seqq., 196–9, 203, 211, 241 seqq., 311; *idem, Gresham on Foreign Exchange*, Cambridge, MA, 1949, pp. 95 seqq., 112 seqq., 128, 141 seqq., 161 seqq.; *idem, Money, Banking and Credit in Medieval Bruges*, Cambridge, MA, 1958, pp. 53–4, 66, 81–2, but De Roover confuses usury and interest; Wilson, op. cit., pp. 303–6, 308, 310, 313; R. H. Tawney and E. Power, *Tudor Economic Documents, being Select Documents Illustrating the Economic and Social History of Tudor*

Englishmen originally effected gages by a grant of the land or other premises to the gagee, either in fee (simple or tail), or for years or for up to three lives, but all with a covenant or clause of defeasance that invalidated the grant if the principal were repaid in due form on or by the due day. The gagee then usually rented the premises back to the gagor. If the rent paid by a gagor were applied solely to the reduction and redemption of the debt, there was no mortgage, but a *vivum vadium*, vifgage or livegage, which was non-usurious and lawful, always provided the full agreed price had really been paid. But the *mortum vadium* or mortgage proper, where all the rent finally went to the mortgagee's account, was usurious and unlawful, as declared in the Act of 1495. The great exceptions to this rule, however, were, first, where the mortgage was for less than one year, for then the mortgagee could not reap the profit, harvest or increase; and, second, where the mortgagee restored his profits to the mortgagor on repayment of the principal. In view of this possibility, for the creditor to enter into a *mortum vadium* was not in itself unlawful, but to take and keep all the rent arising from it was. In the early modern period, usurious mortgages for a year or more were hardly found, partly because they could be camouflaged by shifting the use, so that the creditor had no legal estate in the land, and partly because a straightforward long mortgage would be given only as a last resort by men in dire financial distress. The contract most dangerous for the mortgagor was one for 'a monethes day', with ample gage and a plain bill of sale if the day were not kept. Most mortgages were for six months or less. Then, if not redeemed on time, the mortgagee could lawfully either foreclose or take interest for forbearing to, and then also charge a continuance fee. This corresponded to the practice in loan contracts with *poena conventionalis,* and as we have seen in Lord Pembroke's dealings with Knighton manor, such a loan could be converted into a quasi-mortgage. A succession of agreements for renewal often made nominally short mortgages last a long time, for up to six years or more. True interest could be claimed by any gagee, as by any lender. Interest upon interest (compound interest) was not forbidden by statute, but could be relieved against in Chancery as oppressive, which it was in all but the rare cases where the gage had been assigned for a price that covered also any interest as yet unpaid, always provided the assignment had not been made with the sole intent of creating

England, 3 vols, 1937, vol. iii, pp. 94, 107, 305–7, 349; cf. M. Grice-Hutchison, *Early Economic Thought in Spain 1177–1740*, 1978, p. 46; R. Pauli, 'Drei Volkswirthschaftliche Denkschriften aus der Zeit Heinrichs VIII. von England', *Abhandlungen der Königlichen Gesellschaft der Wissenschaft zu Göttingen*, 1878, xxiii, pp. 19, 20; R. Porder, *A Sermon of Gods fearefull Threatnings for Idolatry ... with a Treatise against Usurie* (1570) n.d. fos 55–7, 63ᵛ, 64, 81ᵛ–3; H. Robinson, *Englands Safety in Trades Encrease*, 1641, pp. 38 seqq.

interest upon interest.[24] The disadvantage to the gagor of what was to all intents and purposes a long-term gage was that when land values started increasing by leaps and bounds, the gagee stood to gain much by foreclosure, for the property had become worth much more than the sum advanced on it. To guard against such inequitable foreclosure, from about 1568 onwards Chancery developed the doctrine of equity of redemption. By this, the gagee was debarred from foreclosing if the estate were worth significantly more than the loan; and the gage might be renewed, for a reasonable period, by decree, on payment of lawful interest, always provided the original agreement had allowed for renewal and continuance, and that the rent and interest to date had duly been paid. The gagor was protected from the worst and the gagee compensated by a further stream of payments. But after about 1650, as land values tended to fall rather than rise, equity of redemption was increasingly disfavoured in Chancery on the grounds that it had become a distinct kind of inheritance, with repayment postponed indefinitely, so that gagees became effectually bailiffs to the gagors.[25] Gages, including longer ones, had by now become

---

24 Croke, *Reports ... James*, pp. 507–9; R. Brook, *Some New Cases of the years and time of King Henry VIII, King Edward VI and Queen Mary*, 1651 and var. edns, p. 188; Glanvill, *The Treatise on the Laws and Customs of the Realm of England commonly called Glanvill*, ed. G. D. G. Hall, 1965, p. 124; J. E. Kew, 'Mortgages in mid-Tudor Devonshire', *Devonshire Association, Report and Transactions*, 1967, xcix, p. 167; W. S. Holdsworth, *A History of English Law*, 3 vols, 1909, vol. ii, p. 490; vol. iii, pp. 110–11; Stat. 11 H. 7 c. 8; Yale, *Lord Nottingham's Chancery Cases*, vol. i, pp. 186–7; A. P. Usher, *The Early History of Deposit Banking in Mediterranean Europe*, vol. i, Cambridge, MA, 1943, pp. 138–9; W. D. Evans, *A Collection of Statutes connected with the general administration of the law*, 8 vols, 1817, vol. ii, p. 832; Melton, op. cit., pp. 54–5, 127 seqq., 133 seqq., 154–5; J. L. Barton, 'The common law mortgage, *Law Quarterly Review*, 1967, 83, 237–8; T. F. T. Plucknett, *A Concise History of the Common Law*, 1956, pp. 604–7; N. Jones, op. cit., pp. 127–9; L. Stone, *The Crisis of the Aristocracy 1558–1641*, Oxford, 1965, pp. 524–6; M. E. Finch, *The Wealth of Five Northamptonshire Families 1540–1640*, Northamptonshire Record Society, 1956 (1954–55) xix, pp. 11, 83–6, 96, 104, 109; J. Bankes and E. Kerridge, *The Early Records of the Bankes Family at Winstanley*, Chetham Society, 3rd series, 1973, xxi, pp. 20, 23, 36; Anon., 'Mortgage of the Manor of Foxton Co. York', *Yorkshire Archaeological Journal*, 1917, 24, 98–101; PRO, Court of Requests, Proceedings, 107/3; Chancery Proceedings, ser. i, Jas B.6/62; Wilson, op. cit., p. 295; R. Crowley, *One and Thyrtye Epigrammes*, n.d., in *The Select Works of Robert Crowley*, ed. J. M. Cowper, Early English Text Society (EETS), extra series, 1872, xv, p. 49; J. P. Cooper, *Wentworth Papers 1597–1628*, Royal Historical Society, Camden 4th series, 1973, xii, p. 222; Anon. [Keck], *Cases Argued and Decreed in the High Court of Chancery from the 12th year of King Charles II to the 31st*, 1697 and var. edns, pp. 29, 61–4, 67–8, 93–4, 105–6, 258. For examples of mortgages, BL, Add. MS 31885, fos 88 (89) seqq.

25 Anon. [Keck], *Cases Argued and Decreed*, pp. 107–8, 148; Melton, op. cit., pp. 127–9; Plucknett, op. cit., pp. 608, 690; R. W. Turner, *The Equity of Redemption: Its Nature, History and Connection with Equitable Estates Generally*, Cambridge, 1931, pp. 24 seqq., 48 seqq., 65 seqq.; Simpson, op. cit., pp. 119–20; E. C. Wilmot, *A Succinct View of the Law of Mortgages*, 1819, pp. 7, 25 seqq., 33 seqq., 46–7, 102; Kew, art. cit., p. 166; D. E. C. Yale,

commoner on all kinds of freehold estates, and especially on copyholds of inheritance, whose titles were easily proved, and even on reversions of such copyholds. The copyholder simply surrendered to the use of the gagee, for life, lives or years, on condition that in event of redemption the surrender would be null and void.[26] But, copyholds apart, a gage was still an excessively awkward, complicated and potentially hazardous way of raising money on landed estates. It was better simply to sell a lease for years for a lump sum and at a peppercorn rent. Yet the simplest, most straightforward course, and the one that still remained the commonest, was to sell rent-charges, that is, rents seck with powers of distraint for non-payment. Either way, by lease or by rent-charge, there was no loan and hence no hint of usury, and Chancery suits about this or about foreclosure and redemption were tribulations that could be banished from mind.[27]

As we have seen, the condemnation of usury stems from the earliest times. Aristotle remarks how strongly and justifiably it was disliked in his day, and comments that money was not intended for this, but for buying and selling; usury merely produced money out of money, and so of all the ways to wealth was the most unnatural. Amongst the ancient Jews,

---

Lord Nottingham's 'Manual of Chancery Practice' and 'Prolegomena of Chancery and Equity', Cambridge, 1965, pp. 15, 285–6; Finch, op. cit. pp. 32–3, 57.

[26] Finch, op. cit., pp. 32–3, 95–6, 131, 163–4, 168, 186, 198–9; Plucknett, op. cit., pp. 607–8; Stone, op. cit., pp. 527–8; Lord Leconfield, *Sutton and Duncton Manors*, 1956, pp. 4, 31, 36, 41–2, 85, 87, 89–92, 98; N. S. B. Gras and E. C. Gras, *Economic and Social History of an English Village*, Cambridge, MA, 1930, pp. 590–91; W. M. Marcham and F. Marcham, *Court Rolls of the Bishop of London's Manor of Hornsey 1603–1701*, 1929, pp. 1, 2, 5, 10; Anon., 'Chancery Proceedings *temp.* Elizabeth', *Collections for the History of Staffordshire*, 3rd ser. (1926) 1928, pp. 64–5; H. Fishwick, *Pleadings and Depositions in the Duchy Court of Lancaster at the Time of Henry VII and Henry VIII*, 2 vols, Record Society for Lancashire and Cheshire, xxii, xxv, 1896–97, vol. [i], p. 101; BL, Add. Ch. 10229; Add. MSS 18458, fo. 58; 23955, fos 3(1), 21–2 (19, 20); 23956, fo. 2; 38487, fo. 22^v; Add. R. 9283, 26341; Harl. MS 2239, fo. 3; Bristol University Library, Hannington Ct Bk 13 Oct. 14 Chas, 9 May 15 Chas, 27 Apr. 16 Chas; Bedfordshire Record Office (hereafter RO), BS/319 Ct R. Woodmanley 2 Sept. 1643; Hertfordshire RO, Ashridge Coll. 1436, 1441; Suffolk RO (Ipswich) 51/10/17.3 Ct Bk Stradbroke and Stubcrofte 1651–65, fos 42, 47; V.5/23/2.1, fos 35, 38; Middlesex RO, Acc.446/ M102 Ct R. Harmondsworth 3 Oct. 8 Chas; Leicestershire RO, 4D/51/1 Ct Bk Cas. Donington 26 Oct. 1635; Northamptonshire RO, Misc. Led. 145, pp. 141, 211; Montagu Coll. Nfk box P pt 1 Ct R. Foxley cum Bawdeswell 2 Oct. 27 Eliz., 9 Dec. 30 Eliz.; Westmoreland Coll. 2. ix. 4 (B7–B11); 5. v. 1 Ct R. Farcet 13 Sept. 21 Jas; Finch-Hatton Coll. 119, fos (23^v–4) Naneby; 562; 1352, fo. 2; 1353; 1359; 1361; 1363; 1365; 1368; 1371; 1372; 1374; 1376; Shak. Bpl., Manorial Docs, Atherstone copy Ct R. 11 Oct. 1632; Rowington custumal; Wilton Ho. Ct R. Manors 1689–1754 box 1, vol. 3, pp. 42, 51–3, 56, 60, 67, 69, 71–3, 75; PRO, D. L., Sp. Commn 1040; Ct R. bdl. 83 no. 1137 mm. 1, 3; Misc. Bk 117, fo. 144^v; Req. Proc. 107/3; Chanc. Proc. ser. i Jas B6/62; B15/6.

[27] Stone, op. cit., p. 524; Finch, op. cit., pp. 9, 24, *55*, 58, 69, 72, 79, 85, 91–2, 94–5, 127, 164, 186; H. J. Habbakuk, 'The long-term rate of interest and the price of land in the seventeenth century', *Economic History Review*, 2nd series, 1952, 5, p. 38; Plucknett, op. cit., p. 572; N. Jones, op. cit., pp. 129–30.

however, usury was not only hateful and unnatural, it was a sin specifically condemned by God: 'If thou lend money to any of my people with thee that is poor, thou shalt not be to him as a creditor; neither shall you lay upon him usury.'[28] Again, God commands, 'And if thy brother be waxen poor ... take thou no usury of him or increase; but fear thy God: that thy brother may live with thee. Thou shalt not give him thy money upon usury, nor give him thy victuals for increase'.[29] The Psalmist asks, 'Lord, who shall sojourn in thy tabernacle? Who shall dwell in thy holy hill?', and the answer is, in part, 'He that putteth not out his money to usury'.[30] The Psalmist and the prophets denounce usury along with assassination and other heinous crimes.[31] The Jews were God's chosen people and all brothers one to another, but the Gentiles were not their brothers, and Jews were not forbidden to lend on usury to them. This was God's explicit rule: 'Thou shalt not lend on usury to thy brother; usury of money, usury of victuals, usury of any thing that is lent upon usury: unto a foreigner thou mayest lend upon usury; but unto thy brother thou shalt not lend upon usury.'[32] This discrimination between Jew and Gentile was characteristic of Jewish practices and beliefs. A Jew, for example, might not enslave a brother Jew, but might freely take bondmen and bondmaids from amongst other races.[33]

The Christian position on usury springs from the Jewish, but is fundamentally different, for Christianity transcends races, no one of which is chosen by God above the others. It follows that in the eyes of Christians any Jew who takes usury from anyone is sinning. John Calvin gives a plausible explanation of the two different positions before and after Christ's mission, for previously God had allowed Jews to take usury of Gentiles because the Gentiles themselves took usury.[34] (Doc. 1)

> *Quoniam gentes poterant exigere foenus a Judaeis; nisi fuisset mutuum illud, jus et reciprocum, ut loquuntur, deterior fuisset conditio populi Dei quam gentium. Permisit ergo Deus suis exigere foenus, sed non inter se.*

> Since the Gentiles were able to exact fenory from the Jews, unless that had been mutual, just and reciprocal, as the saying is, the condition of God's people would have been worse than that of the Gentiles. Therefore God allowed his people to exact usury, but not among themselves.[35]

---

[28] Aristotle, *Politics*, bk 1, cap. 10; Exodus xxii. 25.

[29] Leviticus xxv. 35–7.

[30] Psalm xv. 1, 5.

[31] Nehemiah v. 7, 10; Psalm xv. 5; Ezekiel xxii. 12.

[32] Deuteronomy xxiii. 19, 20; and see Nehemiah v. 7.

[33] Leviticus xxv. 39, 40, 42, 44–6.

[34] J. Calvin, *Commentarii Libros in Mosis necum in Librum Josue*, Amsterdam, 1567, p. 527.

[35] J. Calvin, *Praelectiones Librum Prophetiarum Jeremiae et Lamentationes necnon in Ezechielis Propheta viginti capita priora*, Amsterdam, 1567, p. 170.

This hardly rings true. Richard Capel provides a more convincing explanation: usury is a sin. When the Jews were permitted to practise usury upon strangers, this was a permission of sin. It is not true that the law of Moses against usury was merely a judicial law, for such laws are known by some intelligence from the books of Moses. Heathens of all sorts cry out against usury. It is condemned by instinct and the light of nature.

> Therefore it could not be a politicall law of Moses. Besides, we have it forbidden in the New Testament, when judicialls were out of date; lend, saith the Lord Jesus, looking for nothing again ... Now usury being no act of mercy or kindnesse, but rather the contrary, it cannot but follow, that the permission to lend upon use to the stranger, must not be meant of ordinary strangers, to whom they were to show all kindness and compassion, but the *strangers* of those cursed Nations whom they were bound to bite and eate out; and if this permission to put money to the *stranger* were not looked upon as a punishment, why is it denied to a brother?

Other men put it in a nutshell: God appointed his people to destroy the Canaanites and usury was a weapon against them.[36] Over a millennium earlier St Ambrose had already hit the nail on the head:

> *Sine ferro dimicat qui usuram flagitat: sine gladio se de hoste ulciscitur, qui fuerit usurarius exactor inimici. Ergo ubi jus belli, ibi etiam jus usurae.*

> He fights without force of arms who demands usury: he wreaks vengeance on the enemy who is an exactor of usury from the foe. Therefore where there be a right of war, there also is a right of usury.[37]

Before we go on, we do well constantly to bear in mind that Christians distinguished between divine law and worldly law, which was only needed because the kingdom of God had not yet come on Earth, and wayward men had to be compelled to a degree of righteousness.[38] Christ enjoins us,

---

36 R. Capel, *Tentations: their nature, danger, cure; to which is added a Brief Dispute touching Restitution in the Case of Usury*, 5th edn, 1655, 1st pagination, pp. 266–7; 2nd pagination, pp. 290–91; R. Bolton, *A Short and Private Discourse hetweene Mr Bolton and one M. S. concerning Usury*, 1637, p. 21; N. Holmes, *Usury is Injury, cleared in an examination of its best apologie alleaged by a countrey Minister, out of Dr Ames, in his Cases of Conscience, as a party and patron of that apologie*, 1640, p. 41; G. Powel, *Theologicall and Scholasticall Positions concerning Usurie*, Oxford, 1602, p. 21; A. Willet, *Hexapla in Exodum: that is, a sixfold commentary upon the second booke of Moses called Exodus*, 1608, p. 514; H. Smith, *The Works of Henry Smith; including sermons, treatises, prayers and poems*, 2 vols, Edinburgh, 1866, vol. i, p. 97.

37 St Ambrose, *De Tobia*, lib. 1, cap. xv, para. 51, in *Sancti Ambrosii Mediolanensis Episcopi Opera*, 8 vols, Venice, 1781, vol. i, pp. 738–9. (I have abided by original vol. and page nos.)

38 M. Luther, *An die Pfarrherrn wider den Wucher zu predigen Vermanung* (1540), in

'Lend, hoping for nothing again ... And if ye lend to them of whom ye hope to receive, what thank have ye? for sinners also lend to sinners, to receive as much again'.[39] St Thomas Aquinas thus spoke for all Christians when he condemned usury as a charge for the mere act of lending sterile money or consumable goods, and showed how sharp was the difference between usuries and licit transactions like letting houses. Usurers should be made to return their ill-gotten gains.[40] (Doc. 2) All Christians have always believed usury (fenory or ocker) to be a sin. St Ambrose (c. 340–97) denounced *foeneratores* – usurers – over and over again. They were *viperae* – vipers. True interest he allowed, but stressed the dangers of usury masquerading as interest. His teachings were followed by the Schoolmen, in particular by Alexander Hales (d. 1249), Hostiensis (d. 1271), St Thomas Aquinas (c. 1225–74), John Duns Scotus (c. 1265–1308), Richard Middleton (*fl.* 1280), William Ockham (c. 1290–1349), St Bernardine of Siena (1380–1444) and St Antonine (1389–1459). They distinguished between usury and interest and between the various extrinsic titles under which interest could be claimed, as emergent loss, cessant gain, forbearance (*poena conventionalis*) and risky ventures like bottomry and partnership (*periculum sortis*). Almost the only disagreement concerned claims for cessant gain from the very outset of the loan, which was all too often used to cloak usury; and then it was only that Scotus thought Hostiensis had viewed it too leniently and that it was better avoided altogether. What mainly concerned all the Schoolmen, however, was that usurers be punished and, especially, that they be compelled to make full restitution. Bernardine deals with this subject with characteristic thoroughness.[41] (Doc. 3) Duns

---

M. Luther, *Alle Bücher und Schrifften*, 8 pts (vols) Jena, 1555–58, vol. vii, fo. 401; H. Zwingli, *Von göttlicher und menschlicher Gerechtigheit wie die zemmen und standind: ein predge Huldrych Zwinglis an S. Johannes toufers tag gethon MDXXIII*, in *Huldreich Zwingli's Werke*, ed. M. Schuler and J. Schulthess, 7 vols, Zurich, 1828–42, vol. i, p. 454.

39 Luke vi. 34–5 (Authorized Version).

40 Aquinas, *Summa Theologica*, II–ii, quaestio 78, art. 1, concl., in *Opera*, vol. xxii, pp. 322–3; and see *Opera*, ad secundum didendum, p. 323; *idem, In Duo Praecepta Caritatis, et Decem Legis Praecepta expositio Psalm. XIV*, in *Opera*, vol. viii, p. 20; *idem, Questiones Disputatae de Malo*, qu. 13, art. 4, and resp., art. 1–14, *Opera*, vol. xv, 208 seqq.; *idem, Questiones Quodlibetales*, quodlibet III, art. 19, *Opera*, vol. xvii, pp. 273–4.

41 St Ambrose, *De Tobia*, in St Ambrose, *Sancti Ambrosii Mediolanensis Episcopi Opera*, 8 vols, Venice, 1781, vol. i, pp. 720 seqq., 733–4, 738–9; *idem, Epistolarum Classis I: Epistola xix*, in *Opera*, vol. iii, p. 889; *idem, De Excessu Fratris sui Satyri*, in *Opera*, vol. iv, p. 172; *idem, Expositio Evangelii Secundum Lucam*, in *Opera*, vol. ii, p. 1040; *Enarrationes in XII Psalmos Davidicos*, in *Opera*, vol. ii, pp. 93–4; Antonine, *Summa Major*, fos 20ᵛ seqq.; Aquinas, *Opera*, vol. viii, p. 20; vol. xv, p. 208 seqq.; vol. xvii, pp. 273–4; vol. xxii, pp. 322–5; St Bernardine, *Opera*, vol. i, pp. 29, 144–6, 152 seqq., 162, 166, 168–9, 178–9, 181, 185; vol. ii, pp. 96, 207 seqq., 256–8; vol. iii, 220–23, 236–7, 273; vol. v, p. 93; Alexander (of) Hales, *Summa Theologice*, Leiden, 1516, fos 141ᵛ–3; Duns Scotus, *Quaestiones*, dist. XV, qu. ii, in *Opera Omnia*, vol. xviii, pp. 292–3, 321, 324–5, 328, 333;

Scotus[42] and Ockham[43] had said much the same in fewer words. So had Middleton. After distinguishing sharply between a trading agreement and a loan contract, he went on to show that in trade both parties expected to gain, whereas in lending at usury, only the usurer could profit. Nor would it aught avail the usurer to try to put his gains to good uses, for 'The corrupt tree bringeth forth evil fruit' – *Mala arbor malos fructus facit*.[44] Looking at it the other other way round, Bernardine said, '*Nolite vele eleemosynas facere de foenore et usuris*' – 'Crave no alms from usurious gains'.[45]

In all ages Christians of all kinds have said the same as Ambrose and the medieval Schoolmen. Wolfgang Musculus pointed out that Christ's injunction was to be taken literally.[46] Bernardine de Picquigny asks what reward was to be expected from God, 'Even if thou shall hast given a loan to those from whom you coveted no more than an equal favour?' – '*Et si mutuum dederitis iis tantum a quibus parem expetatis gratiam*'.[47] Luther affirms the same: '*Jr solt leihen und nichts davon gewarten. Das ist, jr solt leihen denen, die euch nicht wider leihen mügen oder wollen*' – 'You should lend and expect nothing. That is, you should lend to those whom you neither can nor wish to borrow back from'.[48] This agrees with the exposition made by St Bernardine,[49] who also puts the matter succinctly, thus: '*Mutuum autem, si non est gratuitum, non est jam mutuum, sed usura*' – 'Indeed, a loan if not gratuitous, is then no loan, but usury'.[50]

Hostiensis, *Summa Hostiensis*, fos 443^v seqq.; *idem*, *Summa Aurea*, fos 250–52; Middleton, *Sententiarum Questiones Persubtilissime*, lib. iv, *Sententiarum Resolute Questiones*, dist. xv, art. v (fos 74^v–5; W. (of) Ockham, *Opus Nonaginta Diernum*, in Guillelmi de Ockham, *Opera Politica*, eds J. G. Sikes, B. L. Manning, H. S. Offler, R. F. Bennett and R. H. Snape, 3 vols, Manchester, 1940–56, vol. i, pp. 315, 319 seqq.; Noonan, op. cit. pp. 118–19.

[42] Duns Scotus, *Quaestiones in Quartum Librum Sententiarum*, dist. XV, quaes. ii, pp. 292– 3, 321, 324–5, 328, 333.

[43] Ockham, *Opus Nonaginta Diernum*, pp. 305–6, 315, 320–23, 331.

[44] Middleton, op. cit., lib. IV, dist. xv, princ. 5, qu. 6 (fo. 75^v); Matthew vii. 17.

[45] Bernardine, *Quadragesimale de Religione Christiana*, sermo VII, art. II, cap. iv, in *Opera*, vol. i, p. 29.

[46] W. Musculus, *De Usuris ex Verho Dei*, Tübingen, 1558, sig. A. 5, B. iiii, D. 5.

[47] Bernardinus a Piconio (Henri Bernardine), *Opera Omnia Bernardini a Piconio*, 3 vols, Paris, 1870–74, vol. ii, p. 85.

[48] M. Luther, *Grosser Sermon vom Wucher* (1519), in M. Luther, *Alle Bücher und Schrifften*, 8 pts (vols), Jena, 1555–58, vol. i, fo. 193. For vol. i I used the 4th reprint.

[49] Bernardine, *Quadragesimale de Religione Christiana*, sermo XXXIII, art. I, cap. iii, and art. II, cap. iii (*Opera*, vol. i, pp. 144–6); *idem*, *Quadragesimale de Evangelio Aeterno*, sermo XXXVI, ad. init., art. I, cap. ii; art. II, cap. i, ii; art. III, pass.; sermo XXXVII, art. I, cap. ii, iii; sermo XXXVIII, pass.; sermo XXXIX, art. I, cap. iii (*Opera*, vol. ii, pp. 207 seqq.); sermo XLIII, ad init.; art. I, cap. i, ii, iii; art. II, cap. i, ii, iii (*Opera*, vol. ii, pp. 256–8); *idem*, *Duo Adventualia*, sermo XXV, prima pars principalis, tertia pars principalis (*Opera*, vol. iii, pp. 220–23); sermo XXXIII, prima pars principalis (*Opera*, vol. iii, p. 273).

[50] Bernardine, *Quadragesimale de Evangelio Aeterno*, sermo XXXVII, art. I, cap. ii, in *Opera*, vol. ii, p. 213.

Before we pursue our study of usury any further, it is necessary to advert to the position of the Jews, in order to explain English and, even more, continental attitudes to them. In the early Middle Ages most of the usurers in England were Jews practising under special royal dispensation. Not being Christians, they were debarred from the public exercise of lawful trades and occupations, but were allowed to practise them within their own community, which needed rabbis, physicians, surgeons, lawyers, butchers, bakers and so on. Thus, while by no means all Jews were usurers, all lived by usury directly or indirectly, so the stigma attaching to usurers was extended to the Jews as a whole, and heightened by a general dislike of foreigners and foreign ways and beliefs.

Although usury was illegal by the common law and by the Statute of Merton (1236), and there were few English usurers before 1275, some Englishmen wished to borrow upon usury, and their want was supplied by Jews who started to infiltrate in the eleventh century. Edward the Confessor, though offering his protection to the Jews, prohibited usury and forbade usurers his realm. Convicted usurers, amongst whom figured some Englishmen, were to forfeit all their goods and possessions and be deemed outlaws. But when they later had the chance, Jews had no scruples in practising usury upon the English, making loans, often for short terms, secured on bonds, at effective rates of usury that averaged, and often greatly exceeded, 40 or 50 per cent. Those foolish or desperate enough to fall into the usurers' toils, found it almost impossible to escape. Usurers were envied, despised, feared and hated, especially by those who used their services. It was all too easy to lead the common people into the detestable sin of anti-Semitism, so the English generally came to loathe the Jews and seldom missed a good opportunity of attacking them. The kings, however, protected the Jews and so held them at their mercy, in order to mulct them of a large part of their ill-gotten gains. As has so often been remarked, kings used the Jews as a sponge to soak up their subjects' wealth. Not until 1275 was the *Statutum de Judaismo* passed forbidding the Jews to practise usury. Few of them were ever converted to Christianity, opening the way for them to adopt lawful pursuits, and in 1290 all those of Jewish faith were banished.[51] Needless to say, expelling the Jews did not extirpate

---

[51] Holdsworth, op. cit. (1922–52 edn), vol. viii, p. 102; R. Schmid, *Die Gesetze der Angelsachsen*, Leipzig, 1858, p. 18; F. Liebermann, *Die Gesetze der Angelsachsen*, 3 vols, Halle, 1903–16, vol. i, p. 668; Glanvill, p. 89; Bracton, Henrici de, *De Legibus Consuetudinibus Angliae*, ed. T. Twiss, Rolls Series, 6 vols, 1878–83, vol. ii, p. 244; E. Coke, *The Institutes of the Lawes of England*, 4 pts (vols) 1628, 1629, 1642–44 and var. edns, vol. ii, pp. 506–7; D. M. Stenton, *English Society in the Early Middle Ages*, Harmondsworth, 1951, pp. 190 seqq.; J. Shatzmiller, *Shylock Reconsidered: Jews, Moneylending and Medieval Society*, Berkeley and Los Angeles, CA, and London, 1990, pp. 48, 91; P. Elman, 'The economic causes of the expulsion of the Jews in 1290', *Economic History Review*, 1936–37, 7, 145 seqq.; A. E. Bland, P. A. Brown and R. H. Tawney, *English Economic History: Select Documents*, 1914, pp. 44 seqq.

usury; it merely led to it being conducted mostly by professedly Christian English people.

Nevertheless, so closely had the Jews been identified with usury, that in common parlance the words 'Jew' and 'usurer' were synonymous. Three hundred years after they had gone, to Judaise still meant to be a usurer; the saying was, 'Usurers should have orange-tawny bonnets, because they do judaise'.[52] A fictitious learned preacher could still have these words put into his mouth: 'What is the matter that Jewes are so universallye hated wheresoever they come? Forsoothe, usurie is one of the chief causes, for they robbe all men that deale with them, and undoe them in the ende. And for thys cause they were hated in England, and so banyshed worthelye.'[53] In 1605 the Lord Chancellor, Sir Thomas Egerton, sitting in the Court of Star Chamber, denounced all manner of usury as 'Judaisme' and all usurers as 'mercatores Judaizaates'. The early modern English had still not entirely forgotten their wicked hatred of the Jews.[54]

But the Jews were not expelled from the Continent and there they were still widely permitted to practise usury, so anti-Semitism continued unabated or even grew in malignancy, which must be borne in mind when reading the works of Martin Luther and other continental writers.

---

[52] F. Bacon, *Essays*, 'Of Usury'; *idem*, *The Works of Francis Bacon*, eds J. Spedding, R. L. Ellis and D. D. Heath, 14 vols, 1862–83, vol. xiv, p. 415.

[53] Wilson, op. cit., p. 232.

[54] J. Bentham, *The Christian Conflict*, 1635, p. 329; Fenton, op. cit., p. 72; J. Hooper, *Early Writings*, ed. S. Carr, Parker Society, 1843, p. 393; J. Pilkington, *The Works of James Pilkington, B.D.*, Parker Society, 1842, pp. 39, 40, 150, 464; W. P. Baildon, *Les Reportes del Cases in Camera Stellata, 1593–1609*, p.p. 1894, p. 237; Anon., *A Supplication of the Poore Commons, 1546*, ed. J. M. Cooper, in *Four Supplications 1529–1553*, ed. F. J. Furnival, EETS, extra ser. 1871, xiii, p. 82; Anon., *The Death of Usury*, p. 10; Anon., *Usurie Arraigned and Condemned*, 1625.

CHAPTER TWO

The Reformation

The Reformation made no real or substantial change to fundamental Christian teaching about usury, nor to any of the Christian attitudes to it, remedies for it, or laws against it. The Protestant reformers were all substantially orthodox concerning usury and interest. Martin Luther was the greatest reformer and preached and wrote at length on these subjects, mostly in German. Melanchthon dealt with them meticulously in Latin, and Zwingli added some worthwhile remarks in German; but Calvin, valuable as was his publication of scholarly expositions of Latin and Old Testament terminology, had little to say that was both new and significant. One reason why such disproportionate attention was paid to him was that he wrote in Latin and Luther in German, which few outsiders could read.

The attitudes of the reformers to usury and interest have been much misrepresented. R. H. Tawney says continental 'universities and divines gave, as is their wont, a loud but confused, response' to enquiries on these subjects; but the only confusion is strictly his own and arises from his inability to distinguish interest from usury.[1] He does Luther a grave injustice when he accuses him of incoherence and likens him to 'a savage introduced to a dynamo or a steam-engine' when confronted with commercial and financial complexities.[2] Tawney is correct in pointing out that Luther's doctrines on these matters 'are drawn from the straitest interpretation of ecclesiastical jurisprudence', but wrong in asserting they were 'unsoftened by the qualifications with which canonists themselves had attempted to adapt its rigours to the exigencies of practical life'.[3] The canonists had made no such attempt, and had no reason to do so, for they distinguished between usury and interest; and there were no qualifications for Luther or anyone else to consider. Tawney completely misrepresents Luther when he accuses him of denouncing investment in rent-charges and the payment of interest in compensation of emergent loss, both of which the canon law permitted.[4] As we shall see, Luther expressly allowed them both. The truth is, Tawney had never read much of Luther, and even if he had, would not have been able to understand him; he could not have crossed the *pons asinorum* formed by the distinction between usury and interest. Pascal had studied Luther, and struggled halfway across the asses' bridge, but

---

1 R. H. Tawney, *Religion and the Rise of Capitalism*, Harmondsworth, 1938, p. 86.
2 Ibid., p. 92.
3 Ibid., p. 97.
4 Ibid.

could go no further.[5] Luther did not denounce all *Wiederkauf* (redemption), only usury concealed under that name:

> *Es stehen aber der Klöster und Stiffte güter zur teil, und Pfründen fast vill auff dem Wucher, der sich jtzt in aller Welt nennet den Widerkauff.*

> There are, however, monastic estates and foundations, in part, and clerical livings, almost wholly, that stand on the usury that now dignifies itself throughout the world with the name of redemption.[6]

The slur on Luther's character intended by Pascal when he says, 'Luther himself, when entrusted with 500 guilden as an endowment for poor biblical scholars at Wittenberg, had no scruples against asking how best he could lay it out at interest', is seen to fall short of the mark as soon as the difference between interest and usury is appreciated.[7] But it is not even true that the money was to be lent at interest, which anyway was technically impossible; it was to be used to buy rent-charges. What Luther agreed with Melanchthon and other university colleagues to do, and really did, was to ask Lazarus Spengler, a syndic of Nuremberg, to put the money to the purchase of rent-charges. Luther himself writes to the benefactrix, Dorothea Jörger, that he and his colleagues had decided,

> because it was to be expended on such a good and needful work, that it should be put out on rents, wherewith it might be permanently and fully helpful. For one can be of great help to two people a year with such rents, so long as care be taken that it shall be well laid out, which we of the University of Wittenberg will take care to oversee.

> *weil es an solch nötig nutzlich werck sol angelegt werden, das es auff Zins würde ausgethan, damit es ewig und vilen möcht behilflich sein. Denn man zwo Personen Järlich mit solchen Zinsen ein gute hülff thun kan, so lang es gemerckt wirt wol angelegt sein, welche wir der Universitet zu Wittemberg auffzusehen wolten befehlen.*[8]

Spengler was chosen because he was known and trusted. Luther addresses him as '*lieber Herr und Freund*', '*lieben Herrn und trewen Heilande*' – as 'a dear friend and true saviour'.[9] It is both untrue and unfair to say, as Tawney does, that Zwingli 'in his outlook on society, stood midway between Luther and Calvin' or that he condemned interest 'as in itself contrary to the laws of God'.[10] It is unjust to Melanchthon to say that

---

[5] R. Pascal, *The Social Basis of the German Reformation: Martin Luther and his Times*, 1933, pp. 184–5, 190.

[6] M. Luther, 'Ordnung eins gemeinen Kastens' (1523), in M. Luther, *Alle Bücher und Schrifften*, 8 pts (vols), Jena, 1555–58, vol. ii, fo. 250.

[7] Pascal, op. cit., p. 190.

[8] Luther, *Werke: Briefwechsel*, 14 vols, Weimar, 1930–70, vol. vi, pp. 273–4.

[9] Luther, 'Dem erbarn fursichtigen Lasaro Spengler der Stad Nurmberg syndico', *Alle Bücher und Schrifften*, vol. v, fo. 168.

[10] Tawney, *Religion*, p. 104.

'with some hesitation' he sanctioned 'a modest rate on loans to the rich'.[11] Tawney likewise misrepresents Calvin by accusing him of dismissing 'the oft-quoted passages from the Old Testament and the Fathers as irrelevant, because designed for conditions which no longer exist'. That Calvin argued 'the payment of interest for capital is as reasonable as the payment of rent for land' did not represent 'a fresh start', for in this no difference can be found between Calvin and Luther or between Luther and the canonists.[12]

We have to rid our minds of the euphemism, nowadays no longer generally recognized as one, by which usury, in the sense of fenory or ocker, is called 'interest', and admit that this so-called 'interest' is often really usury, that is, payment for the mere use of money lent on collateral security. Calvin expatiates on this theme when examining Ezekiel xviii. 7, 8:

> *Hic inter alia peccata Ezechiel foenus commemorat. Nomen usurae proprie non convenit huic loco. Neshek deductum est a mordendo: et sic Hebraei foenus appellant, quia arrodit, et paulatim consumit miseros homines.*

> Here, among other crimes, Ezekiel numbers *foenus*. The word usury is not properly apt in this passage. *Neshek* is derived from the word for biting and is the name the Hebrews give to fenory, because it gnaws away and progressively devours wretched men.[13]

Calvin borrowed this interpretation, from Martin Bucer probably,[14] and it is correct. There was nothing new in taking the word 'usury' in its broad sense. Erasmus normally employed *usura* in the narrow sense, but, long before Calvin's day, had drawn attention to the narrow and broad senses of the word and to the confusion caused by them:

> *Andabatarum pugna. Expedit interdum ejusdem rei diversa explicare nomina, quod aliud sit alio significantius: velut usura, nobis ab utendo dicitur, et ad alias quoque res accommodatur, quibus ad tempus utimur, quum aliud sonet usura quum vetamur proximo dare ad usuram ... id est, partus, quod pecunia mutuo data, pariat lucrum ei qui dedit. Foenus autem dicitur a ferendo, quae vox magis quadrat in terram, quae plus reddit in messe, quam acceperat in semente.*

---

11 Ibid., p. 107.

12 Ibid., pp. 107–8.

13 Calvin, *Praelectiones in Librum Prophetiarum Jeremiae et Lamentationes necnon in Ezechielis Propheta viginti capita priora*, Amsterdam, 1567, p. 169; but cf. T. Pie, *Usuries Spright Coniured or a Scholasticall Determination of Usury*, 1604, p. 45.

14 C. Hopf, *Martin Bucer and the English Reformation*, Oxford, 1946, p. 124; M. Bucer, *Scripta Anglicana fere omnia*, Basle, 1577, p. 794; Anon., *The Death of Usury, or the disgrace of usurers*, Cambridge, 1594, p. 1; and see W. Gesenius, *Hebräisches und Aramäisches Handwörterbuch über das Alte Testament*, ed. F. Buhl, Leipzig, 1921, per indice; B. Gordon, 'Lending at interest: some Jewish, Greek, and Christian approaches, 800 B.C. to A.D. 100', *History of Political Economy*, 1982, **14**, 407.

> A fight between blindfolded gladiators. It is useful now and then to explain the diverse names attached to the same thing, because the one be more significant than the other: for instance, usury, it means to us 'the using', and to others, what we are using at the moment, while, to yet another, usury is the word spoken when we prohibit giving to a neighbour at usury ... that is, the gain arising from a loan of money, the profit accruing to him who gave it out. Fenory, however, means, in ordinary speech, the harvest from land that renders more at the gathering in than was bestowed at the sowing.[15]

In this way, *foenus* (*fenus* or *faenus*) became late Latin for what in English is known, strictly and correctly, as fenory or ocker, or, by circumlocution, as 'biting' or 'harsh and unconscionable' usury, but colloquially and generally simply as 'usury'. What Ezekiel denounced was not usury in the ancient, broad sense, but usury in the narrow, generally understood sense.

Again, commenting on Exodus xii. 25, Leviticus xxv. 35–8, and Deuteronomy xxiii. 19, 20, Calvin draws our attention to the way the Latin *nomen usurae* became misused to apply to what was correctly called *foenus*, and remarks that the Israelites fell into similar tergiversation, whereby *therbith*, meaning increment, was used as an euphemism for *neshek*, meaning fenory.[16] And further,

> *Ubi vertimus, Non eris sicut foenerator, in voce Hebraica* nashac *aliqua est ambiguitas: quia verbum* nashac *interdum generaliter accipitur pro mutuum dare, absque sinistra nota: hic vero dubium non est quin pro foeneratore sumatur, qui miseros arrodit.*

> Where we have translated the words, 'Thou shalt not be to him as an ockerer', in the Hebrew word *nashac* there is some ambiguity, for it is sometimes used to mean to lend, without any bad sense, but here it is undoubtedly applied to an ockerer who grinds poor wretches.[17]

Similarly, when David denounced fenory, he used the word *neshek*, which derives from the word 'biting', and so clearly refers only to fenory, showing that usuries were condemned only when they entailed robbery and plunder. But this biting usury is what most people call simply 'usury'.[18] In the usual and narrow sense, all usury is biting: it eats up the borrower's resources. As Capel puts it,

---

[15] Erasmus, *Ecclesiastes sive Concionatur Evangelicus sive De Ratione Concionandi*, lib. ii, in Erasmus, *Opera Omnia*, 10 vols, Leiden, 1706, vol. v, col. 932 (E–F); and see *idem*, *De Puritate Tabernaculi sive Ecclesiae Christianae*, in *Opera Omnia*, vol. v, cols 298 (B), 306 (C)–307 (A); *idem*, *Ecclesiastes*, col. 897 (C–D); *idem*, *Collectanea Adagiorum Veterum*, in *Opera Omnia*, vol. ii, chilia ii, cent. vi, Prov. lx, col. 610 (E).

[16] J. Calvin, *Commentarii in Libros Mosis necum in Librum Josue*, Amsterdam, 1567, p. 527.

[17] Ibid., p. 528.

[18] J. Calvin, *Commentarii in Librum Psalmorum*, Amsterdam, 1567, p. 47.

It is true that Ainsworth in his translation renders it *biting* usury, not that there is any usury not biting, but that all usury doth bite ... He observes that it is fitly called *biting*, because usury bites and consumes the borrower and his substance, and very few takers of usury save their owne by it, but the most of them are utterly undone and bitten as 'twere to death by it ... John Rainold ... holds this distinction betwixt *biting* and *not biting* usury ... to be but a mere flam.[19]

As for the distinction, all too often slurred over, between *usura* and *foenus*, and the introduction of 'interest' as a euphemism for fenory, Calvin gives a good explanation: *foenus* was so fiercely hated that the word itself became too disgraceful for usurers and their clients, so that *usura*, which was still proper and acceptable, was substituted as an euphemism.[20] (Doc. 4)

From all this, Calvin concludes,

> *Ita nomen usurae, quum re ipsa tantundem valeat ac foenus, integumentum est rei odiosae: quasi vero talibus cavillis se a Dei judicio expediant, ubi sola integritas ad defensionem valet.*

> Thus the word *usura*, since the thing itself is equivalent to *foenus*, is a covering for an odious thing: as if such cavillings would excuse oneself from God's judgement, where integrity alone serves for defence.[21]

But this use of the words *usura* and *foenus* derives directly from Roman civil law. This, in some form at least, had long been practised in the Rhineland and thereabouts, in southern France and Geneva, and had recently gained a footing in Scotland, especially in private law. Roman civil law had also recently been adopted in the *Reichskammergericht* as something of an interstate or common law for all Germany, but took little or no hold in Saxony and other northern parts where the *Sachsenspiegel* system of customary law and its Germanic terminology reigned as strong as ever.[22] It was Roman civil law that Calvin studied in the university of Orleans, and perhaps in that of Bourges.[23] In adopting this Roman usage,

---

19 R. Capel, *Tentations: their nature, danger, cure; to which is added a Brief Dispute touching Restitution in the Case of Usury*, 5th edn, 1655, 2nd pagination, pp. 291–2; and see Pie, op. cit., pp. 22, 45; H. Smith, *The Works of Henry Smith; including sermons, treatises, prayers and poems*, 2 vols, Edinburgh, 1866, vol. i, pp. 90–91.

20 Calvin, *Praelectiones*, p. 170. Cf. Emperor Justinian, *Corpus Juris Civilis*, eds P. Krueger, R. Schoell and W. Kroll, 3 vols, Berlin, 1906–12, vol. i, pp. 132, 320 seqq.

21 Calvin, *Commentarii in Libros Mosis*, p. 527.

22 Capel, op. cit. 2nd pagination, pp. 293–4; P. Vinogradoff, *Roman Law in Mediaeval Europe*, 1909, pp. 19 seqq., 32 seqq., 46 seqq., 59 seqq., 80–81, 84–5, 106 seqq., 112–15, 125 seqq.; St T. Aquinas, *Summa Theologica*, II, ii, qu. 78, art. I, ad tertium dicendum, in St T. Aquinas, *Opera*, 28 vols, Venice, 1775–88, vol. xxii, p. 323.

23 T. Beza, *The Life of John Calvin*, in J. Calvin, *Tracts relating to the Reformation*, vol. i, ed. H. Beveridge, Edinburgh, 1844, pp. xii, xiii; St Bernardine, *Quadragesimale de Evangelio Aeterno: Caritatis et ... de Usura*, sermo XXXVIII, art. III, cap. iii, in St Bernardine, *Opera*, 5 vols, Venice, 1745, vol. ii, pp. 222–3.

Calvin was preceded by Bucer,[24] and much earlier by St Ambrose (340–97), who was steeped in Roman civil law and preferred *foenus* rather than *usura* when intending the narrow sense.[25] Beza frequently follows the same usage, as in his poetic rendering of the response to the question in Psalm 15, 'Lord, who shall sojourn in thy tabernacle?': '*Infames numerat nullos qui foenore nummos*' – 'He considers none of those who put money out to fenory'.[26] Heinrich Bullinger employs the same terminology, by which usury included not only the lending of money and goods, but also the letting of goods or real estate, so that it was only the abuse of the word 'usury' that made it into something dishonest.[27] (Doc. 5)

According to this terminology, and according to civil law, usury included letting land to farm, stock-and-land leases and letting sheep or cows to farm, all of which were always freely allowed by Christians and never considered usurious in the usual and narrow sense.[28] Both Bucer, the reformer at Strasburg,[29] and Oecolampadius, the one at Basle, adopted this broad sense. After quoting, in part, Ezekiel xii. 12 as '*Usuram et foenus accepisti*' – 'Thou hast taken usury and *foenus*', the latter comments,

> *Usuram autem maxime notat. In qua consideretur inclementia erga proximum, potius quam recepisse aliquid ultra sortem, et animus avarus pontissimum arguit foeneratorem.*

> But most of all he notes usury, in which abides harshness against one's neighbour, rather than to have taken anything above the

---

[24] Hopf, op. cit., pp. 122–5; Bucer, *Scripta Anglicana*, p. 789; *idem, Enarrationum in Evangelia Matthaei, Marci, et Lucae*, Strasburg, 1527, fo. 181ᵛ.

[25] St Ambrose, *Epistolarum Classis I*, Epistola xix, in St Ambrose, *Sancti Ambrosii Mediolanensis Episcopi Opera*, 8 vols, Venice, 1781, vol. iii, p. 889; *idem, De Excessu Fratris Sui Satyri*, lib. I, para. iii (*Opera*, vol. iv, p. 172); *idem, Expositio Evangelii Secundum Lucam*, lib. VIII, para. 93–4 (*Opera*, vol. ii, p. 1040); *idem, Enarrationes in XII Psalmos Davidicos*, para. lxii (*Opera*, vol. ii, pp. 93–4); *idem, De Tobia*, lib. I, cap. ii, para. 7, 8; cap. iii, para. 9, 10; cap. iv, para. 12, 13; cap. v, vi, vii; cap. xii, para. 40, 42 (*Opera*, vol. i, pp. 719 seqq., 733–4).

[26] T. Beza, *Poemata: Psalmi Davidici XXX; Sylvae; Elegiae; Epigrammatica, sine loco*, 1576, pp. 33–4; but see also C. Marot and T. de Bèze, *Les Pseaumes de David*, Amsterdam, 1700; *idem, Les Psaumes de David*, Hamburg, 1716, p. 25.

[27] H. Bullinger, *Sermonum Decades quinque, de potissimis Christianae Religionis captibus, in tres tomes digestae*, Zurich, 1557, fos 93ᵛ–4.

[28] Bernardine, *Quadragesimale de Evangelio Aeterno*, sermo XXXVI, art. I, cap. iii; sermo XXXVII, art. I, cap. ii, iii; sermo XL, art. I, cap. i, iii; art. II, cap. i, ii (*Opera*, vol. ii, pp. 208, 213–14, 233–6); St T. Aquinas, *Questiones Disputatae de Malo*, qu. 13, art. IV, resp., art. iv (*Opera*, vol. xv, p. 211); Alexander (of) Hales, *Summa Theologice*, Leiden, 1516, fo. 143 (questio L, membrum 3); R. Middleton (Ricardus de Media Villa), *Sententiarum Questiones Persubtilissime*, 4 bks, Venice, 1507–09, lib. IV, dist. xv, art. v, qu. 5 (fo. 75); W. T. Mellows and P. I. King, *The Book of William Morton, almoner of Peterborough Monastery 1448–67*, Northamptonshire Record Society 1954 (1951–53) xvi, pp. 14, 15, 54, 104, 155; cf. Intro. by C. N. L. Brooke, pp. xxxv–vi.

[29] Bucer, *Enarrationum*, fo. 181.

principal, and such an avaricious spirit betokens an overvaunting ockerer.[30]

Most learned Christians, however, usually or commonly equated the words *usura* and *foenus*, as did those great men Sts Bernardine[31] and Thomas Aquinas.[32] Melanchthon, too, writes, under the title 'De Usuris':

> *Usura seu foenus hoc est, cum dans mutuo pecuniam et non emens fundum, vel certum reditum in fundo, sed exploratum habens, quando sit recepturus pecuniam, seu sortem, insuper tamen paciscitur et aufert lucrum aliquod supra sortem, tantum ratione mutuationis, seu propter officium mutuationis.*

> Usury or fenory is this, when granting money in a loan, and not buying a landed estate or fixed rent in a landed estate, but when one is assured the money or principal will be repaid, it is nevertheless additionally agreed that one take some gain over and above the principal, merely by reason of the loan or on account of the service of lending.[33]

This usage conforms more closely to that of the practical, everyday world. Melanchthon here equates *usura* and *foenus* and treats them both as equivalent to what the common man called usury or ocker. Elsewhere he usually contents himself with distinguishing usurious loans from those made without any thought of gain.[34] In so doing, he conforms to the general German practice, exemplified in the writings of Luther and Zwingli, of simply distinguishing Christian lending from *Wucher*, meaning ocker, fenory or usury in the narrow popular sense. Luther anticipated Calvin in noticing how the euphemistic use of the word *interesse* had crept in: '*Es ist ein Wörtlin, das heisset auff Latin,* Interesse. *Das edle, thewre, zarte Wörtlin*' – 'There is a little word that is called in Latin *Interesse*. That

---

30 J. Oecolampadius, *Commentarii Omnes in Libros Prophetarum*, 2 vols in 1 (Geneva), 1553–58, vol. ii, pp. 117–18.

31 St Bernardine, *Quadragesimale de Religione Christiana*, sermo VII, art. II, cap. iv; sermo XXXIII, art. I, cap. iii; art. II, cap. iii; sermo XXXV, art. I, cap. ii, art. II, ad init.; art. III, cap. i; cap. iv, ad init.; cap. v, ad init. (*Opera*, vol. i, pp. 29, 144, 146, 153–4, 157–8); *idem*, *Quadragesimale de Evangelio Aeterno*, sermo XVI, art. III, cap. ii; sermo XXXVI, art. ii, cap. ii; art. III, cap. viii; sermo XXXVIII, art. iii, cap. iii; sermo XXXIX, art. I, ad init. (*Opera*, vol. ii, pp. 96, 208, 211, 222, 224–5); *idem*, *Duo Adventualia*, sermo XXXV, tertia pars principalis (*Opera*, vol. iii, p. 223).

32 Aquinas, as Chapter 1, note 40; and see in addition *idem*, *Opera*, vol. xxviii, p. 341.

33 P. Melanchthon, *Conciones Explicantes Integrum Evangelium: S. Matthaei (Breves Commentarii in Matthaeum)*, in P. Melanchthon, *Operum Reverendi Viri Philippi Melanthonis*, 4 pts (vols), Wittemberg, 1562–67, vol. iii, p. 311; and see *idem*, *Philosophae Moralis Epitomes*, in P. Melanchthon, *Opera quae supersunt Omnia*, 28 vols, Halle and Brunswick, 1834–60, vol. xvi, cols 128–30.

34 P. Melanchthon, *Enarratio Psalmi Dixit Dominus, et aliquot Sequentium scripta Anno MDXLII et sequenti*, in *Operum*, vol. ii, pp. 771–2; *idem*, *Conciones Explicantes*, in *Operum*, vol. iii, pp. 312–13.

grand, precious, delicate little word.' He himself uses it occasionally, but only euphemistically, to give colour in argument. He almost always called *Wucher* by its real name.[35]

Martin Bucer brought a different approach to the subject of the legality of usury, when the word was used in its broad sense. In an inevitably circumlocutory, opaque way, Bucer seems to justify usury, as he defines it, when it was a reward for risking capital, which most people called gain or interest under the title of *periculum sortis*.[36] (Doc. 6)

Usura or usury might be used either in a broad or a narrow sense, while *Wucher* or ocker, had only a narrow and derogatory one. Depending on whether usury were taken as broad or narrow, the same set of beliefs would manifest themselves in one or the other of two sets of terminologies. Those who took the broad sense, had then often to distinguish it from usury in the narrow sense by referring to it as 'biting usury' and then to catalogue all legitimate forms of usury under the extrinsic titles to interest allowed by canon law and by all Christians, and at the same time take care to avoid using 'interest' as an euphemism for unlawful usury. But those who used the word 'usury' in the broad sense, which included rents from land as well as legitimate interest under any of the titles, though etymologically correct, ran into great practical difficulties, for they had then to find circumlocutions to enable them to distinguish, and stigmatize, fenory, ocker, or 'biting' usury. In their terms, usury as such was not at all forbidden by God; He allowed usury to those who were lawfully entitled to it, and forbade only biting usury, to which there could be no lawful title. Calvin was thus forced into trying to specify all over again what was lawful and what unlawful usury, what allowed by Scripture and what not. Since he only admits the use of the words *usura* and *foenus*, and then *usura* in the broad sense, and rigorously eschews both the term 'interest' and the names of all the lawful entitlements to it, when faced with the problem of imposing legal limits on rates of interest, in order to prevent the exaction of excessive and harsh rates of 'interest' as a cover for 'biting' usury, he can do so in no form of words other than one that specifies a legal limit on the rate of usury. His difficulties are well exemplified in a letter he wrote in response to an enquiry about usury, where he was forced to resort to long-winded circumlocution when he tried to define usury in its narrow sense.[37] (Doc. 7)

Calvin's terminology was confusing to most people and has lured some writers into the error of supposing that Calvin allowed all usury in the narrow, normal and popular use of the term. But this was very far removed

35 M. Luther, *Grosser Sermon vom Wucher*, in *Alle Bücher und Schrifften*, vol. i, fos 195–6; and see fo. 193ᵛ.

36 Bucer, *Enarrationum*, fos 181ᵛ–2.

37 J. Calvin, *Epistolae et Responsa*, Geneva, 1575, pp. 355–7.

from his beliefs and teachings. He was in step with Luther, Melanchthon and Zwingli in condemning what most people called usury, ocker or *Wucher* and in allowing what was correctly and honestly called interest. He only allowed usury provided it was conducted under strict provisions and in full accordance with a true Christian conscience. This, however, made little or no practical difference, for no one ever complained of usury conducted in this ideal way.

This terminological division and this essential theological unity are displayed in all Calvin's work on the subjects of usury and interest. To avoid using the term *titulus morae*, he is compelled to say:

> *Debitor si tergiversando tempus extraxerit cum dispendio et molestia creditoris, an consentaneum erit eum ex mala fide et frustratione lucrum capere? Nemo certe (ut arbitror) negabit usuras creditori solvendas esse praeter sortem ut pensetur ejus jactura.*

> If the debtor have shiftily defaulted on the time, to the loss and trouble of the creditor, will it be reasonable that he should profit from his bad faith and deception? Surely no one, I think, will deny that usuries over and above the principal ought to be paid to the creditor to compensate his loss.

To avoid using some such term as rent-charge or rent seck, Calvin has to say:

> *Si quis locuples qui erit in suis nummis, fundum emere volens partem aliquam summae ab altero mutuetur: qui pecuniam numerat, annon poterit ex fundi reditu fructum aliquem percipere, donec sors repraesentata fuerit?*

> If any responsible moneyed man, wanting to buy a landed estate, should borrow some part of the sum from another, may not he who pays out the money receive some income from the rent of the land until the principal be repaid?

It follows inexorably from the terminology Calvin adopts, that not all usury is ungodly:

> *Verum excipient qui contra sentiunt, simpliciter standum esse Dei judicio, qui generaliter omne foenus populo suo interdicit. Respondeo, nonnisi de pauperibus haberi sermonem, ideoque si cum divitibus negotium sit, liberum jus foenerandi permitti: quia Legislator rem unam notando, alteram de qua subticet, videtur non damnare. Si rursus objiciant, foeneratores a David et Ezechiele in totum damnari, sententias illas ad normam charitatis exigi debere arbitror: ideoque non damnari nisi improbas exactiones, quibus creditor, posthabita aequitate, debitorem suum onerat ac premit ... Unde sequitur usuras hodie non esse illicitas, nisi quatenus cum aequitate et fraterna conjunctione pugnant.*

> It is true, those who entertain the contrary opinion simply abide by the judgement of God when He generally prohibits fenory to His

people. My answer is, the passage has to do only with the poor, and therefore if we have to do business with the rich, to take fenory is freely allowed. Because the Lawgiver in alluding to one thing, is not to be taken to condemn another He says nothing about. If in return they object, that usurers are totally condemned by David and Ezekiel, I think their opinions ought to be judged in the light of the rule of charity and therefore usurers are not to be condemned unless they make wicked exactions, where the creditor, having cast off charity, burdens and oppresses his debtor ... From this it follows, usuries are not nowadays unlawful, unless and in so far as repugnant to equity and brotherly association.[38]

It is interesting that Calvin does not press the argument to its logical conclusion, that it is no sin to lend on fenory to a pauper, provided it is done with the sincere intention of helping him.[39]

Calvin's views might be roughly summed up as follows. Usury is all right in the broad sense, but not in the narrow, especially not when exacted from the poor. This perhaps justifies Fenton's wisecrack, that, 'Calvin deals with usurie as the apothecarie with poyson'.[40] A rich man in his right senses will not pay fenory; he will take a loan with formal contracts and covenants and after agreement on contingent entitlements to genuine interest. Nevertheless, usury was practised on the extravagant rich,[41] especially on wild youths and reckless landowners.[42] Calvin's suggestion that usury might rightly be taken from the rich is absurd. The argument, that simply because usury was disallowed on the poor, it must be allowable on the rich, contains a plain *non sequitur*, as Jewel and others, notably Capel, pointed out.

Besides, what was lent to the rich could not be lent to the poor, and usurers preferred rich clients. The Mosaic law, says Capel, is that usury be not done upon the poor Jews. We are forbidden to rob the poor, but this does not mean we may rob the rich. Whether against rich or poor, usury is a sin. It is a sin to oppress the poor, 'Yet I hope it is a sinne to oppresse the rich, though or because he is rich'.[43] All that the rest of Calvin's verbiage amounts to is, genuine interest is allowable; his research resulted in the discovery of what everybody else knew already.

---

[38] Calvin, *Commentarii in Libros Mosis*, p. 528.

[39] Middleton, op. cit., lib. IV, dist. xv, art. v, qu. 5 (fo. 75); Smith, *Works*, vol. i, pp. 97–8.

[40] R. Fenton, *A Treatise of Usurie*, 1611, p. 61.

[41] Bernardine, *Quadragesimale de Religione Christiana*, sermo XXXV, art. I, cap. i (*Opera*, vol. i, p. 152).

[42] D. North, *Discourse upon Trade; principally directed to the cases of the interest, coynage, clipping, increase of money*, 1691, pp. 6, 7.

[43] J. Jewel, *The Works of John Jewel*, ed. J. Ayre, Parker Society, 4 vols, 1845–50, vol. iv, p. 1294; Capel, op. cit., 1st pagination, p. 267; 2nd pagination, p. 292; Anon., *The Death of Usury*, pp. 28–9, 31–3.

When Calvin tries to reconcile his terminology with that of the Bible and of the generality of Christians, he runs into difficulties. Ezekiel (xviii. 17 and xxii. 12) seems to condemn all remuneration for all kinds of loans. Now this is precisely the broad sense of 'usury' that Calvin has bound himself to follow, even though this entails allowing and approving some kinds of it. In this quandary, he has to resort to putting a gloss on Ezekiel, saying,

> *Sed non dubium est quin ad injustas et captiosas lucrandi artes respiciat, quibus divites egenam plebem rodebant ... Hic inter alia peccata Ezechiel foenus commemorat. Nomen usurae proprie non convenit huic loco.*

> But he is doubtless considering rather the unjust and crafty artifices by which rich men gnawed away the poor and needy ... Here, among other crimes, Ezechiel numbers fenory. The word usury is not properly suited to this passage.[44]

According to St Luke vi. 35, Jesus said, '*Mutuum date, nihil inde sperantes*' – 'Lend, hoping for nothing again', which seems to enjoin us to hope for nothing back, or at least nothing beyond the principal. According to Calvin, the 'nothing' is not to be taken to refer to usury or anything over and above the principal.

> *Haec sententia perperam restricta fuit ad usuras ... Nunc videmus particulam. Nihil perperam de foenore exponi quod ad sortem accedit: quum quantum hortetur Christus ad gratuita officia.*

> This sentence was erroneously restricted to usuries ... Now we see the word *Nihil* to be wrongly expounded concerning fenory, which is added to the principal, when at the most Christ is exhorting us to do our duty freely and for nothing.[45]

Again, from Ezekiel and Psalm 15,

> *Videtur itaque ... foenus per se esse illicitum. Sed quia Lex Dei complectitur summam et perfectam justitiam, ideo tenendum est, foenus nisi cum Lege Dei pugnet, non esse prorsus damnabile: alioque ignominia, ut apparet, irrogatur Legi Dei, nisi praescribat nobis veram et integram juste vivendi regulam. Atque in Lege ea est perfectio, ad quam nihil possit accedere. Si ergo volumus statuere an foenus sit illicitum, necesse est venire ad normam Legis, quae fallere non potest. Atque non reperiemus quodlibet foenus esse Legi contrarium. Hinc ergo sequitur, necque semper foenus posse damnari.*

> It seems ... fenory is in itself unlawful. But because God's law embraces complete and perfect justice, it must be held that fenory is not

---

44 Calvin, *Commentarii in Librum Psalmorum*, p. 47; idem, *Praelectiones*, p. 169.

45 Calvin, *Commentarii in Quatuor Evangelistas necnon in Acta Apostolorum*, Amsterdam, 1567, p. 74. I have used Authorized Version for translation. Revised Version has 'Lend, never despairing', the import of which escapes me, unless taken as never despairing of repayment, which would seem against the sense.

altogether to be condemned, unless it opposes God's law. Yet, as is obvious, ignominy is heaped upon the law of God, unless He is prescribing us a true and complete rule for living justly. But yet in this law there is perfection, to which nothing can be added. If, then, we wish to determine if fenory be illicit, it is necessary to resort to the rule of secular law, which cannot deceive. And yet we would not discover all fenory whatsoever to be against law. Hence it consequentially follows that fenory is not always to be condemned.[46]

But this isolates, and places undue emphasis on, the exception that proves the rule.

In practice, Calvin found his terminology and approach to the question of usury and interest made it difficult for him to decide whether a particular credit transaction was licit or not. Thus when a member of the French Reformed Church enquires, 'Whether it be lawful, and when I may put out my money unto interest?', presumably meaning usury in the broad sense, Calvin answers:

> I would never advise any man to put his money out to interest, if he can employ it any ways else. Yet when a man's whole estate doth lie in ready money, he may well contract with such and such persons, that upon such and such terms it may be lawful for him to receive benefit and profit thereby. But he must be very careful, that he do not let loose the reins to demand, and take excessive gains, as is the custom and practice of too, too many, nor should he grieve or grind the face of that poor man with whom he hath contracted, nor endammage the publick interest by his own private benefit. Wherefore upon the whole, I dare not approve of any interest, till I do first know how, and upon what terms, articles and conditions, and with what persons you do transact herein.

In reply to another enquiry, '*Si les ministres peuvent bailler argent à profit*' – 'If ministers might lend money at a profit', Calvin first admits, '*Je n'oseroys pas affermer qu'il ne soit licite*' – 'I would not dare to declare it not licit', then declines to give a direct answer, lest it lead to misunderstanding:

> *Le plus seur et expédient seroit de ne point entrer en telles pratiques ou contracts ... Ainsi quand ung ministre se passera de faire tel profict, ce sera bien le meilleur ... Mais pource que cela est plus supportable que de marchander ou mener quelque train dont il soit distrait de son office, je ne voy point le fait doive estre condamné en général. Mais cependant je vouldroys bien qu'on y gardast telle modération que ce ne fut point pour en tirer profit certain, mais qu'on se contentast, en baillant son argent à quelque marchant homme de bien, de se rapporter à sa foy et sa loiauité à ce qu'il en fist profit équitable, selon que Dieu feroit prospérer son labeur.*

The surest and most expedient thing would be not to enter at all into such practices or contracts ... So, when a minister would stand to

---

[46] Calvin, *Praelectiones*, p. 170.

make such a profit, this would be much the best ... But because that is more tolerable than engaging in trade or taking some course by which he would be distracted from his office, I do not see at all why this action should be generally condemned. But, nevertheless, I would certainly hope that one take care to use such moderation that this never be done to draw an assured profit, but that one content oneself, in lending one's money to a merchant of means, to conform with one's faith and uprightness, that he make a fair and equitable profit, according to how God shall prosper his work.[47]

Considering he was handling the matters at arm's length, these replies were not unreasonable, but still betray the difficulty he found himself in when called upon to decide a specific case. Nevertheless, these letters make clear that the only forms of usury Calvin would approve were not usury in the narrow sense, but contracts such as partnership, where the investor's return was uncertain, where it was not ocker.

Bullinger's adoption of Bucer's terminology and approach led him into similar difficulties. Having succeeded Zwingli in Zurich, he found that reality compelled the passage of the *Zins-und Wuchermandate* of 1545 and 1548, by which *Wucher*, and so called, was strictly forbidden. Then, in 1558, a maximum rate was laid upon domestic interest payments. Despite all their theorizing, when it came to practical action, the clergy of the Reformed Church had to admit, '*Wir verstehen nicht so viel von weltichen Dingen, und lasend wir gar gern andrer dervon reden, die es bas verstand als wir*' – 'We do not understand worldly matters very much, and are perfectly happy to leave the judgement of them to others who understand them better than we do'.[48]

But all Calvin's difficulties are of his own making; they arise solely from his insistence on rigidly adhering to the broad sense of 'usury'. We should be deluding ourselves if we for one moment imagined that Calvin regarded ocker (usury in the narrow and common sense) with anything but the utmost loathing.

Roman civil-law terminology was so impossibly difficult and cumbersome to apply in the real world, that Calvin's followers mostly eschewed it. The French Reformed Church employed *usure* in the common and narrow sense. The Dutch Reformed Church used the words *woucker*, *woecker* and *woekerie*, meaning ocker, and *woeckener*, meaning ockerer. These were always, and still are, the Netherlands words for these things, just as *woekerdier* means an animal parasite and *woekerplant* a vegetable

---

47 J. Quick, *Synodicon in Gallia Reformata, or the Acts, Decisions, Decrees and Canons of those famous National Councils of the Reformed Church in France*, 1692, pp. 76, 79, 80; J. Calvin, *Lettres de Jean Calvin*, ed. J. Bonnet, 2 vols, Paris, 1854, vol. ii, pp. 451–2; *idem*, *Letters of John Calvin*, ed. J. Bonnet, 4 vols, New York, 1972, vol. iv, pp. 252–3.

48 E. Dollfus-Zodel, *Bullingers Einfluss auf das züricherische Staatswesen von 1531–1575*, Zurich, 1931, p. 44.

one. The new usage never caught on widely. Even English versions of the Geneva Bible, including the so-called Breeches Bible (1560), gave the relevant part of Psalm 15 as 'He that giveth not his money to usury'. This hardly differs from Luther's '*Wer sein Geld nicht auff Zinsen gibt*', or from the Jesuit Bellarmine's '*Qui pecuniam suam non dedit ad usuram*', or from Beza's '*Qui d'usure se gardera*' and '*Qui ne donne point son argent à usure*'. Beza and his associates, when writing in Latin, commonly used *foenus*, and one edition of the Bible (1581), whose translators referred to Beza's work, used *foenori* in Psalm 15. But, as Divine says, 'As much as they differed in matters of theory, the systems of Calvinism and scholasticism are one in their practical conclusions'.[49] Whatever terminology they preferred, all Christians of all denominations whatsoever vied with each other in denouncing usury in the common, narrow sense of the word. If, in this matter, Protestants were distinguished from others, it was only in that they bent themselves to study the subject all over again and mostly preached about usury and interest in ways and words that the common man could readily understand. They were the new brooms that swept clean.

Christ's injunction that we should 'Lend, hoping for nothing again' (Luke vi. 35), Luther explained to his flock in these words:

> *Ir solt leihen also, das ir nichts davon hoffet, das ist, ir solt frey dahin leihen und wagen, obs euch wider werde oder nicht: wirds wider, das mans neme; wirds nicht wider, das geschenckt sey ... Denn wer also leihet, das ers besser oder mehr widernemen wil, das ist ein öffentlicher und verdampter Wucher.*

> You should so lend, that you hope for nothing therefrom, that is, you should lend for free and risk whether it comes back to you or not: should it come back, then one takes it; should it not come back, it be a gift ... For who so lends that he wants it back better or more, that is open and damnable ocker.[50]

He continues:

---

[49] J. H. Hessels, *Ecclesiae Londino-Batavae Archivum*, 3 vols, Cambridge, 1887–97, vol. iii, pp. 213, 221–2, 224–5, 228, 391, 398, 401–4, 421, 425, 427, 430, 443, 467; T. F. Divine, *Interest: An Historical and Analytical Study in Economics and Modern Ethics*, Milwaukee, WI, 1959, p. 88; Marot and de Bèze, *Pseaumes*, Ps. xv; *idem*, *Psaumes*, p. 25; Beza, *Poemata*, 33–4; R. Bellarmine, *Explanatio in Psalmos*, Leiden, 1858, pp. 58–9; Psalm XV, in *Biblia*, Dordrecht, 1729; *Biblia Sacra Utriusque Testamenti*, Zurich, 1539; *Biblia Sacrosancta Testamenti Veteris et Novi*, Zurich, 1543; *Bibliorum Codex Sacer et Authenticus, Testamenti Utriusque Veteris et Novi*, Zurich, 1564; *Biblia Utriusque Testamenti, sine loco*, 1557; *Testamenti Veteris Biblia Sacra*, 1581; *Testamenti Biblia Sacra sive Libri Canonici*, Geneva, 1530; *The Bible (Breeches Bible)*, Geneva, 1560; *The Bible*, Geneva, 1606; *Testamenti Veteris Biblia Sacra*, Geneva, 1630; Psalm XIV, *Biblia Sacra Vulgate Editionis Sixti Quinti*, Frankfurt on the Main, 1826; *Holy Bible* translated from Latin Vulgate, Douai (1609) 4 vols, 1750.

[50] Luther, *Von Kauffshandlung* (1524), in *Alle Bücher und Schrifften*, vol, ii, fo. 474.

Das ist ein Schalcksauge des Geitzs, das nur auffs Nehesten notdurfft sihet, nicht der selben zu helffen, sondern sich der selben zu bessern und mit seines Nehesten Schaden reich zu werden. Das sind alles öffentliche Diebe, Reuber und Wucherer.

That is the deepest depth of greed, that just looks upon a neighbour's want and need as an opportunity not to help him but to enrich oneself and become wealthy through one's neighbour's loss. Those who do that are all daylight robbers, thieves and ockerers.[51]

Elsewhere he said:

Das Leihen oder Borgen sol geschehen frey ... Das alle sampt Wücherer sind, die Wein, Korn, Gelt und was des ist, jrem Nehesten also leihen, das sie ubers Jar oder benante Zeit dieselben zu Zinsen verpflichten, oder doch beschweren und uberladen, dass sie mehr oder ein anders wider geben müssen, das besser ist, denn sie geborget haben.

The loan or credit should be extended freely and for nothing ... They are fully fledged usurers who lend their neighbours wine, corn, money or whatever it is, so that they bind themselves to pay usuries by the year or at a specified time, or howsoever they load and overburden themselves in having to give back more or better than they borrowed.[52]

Luther comments further, that to lend wine, corn, money or whatever else in order to take back more or better, '*Das sind Jüdische Stücklin und Tücklin*' – 'Those are little Jewish arts and tricks'.[53] Later in life, exhorting Lutheran pastors to preach against usury, Luther explained that, 'Whoever lends and takes back something for the lending, he is a usurer'.[54] (Doc. 8) Not only Christians, but also Solon, Alexander the Great, the Romans, Julius Caesar, Hostiensis, Cicero, Aristotle, Cato and others, the heathens – they all reckoned usurers double-dyed thieves and murderers.[55]

Luther made not the slightest concession to usury. It made no difference whether the borrower were rich or poor:

Es legt ein Bürger sechs Jar lang zu einem Kauffman ein, zwey tausent Gülden, damit sol der Kauffman handeln, gewinnen oder verlieren, und dem Bürger jerlich zwey hundert Gülden gewisser Zinse davon geben, was er aber darüber gewinnet ist sein. Gewinnet er aber nichts, mus er doch die Zinse geben. Und der Bürger thut dem Kauffman

---

51 Ibid., fo. 475ᵛ.

52 Luther, *Grosser Sermon*, 192ᵛ–3. *Zins* means usury (erron. 'interest') when referring to loans, rent when referring to real estate, and tribute when referring to dues. Here I have translated *Zins* as usury, in accordance with Luther's practice equating *Zins* with *Wucher* in his translation of the Bible, see 2 Mose xxii. 24; 3 Mose xxv. 36–7; 5 Mose xxiii. 20–21; Nehemia v. 7; Psalm xv. 5; Hesekiel xxii. 12; Matthaeus xxv. 27; Lukas xix. 23.

53 M. Luther, *Kleiner Sermon vom Wucher*, in *Alle Bücher und Schrifften*, vol. i, fo. 199ᵛ.

54 M. Luther, *An die Pfarrherrn wider den Wucher zu predigen Vermanung*, 1540, in *Alle Bücher und Schrifften*, vol. vii, fos 397–9.

55 Ibid., fos 401ᵛ–2.

*grossen Dienst daran, denn der Kauffman meinet mit zwey tausent
wol drey hundert zu gewinnen. Widerumb thut der Kauffman dem
Bürger einen grossen Dienst daran, denn sein Gelt müsste sonst stille
ligen und kein gewin bringen. Wie dis gemeine Stücklin unrecht sey
und ein rechter Wucher, hab ich im Sermon vom Wucher gnugsam
erzelet.*

A burgess puts out to a merchant for a period of six years, 2000
guilders, with which the merchant is to trade, win or lose, and from it
give the burgess by the year 200 guilders of assured increase, but
what he gains over and above is his. But if he gains nothing, he must
still pay the increase. And in this the burgess does the merchant a
great service, for the merchant means to gain a good 300 with the
2000. Conversely, the merchant does the burgess a great service in
this, for otherwise his money must lie idle and bring no gain. How
this common little trick be unjust and a right usury, I have sufficiently
explained in the Sermon on Usury.[56]

When questioned on the subject, Luther's express word was that,

*öffentlicher Wucherer soll man in pann thun, wie ich dem Edelman
gethan habe, das ist, man soll im nicht das Sacrament geben. – Tum
quidam, Quid, si poeniteret? – Respondit, Das hatt sein mass. Er
muss aber ein Zacchaeus werden, was er zu vill geraubt hatt,
widergeben, denen ers abgeschunden hatt.*

A manifest usurer one should excommunicate, that is, one should not
give him the sacrament. – Then to this, What if he be penitent? – He
answered, He has his mass. But he must become a Zaccheus, give
back in full what he has stolen to whom he skinned it off.[57]

That Luther relentless opposed all usury is beyond doubt. Melanchthon
was no less opposed, and he, too, made a careful distinction between
usury and lending by *contractum mutuationis*, that is, lending or granting
credit gratis, but with a bond stipulating the due date for repayment or
settlement and with the debtor binding himself in an agreed sum of money
either to settle his debt on the due date or to forfeit his bond and so pay
the agreed penalty, or, alternatively, with the creditor's approval, to pay
an agreed or arbitrated rate of interest under *titulus morae* for his
forbearance in not having the debtor's bond forfeited. This meant nothing
was charged for the loan or credit itself and so no usury was taken. Such
non-usurious contracts were standard form in commercial and financial
transactions in England and, evidently, in Saxony, and, presumably, in the
rest of Germany and in the whole of the Holy Roman Empire.[58] (Doc. 9)

---

[56] M. Luther, *Von Kauffshandlung*, fo. 477ᵛ.

[57] M. Luther, *Tischreden*, in *Luthers Werke in Auswahl*, 8 vols, Berlin, 1930–35, vol.
viii, ed. O. Clemen, 276–7 (no. 5216).

[58] P. Melanchthon, *Conciones Explicantes Integrum Evangelium*, in *Operum*, vol. iii,
pp. 312–13.

Melanchthon points out that,

Differunt enim mutuatio piorum et impiorum ... Deinde continet hic locus etiam utilem doctrinam, de contractibus, quod Deus approbet contractus, quia hic et praecipit et ornat promissionibus. Item quod officia contractum recte facta, sint cultus Dei ... Iudicium de contractibus et de usuris, ut de alijs rebus politicis, petendum esse a Magistratu civili, hoc est, ab ipsis legibus recte et sane intellectis, et consentientibus cum ratione ... Etsi enim alicubi permittunt usuras, non tamen approbant, quia Leges non possunt omnibus vicijs mederi.

Lending by the godly and by the ungodly differ indeed. Then here also stands a useful doctrine, of contracts, that God approves contracts, because He is present and joins in and brings honour to the promises. Likewise, what obligations are rightly entered into by contract are to the honour of God ... The trial of contracts and of usuries, like other political matters, is to be administered by the civil magistracy, that is, by their laws correctly and sensibly understood and consistent with reason ... And even if they nevertheless let some usuries pass here and there, though they approve them not, it is because laws cannot rectify all offences.[59]

Melanchthon says the only one to gain from usury was the usurer, and goes on to delineate precisely the demarcation between usury on the one hand and credit and lending by legitimate contract on the other.[60] (Doc. 10) Elsewhere, too, Melanchthon explains usury in the traditional way, as payment for the mere act of lending.[61] (Doc. 11) In a catechism for boys, Melanchthon deals with usury as clearly and simply as possible, and in just the same sense.[62] (Doc. 12) No writer on the subject of usury was more consistent than was Melanchthon. Zwingli differed from Luther, Melanchthon and other reformers on some other points, but not on usury.[63] (Doc. 13)

As we have seen, what other people called *usura*, Calvin called *foenus*, but his condemnation of it was none the less sharp: '*Foenus quidam exercere, quum inter pudendos et turpes quaestus duxerint profani scriptores, multo minus tolerabile est inter filios Dei*' – 'Considering that

---

59 P. Melanchthon, *Enarratio Psalmi*, in *Operum*, vol. ii, pp. 770–71.

60 Ibid., 772–3.

61 P. Melanchthon, *Definitiones Appellationum in Doctrina Ecclesiae Usitatarum*, in *Operum*, vol. i, fo. 356; and see *idem, Philosophiae Moralis Epitomes*, in *Opera quae supersunt Omnia*, vol. xvi, cols 129–30; *idem, Dissertatio de Contractibus*, in *Opera quae supersunt Omnia*, vol. xvi, col. 497.

62 P. Melanchthon, *Catechesis Puerilis*, in *Operum*, vol. i, fo. 18ᵛ.

63 H. Zwingli, *Von göttlicher und menschlicher Gerechtigheit wie die zemmen und standind: ein predge Huldrych Zwinglis an S. Johannes toufers tag gethon MDXXIII*, in H. Zwingl, *Huldreich Zwingl's Werke*, ed. M. Schuler and J. Schulthess, 7 vols, Zurich, 1828–42, vol. i, pp. 438–9; and see Huldrych Zwingli, *Writings*, eds E. J. Furcha and H. W. Pipkin, 2 vols, Allison Park, PA, 1984, vol. i, p. 275; vol. ii, pp. 17, 66, 72, 96, 112, 162.

profane writers judged plying the trade of fenory amongst the shameful and disgraceful ways of making profit, it is so much the less tolerable amongst God's children'.[64] Elsewhere he writes on the subject at greater length, but in the same vein.[65] (Doc. 14) Calvin's implacable opposition to usury (in the narrow sense) he makes plainer still elsewhere: 'An ockerer will always be a brigand.'[66] (Doc. 15)

In short, what divergence there was between Calvin and other Christians in this regard was simply in the use of different terminologies. Understandably, then, French and Dutch Calvinists were meticulous repressors of usury, narrowly understood, and could spend months and years agonizing over the question whether a particular gain resulted from true interest, from an unsolicited gift, or from an *acte d'usure* and thus '*teghen Godes woort*' ('against God's word').[67]

All Protestants condemned usury; all allowed only true and genuine interest.

It is absolutely untrue to allege, as Tawney does, that Luther rejected the qualifications of the canon law regarding interest. First, the canon law made no such qualifications; it simply distinguished and discriminated between usury and interest. It is equally untrue that Luther denounced as unlawful *Zinskauf*, i.e. dealing in rent-charges.

In his open letter to the German nobility in 1520, Luther was dealing with *Zinskauf* as a strictly political matter and warning them against a practice that threatened Germany with ruin.[68] (Doc. 16) Yet it is not even *Zinskauf* as such that Luther is denouncing, but only the form of it then prevalent, which was *Zinskauf* with *Wiederkauf*, with redemption. The reason he gives for this is, '*Ich noch nie keinen rechten Zinskauff auff Widerkauff gesehen oder gehört habe*' – 'I have yet to see or hear of any just *Zinskauf* based on *Widerkauf* (redemption)'.[69] Luther's opinions on worldly matters were not infallible; but in fact the Germans started gobbling up each other well before another hundred years had passed.

As for Luther's opinion on *Zinskauf* from the religious and legal point of view, quite contrary to what has been alleged, he writes, '*Ich acht der Zinskauff sey nicht Wucher*' – 'I own the buying of rent-charges be not

---

64 Calvin, *Commentarii in Libros Mosis*, p. 528.

65 Calvin, *Commentarii in Libros Psalmorum*, p. 47.

66 Calvin, *Praelectiones*, p. 170.

67 Hessels, op. cit., vol. iii, pp. 213, 221–2, 224–5, 228, 391, 398, 401–4, 421, 425, 427, 430, 432, 443, 467; J. U. Nef, *La Naissance de la Civilisation Industrielle et le monde contemporain*, Paris, 1954, pp. 130–33; *idem*, *The Conquest of the Material World*, Chicago and London, 1964, p. 222; cf. H. Hauser, *Les Débuts du Capitalisme*, Paris, 1927, pp. 70–72, 77–8.

68 M. Luther, *An den Christlichen Adel Deudscher Nation* (1520), in *Alle Bücher und Schrifften*, vol. i, fo. 314.

69 M. Luther, 'Ordnung eins gemeinen Kastens', in *Alle Bücher und Schrifften*, vol. ii, fo. 250.

usury'. This he takes for granted. What he denounces in his sermons is merely the abuse of *Zinskauf* as a cloak for usury, for he goes straight on:

> *Mich bedünckt aber sein art sey das jm leid ist das er nicht mus ein Wucher sein. Es gebricht am willen nicht und mus leider from sein.*

> But it seems to me its nature is such as to cause concern lest it be usury. This is not unjustified and must, unfortunately, be to the good.[70]

He had already explained to such doubters the reasons for, and practice of, genuine *Zinskauf*, the abuses it was open to, and how it was being transformed into usury by the exaction of excessive rates, up to ten in the hundred, from petty landholdings.[71] (Doc. 17) Whereas Tawney says Luther opposed rent-charges,[72] we find him in 1519 freely allowing *Zinskauf* paying up to six in the hundred, yet warning of the dangers of overstepping the mark and falling into ungodly usury. This was the danger he was greatly concerned to warn his flock against.[73] He returned to this theme when talking at the table:

> *Man muss ein wenig epiikiam haben. Die Guten seindt nicht ein wenig gestigen, und kann einer jtzt ein Gutt vill hoher geniessen. Drumb lass ich gern zu, was die Recht und Keiser zu lassen: 5 oder 6 von hundertt. Aber 20, 30 und 40, das ist ubermacht. Wollensecker soll from sein und nimpt dennoch das 100 umb 20 an und gewindt an 100: 40. Das ist zu vill. Und Dr Lössel hat von 10 000 jerlich, wie ich hör, 4 000, und dennoch ist ein doctor juris.*

> Landed properties have gone up not a little, and now a man can enjoy a much higher return from property. Accordingly, I readily allow what the law and emperor allow: 5 or 6 in the hundred. But 20, 30, 40, that is overmuch. Wollensecker is supposed to be pious and yet takes in the 100 about 20 and gains in the 100: 40. That is too much. And Dr Lössel has from 10 000 a year, so I hear, 4000, yet he is a doctor of law.[74]

One of Luther's letters, written in 1523, gives a further insight into his attitude to rent-charge or *Zinskauf*, or, more particularly, to it when employed, as it all too often was, as a cover for usury. It is headed and addressed, '*Bedencken vom Zinskauff, an Doc. Gregorium Brücken, Curfürstlicher durchleuchtigkeit zu Sachsen Cantzler*' – 'Thoughts on *Zinskauf*, to Dr Gregory Brücken, Chancellor to his highness the Elector of Saxony'. Luther says he has read through a pamphlet by a certain Dr Strauss of Eisenach and thinks he should acquaint the chancellor with his views on it. These were that it might be well to do away with rent-charge

---

[70] M. Luther, *Kleiner Sermon*, fo. 201ᵛ.

[71] Ibid., fo. 200ᵛ.

[72] Tawney, *Religion*, p. 97.

[73] M. Luther, *Grosser Sermon*, fo. 194; see *idem, Werke: Briefwechsel*, vol. iii, p. 307.

[74] M. Luther, *Tischreden*, p. 241 (no. 4875).

(*Zinskauf*) altogether, it being so much used as a cover for usury, but that Strauss was playing with fire when he urged debtors to refuse to pay usurers. It were better that the matters came to trial by law and be tested by the touchstone of the Gospel.[75] (Doc. 18)

On the very same day Luther wrote to Strauss himself, as follows:

> *Sed et hoc gratulor tibi, quod censum illum redemptionis damnas, sicut et ego damnavi. Verum hoc unum de te addis, quod eos iubes non solvere, qui tales pendunt, facisque eos reos usurae, si illicitas istos census perpenderint seu persolverint, tanquam consentientes usurae.*

> Although I give thanks to thee, that thou condemnest, just as I have condemned, that form of rent-charge based on redemption; but verily thou addest of thine own, that thou tellest those who owe such not to pay, and maketh out such payments to be acts of usury, if they judge those rent-charges to be illicit, or, if they should pay them, to being tantamount to implication in usury.[76]

Then, writing to Johann Friedrich of Saxony in June 1524, Luther says he does not advise the prince to try to stop people engaging in this *Wucherzins* (that is, usurious traffic in rent-charges), for it could not be done by one prince alone.

> *Solchs aber rede ich von den Zinsen, die nicht uber vier oder fünf aufs hundert geben werden, welche nicht wucherische seind der summa halben, sondern dass sie gewiss seind und nicht in der Fahr stehen, wie sie sollten. Wo aber mehr dann fünf aufs hundert gehen, da sollt ein jeglicher Fürst und Oberkeit zutun, dass mans auf Fünfte oder Vierte brächt, mit etzlicher Mass nachlassen an der Hauptsumma, donach sie lang gangen seind, und dasselb mit der Güte, auf dass damit ein Anfang würde, den ganzen Zinskauf zurechte und in seine billige Fahre zu bringen mit der Zeit.*

> But I advise like this about rent-charges that will yield not above four or five in the hundred, which is not usurious in proportion to the principal, but, as they should be, certain and not left variable. Where, however, more than five in the hundred is found, there every prince and authority should see to it that it is brought to five or four, with some remission of the total of the principal, according to how long it has to run, and the same with the landed estates, that thereby a start would be made in eventually bringing *Zinskauf* as a whole into a proper state and fair course.[77]

In fine, taking all these passages together, it is clear Luther had no religious objection to *Zinskauf* as such, but was supremely concerned to stop it being abused by usurers.

---

[75] M. Luther in *Alle Bücher und Schrifften*, vol. ii, fos 275ᵛ–6.

[76] M. Luther, *Werke: Briefwechsel*, vol. iii, pp. 178–9.

[77] Ibid., pp. 305, 307.

Melanchthon's views on *Zinskauf* were similar, but in greater technical detail, distinguishing between alienation, or sale and purchase, on the one hand and mutuation, or lending and borrowing, on the other, and pointing out that *Zinskauf* (rent-purchase or rent-charge) in all its true forms arose from sale and purchase, not from borrowing and lending.[78] (Doc. 19)

Elsewhere Melanchthon puts the matter more succinctly:

> *Iustum est itidem, emtos fructus seu reditus, cum pacto revendendi, iis quibus debentur fideliter solvere, propterea quod omnis vera legitima et non simulata emtio divinitus ordinata et approbata est.*

> In the same way, it is just, incomes or rents be purchased, with covenant of repurchase, by those who faithfully pay what they owe, therefore, when all truly legitimate, and not simulated, this is a purchase divinely ordained and approved.[79]

Melanchthon explains the matter in the same way in his catechism for boys.[80] (Doc. 20)

Zwingli is also in broad agreement with Luther on this question, but fails to distingush as clearly between alienation and lending and borrowing. He sheds invaluable light on the subject, however, by observing that *Zinskauf* was often a cover for what was substantially a mortgage.[81] (Doc. 21)

Yet it was left to Bullinger to explain exactly how livegages operated. (Doc. 22) He justified *Zinskauf* and *vivum vadium*, vifgage or livegage, but became convinced many peasants were being illictly burdened with *Zinswucher* (a usurious rent-charge or mortgage) making legal remedies necessary.[82]

It is quite untrue to allege Luther rejected either the qualifications of usury or the titles to interest made or allowed by canon law. First, canon law made no such qualifications. Secondly, Luther went out of his way to explain to unworldly parsons, and to plain folk, in homely words and phrases they could readily understand, how far removed from usury was the interest earned under the titles of *lucrum cessans* and *damnum emergens*.[83] (Doc. 23)

Melanchthon's view of *poena conventionalis*, is no less clear, and he is one of the few to deal adequately with emergent loss and cessant gain

---

78 Melanchthon, *Enarratio Psalmi*, in *Operum*, vol. ii, pp. 771–2.

79 Melanchthon, *Conciones Explicantes Integrum Evangelium*, in *Operum*, vol. iii, p. 312.

80 Melanchthon, *Catechesis Puerilis*, in *Operum*, vol. i, fos 18ᵛ–19; and see *idem*, *Philosophiae Moralis Epitomes*, in *Opera quae supersunt Omnia*, vol. xvi, cols 130 seqq.; *idem*, *Dissertatio de Contractibus*, in *Opera quae supersunt Omnia*, vol. xvi, col. 499; *idem*, *Ethicae Doctrinae Elementorum*, in *Opera quae supersunt Omnia*, vol. xvi, col. 250.

81 Zwingli, *Von göttlicher und menschlicher Gerechtigheit*, pp. 453–5.

82 Bullinger, op. cit., fo. 94; Dollfus-Zodel, op. cit., p. 44.

83 Luther, *An die Pfarrherrn*, fo. 399; *pace* Tawney, *Religion*, p. 97.

incurred before the due day, not merely after it. He shows that it was allowable to contract for emergent loss or cessant gain incurred before delay, provided only that it was true and not sham interest.[84] (Doc. 24) As we have seen, this last was the most intricate form of interest, much bedevilled and abused by usurers.[85] Melanchthon, indeed, re-emphasizes that such contracts were often a cover for usury: '*Altera quaestio est de pactione eius quod interest ante moram, ubi vocabulum* Interesse *videtur plerumque praetexi ad excusandas usuras*' – 'An agreement for interest before delay, where the term "interest" seems mostly to be a pretence with the aim of excusing usuries, is another question altogether'.[86]

How unjust it was of Tawney to describe Melanchthon's attitude to interest as hesitant, may be shown by two further citations, where he distinguishes clearly and sharply between interest and usury, and allows the one and forbids the other, no matter how well it was disguised.[87] (Doc. 25) In his catechism for boys, Melanchthon, consistent and unhesitating as ever, says the same once again, even more simply, and condemns usury even when dressed up as compensation for fictitious emergent loss.[88] (Doc. 26)

Within the constraints of the wide definition of usury, Calvin manages to justify in cloudy circumlocutions both compensatory interest under *titulus morae* and rent-charges in much the same way as Luther had done. As though differing for the sake of differing, Calvin contradicts Aristotle's argument that usury is unnatural because money itself is sterile.[89] (Doc. 27) In so doing, Calvin exposes his own intellectual weakness, for of course it was not the money lent that begat money, but the trade the money was put to. Aristotle can hardly be faulted for saying that money could produce no crop or litter.[90]

Again Calvin says,

---

84 P. Melanchthon, *Philosophiae Moralis Epitomes*, in *Opera quae supersunt Omnia*, vol. xvi, cols 137–40.

85 Sup., Chapter 1, notes 14, 15.

86 P. Melanchthon, *Prolegomena in Officia Ciceronis*, in *Opera quae supersunt Omnia*, vol. xvi, col. 578.

87 P. Melanchthon, *Definitiones Apellationum*, in *Operum*, vol. i, fo. 357.

88 P. Melanchthon, *Catechesis Puerilis*, in *Operum*, vol. i, fo. 19.

89 Calvin, *Commentarii in Libros Mosis*, p. 528.

90 Aristotle, *Politics*, bk 1, cap. 10; J. Duns Scotus, *Quaestiones in Quartum Librum Sententiarum*, in J. Duns Scotus, *Opera Omnia*, 26 vols, Paris, 1891–95, vol. xviii, p. 333; B. W. Dempsey, *Interest and Usury*, 1948, pp. 8, 9, 175–6; L. von Mises, *Theory of Money and Credit*, Indianapolis, IN, 1981, pp. 106–7; cf. W. Blackstone, *Commentaries on the Laws of England*, 4 vols, Oxford, 1778, vol. ii, pp. 455–6; S. H. Frankel, *Money: Two Philosophies: The Conflict of Trust and Authority*, Oxford, 1977, pp. 59–61; W. H. Hutt, *Individual Freedom: Selected Works of William H. Hutt*, Westport, CT, and London, 1975, pp. 209 seqq.; L. von Mises, *Socialism: An Economic and Sociological Analysis*, 1936, pp. 417–18.

Verum, si dives, qui est in aere suo, ut loquuntur, qui habet satis optimum proventum, vel satis amplum patrimonium, sumat pecuniam a suo vicino: an vicinus ille peccabit si recipiat aliquid lucri ex sua pecunia? Alter qui mutuatur est ditior, et potest absque suo damno carere: sed vult emere fundum, unde fructum accipiet: cur fraudabitur creditor suo iure, si pecunia afferat lucrum alteri, et quidem ditiori?

Yet if a rich man, with his own brass, as the saying goes, and who has an excellent enough income, or a good and ample inheritance, should take up some money from his neighbour; surely that neighbour will not be sinning if he receive some profit from his money? Someone else takes a loan, is the wealthier of the two and able to do without it and take no harm, but wants to buy a landed estate, from which he would receive the increase. Why should the lender be cheated of his just due, if the money profits the other man and he the richer of the two?

This was the exception to prove the rule, and an exception not found in England (unless under an extrinsic title). As John Knewstub observed, Calvin 'hathe sayd the most for the allowance of usurie in some speciall cases', and found some to agree with him, but 'there is no usurie that is nowe in use with us that can be upholden by their doctrine'.[91] Incidentally, in these last remarks of his, Calvin falls for the fallacious notion, apparently put forward much earlier by Peter Olivi,[92] that although money pure and simple and lying unused is sterile, it can be used as capital and is then productive. First, the money itself produces nothing; it is just exchanged for capital stock that may produce a net yield. Secondly, by no means all capital stock is productive; it all depends on the industry and ingenuity of the men in charge of it. English people have had a good chance to see for themselves that capital in 'nationalized' industries is usually not productive, but consumptive; it consumes the means of taxpayers and the victims of currency debasement. And most readers will have run across someone who borrowed money for some venture and proceeded to lose it all.

Aquinas pointed out that what appeared to be the fruit of money lent in this way, really '*non est fructus huiusmodi rei, sed humanae industriae*' – 'not the fruit of any such thing, but of human industry'. Middleton agreed money was sterile, '*nisi per laborem et sollitudinem utentis*' – 'unless through the user's labour and care'. Duns Scotus agreed:

---

[91] Calvin, *Praelectiones*, p. 170; J. Knewstub, *Lectures upon the twentieth chapter of Exodus*, 1577, p. 140.

[92] J.A. Schumpeter, *History of Economic Analysis*, 1954, p. 105; Kirshner, Intro., in R. De Roover, *Business, Banking and Economic Thought in Late Medieval and Early Modern Europe: Selected Studies of Raymond De Roover*, ed. J. Kirshner, Chicago and London, 1974, pp. 28–9; J. Mundy, *Europe in the High Middle Ages, 1150–1309*, 1973, p. 185; A. Biéler, *La Pensée Economique et Sociale de Calvin*, Geneva, 1959, pp. 455, 475–6.

> *Pecunia non habet ex natura sua aliquam fructum, sicut habent aliqua*
> *alia ex se germinantia, sed tantum provenit aliquis fructus ex industria*
> *alterius, scilicet utentis ... Ergo ille volens recipere fructum de pecunia,*
> *vult habere fructum de industria aliena.*

> Money by its nature bears no fruit in the way that other things
> reproduce themselves; but any fruit that comes from it comes from
> another man's labour, that is, from that of the man who uses it ...
> Therefore, whoever seeks to receive the fruit of money, seeks the fruit
> of another man's industry.[93]

Bernardine went into this at somewhat greater length:

> *Dicendum quod de denariis homo suscipit fructum: nam si ex usu*
> *denariorum homo suscipit fructum, non venit principaliter ex denariis,*
> *sed ex ingenio utentium eis: at econverso de domo vel agro: nam, licet*
> *fructus per ingenium hominis capiantur ex eis, principaliter tamen*
> *fructus, atque utilitas ex illis cum ingenio hominis originem habent.*

> The saying is, a man gains from money: now if a man gains profit
> from the use of money, it comes fundamentally not from the money,
> but from ingenuity in using it, and from the management of a house
> or field: now, granting that the gains are taken from these by the
> man's ingenuity, then fundamentally the gains and usefulness got from
> them have their origin in the man's ingenuity.

And St Antonine pointed out that to charge usury on such a loan was to
place an unjust imposition on the borrower's industry. Almost without
exception, this analysis had long been part and parcel of Christian thought
and belief. It is found, for example in Luther's teaching on *Zinskauf*, which
he insists must be based on productive estates.[94] Once again, it is clear
Calvin had nothing that was both new and correct to say on the subject of
usury and interest.

John Jewel, who strongly condemns all usury, even where 'a merchant
taketh up of his neighbour a hundred pounds and must answer again a
hundred and ten pounds', or 'if one rich man lend money to another', or
'if a merchant take money in usury of a merchant, and both be the better,
and both be gainers',[95] nevertheless allows annuities:

> An occupier waxeth old, his occupying is done. He hath in stock two
> hundred pounds: he cometh to a young man, wise, of good credit,
> and of honest dealing, and saith : I give thee this money freely; it shall

---

93 P. Melanchthon, *Commentarii in aliquot Politicos Libros Aristotelis*, in *Opera quae supersunt Omnia*, vol. xvi, cols 428–30; Middleton, op. cit., lib. IV, dist. xv, art. v, qu. vi (fo. 75ᵛ); Aquinas, *Summa Theologica*, II, ii, qu. 78, art. iii (*Opera*, vol. xxii, p. 325); Duns Scotus, op. cit., dist. XV, qu. ii (*Opera Omnia*, vol. xviii, p. 293).

94 Bernardine, *Quadragesimale de Evangelio Aeterno*, sermo XVII, art. I. cap. iii (*Opera*, vol. ii, p. 213); St Antonine, *Summa Major*, 4 vols (pts), Venice, 1503, pt II, bk i, cap. v, # 1 (fo. 21); Luther, *Kleiner Sermon*, fo. 200ᵛ.

95 Jewel, op. cit., vol. ii, pp. 851 seqq.; vol. iv, p. 1294.

be thine for ever, upon this condition, that thou give me twenty marks by the year during my life. This may be done, it is no usury. Wherefore? It is a plain gift with a condition. The principal is gone from me for ever; I have no right unto it; it is none of mine. If I die tomorrow before I receive any penny, my executors cannot claim anything.[96]

Jewel likewise allows *damnum emergens*:

Again, I lend my neighbour twenty pound until a day. He hath it freely and friendly without any usury. Yet I say to him: Neighbour, you must needs keep a day, for the next day after I must discharge a pain, I stand bound for a payment. I have no more but this which you borrow. If I miss, I forfeit five pounds. I pray you be careful for it. The day cometh, my neighbour cometh not: I lack my money, and because I lack it, I lose five pounds. He cometh afterward and offereth me mine own money. Then I say: Neighbour, I have lost five pounds by your negligence and slackness. I hope you will not suffer me to be a loser for my gentleness. This is interest, it is no usury.[97]

Jewel, though at the outset confusing the two meanings of the word 'usury', also approves gains from non-usurious loans, where the lender and borrower share the risk, and especially where the loan is made for charitable purposes.[98] (Doc. 28) William Perkins taught along much the same lines as Calvin and allowed entitlements to interest:

The reasons why a man may take sometimes above the principall, are: 1. That which the debter may give, having himselfe an honest gaine besides, and no man any waies endamaged, that the creditour may safely receive. 2. It is convenient, that he which hath money lent him, and gaineth by it, should shew all possible gratitude to him, by whose goods he is enriched. 3. It is often for the benefit of the creditour, to have the goods in his owne hands which he lent.[99]

Here we see, half-explained in short and simple circumlocution, interest freely given on a non-usurious loan, interest paid on a loan where the lender shares the risk and interest due by title of cessant gain or emergent loss.

Since, then, all Christians allowed interest, the intended slur on Luther's character miscarries when we are told he sought the best terms of interest on the 500 guilders endowed for poor scholars at Wittenberg University.[100] Even for the financial advantage of the Church, he would not allow usurious loans: '*Gottes dienst damit nicht gebessert, sondern verderbet*' – 'The service of God is not bettered thereby, but corrupted'.[101] And the

---

96 Ibid., vol. ii, p. 857.

97 Ibid., pp. 857–8.

98 Ibid., p. 858.

99 W. Perkins, *The Workes of that famous and worthie minister of Christ, in the University of Cambridge, M. W. Perkins*, Cambridge, 1603, p. 64.

100 Pascal, op. cit., p. 190 gives no ref. to support his allegation.

101 Luther, *Grosser Sermon*, fo. 194.

attempt to justify usury by claiming Calvin allowed it within limits fails, for it takes no account of Calvin's peculiar terminology, and neglects to point out that true interest was the only kind of *usura* of money that he clearly permitted. In practice, needless to say, Calvin, like Bullinger and other leaders of the Reformed Churches, left mundane commercial and financial matters to the Magistrate and allowed what the Magistrate allowed. And the Magistrate understood usury in the narrow and generally employed sense. In Calvin's Geneva *arrêtes* made by the city council in 1538 and 1544 expressly forbade usury in the sense of ocker and limited true and legitimate interest on loans of such things as flour, wheat, wine and firewood, to 5 per cent. To take more than the legal limit was to take usury in the narrow sense.[102]

But all forms of legitimate mutuation could be taken advantage of by illicit usurers to conceal, disguise and camouflage their wicked business. Everyone knew how evil and cunning such usurers were.[103] They had disguised *nashac* as *neshek*, *foenus* as *usura* and illicit usury as lawful interest. The common allegation that businessmen invented titles to interest to circumvent the prohibition of usury is trebly wrong: it confuses interest with usury; it imputes blame to blameless people entitled to interest; and it ignores the fact that usurers misused these titles to camouflage usury.

As Luther put it,

> *Zum ersten ist zu wissen, das zu unsern Zeiten ... der Geitz und Wucher nicht allein gewaltiglich in aller Welt eingerissen, sondern auch sich unterstanden hat etlich Schanddeckel zu suchen, Darunter er für billig geachtet, seine Bosheit frey mochte treiben.*

> At the outset it is to be known that in our times ... greed and usury have not only mightily gained ground throughout the world, but have had the temerity to seek out cloaks for abomination, under which it could be made to appear just, that they might be free to carry on their wickedness.[104]

Calvin writes:

---

[102] Biéler, op. cit., pp. 168, 474; R. Bergier, 'Les Taux d'Interêt et Crédit à Court Terme à Genève dans la seconde moitié du XVIe siècle', in *Studi in Onore di Amintore Fanfani*, vol. iv, Milan, 1962, pp. 95–8, 101, 119; E. Choisy, *La Théocratie à Genève au temps de Calvin*, Geneva, n.d., p. 244; *idem, L'Etat Chrétien Calviniste à Genève au temps de Théodore de Bèze*, Geneva, 1902, pp. 145, 442; Anon., *The Death of Usury*, p. 30; Dollfus-Zodel, op. cit., p. 44; Quick, op. cit., p. 34; G. R. Potter, *Zwingli*, Cambridge, 1976, pp. 164–5; K. M. Brown, 'Noble indebtedness in Scotland between the Reformation and the Revolution', *Historical Research*, 1989, 62, 263.

[103] E.g., Bernardine, *Quadragesimale de Evangelio Aeterno*, sermo XXXIX, art. II, cap. ii, iii; art. III, cap. ii, iii; sermo XL, art. I, cap. ii; art. II, cap. ii (*Opera*, vol. ii, pp. 229 seqq.); *idem, Duo Adventualia*, sermo XXIX, prima pars principalis (*Opera*, vol. iii, p. 237).

[104] Luther, *Grosser Sermon*, fo. 188; cf. *idem, Kleiner Sermon*, fos 200ᵛ, 201ᵛ.

*Scimus ubique et semper exosum et infame fuisse foeneratorum nomen
... Semper enim excogitant homines astuti captiunculas quibus Deum
illudant.*

We know the name of usurer has been everywhere and in all times
detested and disreputable ... For crafty men are forever inventing some
little subterfuge or other to deceive God with.[105]

That is why,

Sub nomine therbith *Ezechiel comprehendit illa magis occult genera
foenorum, quum scilicet multis integumentis utuntur avari, et ubi
obstendunt tales fucos, existimant se carere omni culpa.*

Under the name *therbith* Ezekiel comprehends those more secret kinds
of fenory that avaricious men habitually use with many disguises and,
where they display such deceits, think to exonerate themselves of all
blame.[106]

Luther points out that rent-charge purchase or *Zinskauf* could easily
be, and often was, adapted to fit the usurer's wicked ways:

*Darumb das im selben ein hübscher schein und gleissen ist, Wie man
on Sünd ander Leut beschweren, und on Sorge und Mühe Reich werden
müge. Denn in den andern Hendeln ists jederman selbs offenbar, wo
er zu thewr, falsche Wahr, falsch Erb, falsch Gut gibt oder besitzt.
Aber dis behend und new erfunden Geschefft macht sich gar offt einen
fromen und getrewen Schutzherr des verdampten Geitz und Wuchers.*

For in this same thing is a fine appearance and show, how one, without
sin, burdens other people, and becomes rich without any care or
trouble. For in other trades it is the case that every man leaves himself
open, where he gives or takes too dear, false wares, false inheritance,
false land titles. But this artful and new-found business very often
makes itself into a good and trusty protector of damnable greed and
usury.[107]

In his homely style, in words that the man in the Wittenberg marketplace
could readily understand, Luther exposes and denounces the colouring of
usury by dignifying it with the name of 'interest', particularly in disguising
usurious rent-charges. No risk was involved and there could be no just
interest by way of cessant gain or emergent loss unless the claim for it
were impartially assessed, taking into consideration that trade carried the
risk of loss as well as the hope of gain, and that the one had to be balanced
against the other. He then goes on to explain how honest *Zinskauf* should
be regulated in order to avoid abuses.[108] (Doc. 29)

---

105 Calvin, *Commentari in Libros Mosis*, p. 527; cf. C. H. George, 'English Calvinist
opinion on usury, 1600–1640', *Journal of History of Ideas*, 1957, 18, 455, 457–8.

106 Calvin, *Praelectiones*, pp. 169–70.

107 Luther, *Grosser Sermon*, fo. 194.

108 Ibid., fos 195–7.

As for mortgages, Luther was, of course, wholly opposed to them as usurious. That the Pope allowed usurious mortgages in the guise of *contractus redemptionis*, Luther is said to have taken as proof positive that he was the Antichrist.[109]

To explain how *titulus morae* or forbearance could be used to camouflage usury, Luther resumes his everyday story of Hans and Baltzer, explaining how Hans might suffer damages if Baltzer failed to repay at Michaelmas the 100 guilders he had borrowed. He then goes on to show how due compensation could be converted into usury by demanding 'not real but fantastic interest'.[110] (Doc. 30)

Melanchthon, too, while acknowledging the lawfulness and justness of buying rent-charges, denounced the fraudulently usurious buying of them.[111] Immediately after showing the trade in rent-charges to be lawful and just in principle, he added, according to report,

> *At quisquis in emtionibus et venditionibus fraudem struit, et debita precia maligne solvit, fur est, exhauriens alienas facultates, eratque severe puniendus a Magistratu.*

> And whoever commits frauds in purchases and sales and grudgingly pays prices short, is a thief, exhausting the other man's resources, and is to be severely punished by the Magistrate.[112]

Zwingli, likewise, after approving *Zinskauf*, adds: '*Aber die zins, die nit nach der oberkeit bestimmung erkouft werdend, die soll man nit geben anderst denn nach anzal der summ*' – 'But the rent that has not been bought after the authorized procedure, this one should not give over and above the amount of the principal'. No interest was to be paid on simulated or covert rent-purchase.[113]

Calvin notes how fenory was practised under cover of cessant gain:

> *Nam quisquis praesentem habet pecuniam, ubi eam mutuo daturus est, utilem sibi fore causabitur si quod emat, et singulis momentis lucrandi materiam offerri. Ita semper erit compensationi locus, quando nemo creditor sine damno pecuniam alteri numerabit.*

> For whosoever has ready money, where he is bent on giving it out by way of loan, will allege it would be profitable to him if he were to buy something and just at that very moment an opportunity to make profit offers itself. Thus there will always be a pretext for compensation, when no lender will pay out money to another without loss.[114]

---

[109] Luther quoted in Fenton, op. cit., p. 58. I failed to find this reference.

[110] Luther, *An die Pfarrherrn*, fo. 400.

[111] Melanchthon, *Conciones Explicantes Integrum Evangelium*, in *Operum*, vol. iii, p. 312.

[112] Ibid.

[113] Zwingli, *Von göttlicher und menschlicher Gerechtigkeit*, p. 455.

[114] Calvin, *Commentarii in Libros Mosis*, p. 527.

Jewel says, 'No man may excuse his usury by name of interest,' showing he knew this was often attempted.[115]

Luther, who wrote more on these matters than any other reformer, went on to denounce the concealment of usury under cover of trade:

> *Auffs erst, machen etliche kein Gewissen davon, das sie jre Wahr auff Borgen und Zeit thewrer verkeuffen denn umb bahr Gelt. Ja, etliche wollen keine Wahr verkeuffen umb bahr Gelt, sondern alles auff Zeit, und das alles darumb, das sie ja viel Gelts daran gewinnen. Hie sihestu das dis Stück gar gröblich wider Gottes Wort, wider Vernunfft und alle Billigkeit aus lauter freiem Mutwillen des Geitzs sündigt ... Denn nach göttlichem Recht solt ers nicht thewrer borgen oder auff Zeit geben denn umb bahr Gelt.*

> First, some make no conscience of selling their goods dearer on credit and time than for ready money. Yea, some will sell no goods for ready money, but all on time, and that entirely to gain much money from it. Here thou seest that this trick is directly against God's word, against reason and all fairness, out of pure unbounded wantonness of sinful greed ... for according to divine law he shall not sell on credit or give time dearer than for ready money.[116]

But Luther later realized these remarks were open to misunderstanding, in that people might think he opposed honest commercial credit. He sets this to right by adding,

> *Den keufflichen zinse habe ich hiemit nicht gemeinet, denn was ein rechten redlicher Kauff ist, das ist kein Wucher. So weis man (Gott lob) wol, was ein keufflicher zinse ist nach den weltlichen Rechten, nemlich, das da sol sein ein unterpfand und nicht zu viel auffs hundert verkaufft werde, davon jtzt nicht zu reden ist. Ein jglicher sehe für sich das ein rechter redlicher Kauff sey.*

> By this I did not mean trade credit terms for what is a right honest deal; that is no usury. As one knows right well (God be praised) what trade credit is according to worldly justice, namely, that there shall be a security and that not too much be charged in the hundred, about which here and now there is nothing to be said. Let every man himself see to it that there be a right honest deal.[117]

For the rest, the reformers were content to finish as they started, arguing that the exercise of Christian charity was all. As Calvin said,

> *Summa haec sit, modo cordibus nostris insculpta sit, quam Christus praescribit, aequitas regula. Quod quisque sibi fieri vult, ut proximis faciat, longa disputatione de usuris minime opus fore.*

---

115 Jewel, op. cit., vol. ii, p. 858.

116 Luther, *Von Kauffshandlung*, fo. 475ᵛ. Cf. T. Wilson, *A Discourse uppon Usurye by way of dialogue and oracions for the better varietye and more delite of all those that shall reade thys treatise* (1572), ed. R. H. Tawney, 1925, p. 223, where Ockerfoe uses a similar form of words.

117 Luther, *An die Pfarrherrn*, fo. 415ᵛ.

> To sum up, if only there were engraved on our hearts, what Christ prescribes, by the rule of equity, To do as we would be done by, then soon lengthy disputations about usuries would serve very little purpose.[118]

Luther enlarges on the difficulties attendant on cases of disputed emergent loss, and once again through the characters Hans and Baltzer. He ends up by concluding, as most divines did, that such cases should be left to the law courts to decide. He contents himself with pointing out that the courts were in duty bound always to be on their guard against disguised usury.[119] (Doc. 31)

At the same time, the reformers recognized that usury could never be stamped out entirely. As Luther says to his pastors, one might as well expect the world to be without sin of any kind.[120] (Doc. 32) This echoed the view of the early Schoolmen, that usury could never be wiped out entirely. Aquinas said:

> *Leges humanae dimittunt aliqua peccata impunita propter conditiones hominum imperfectorum, in quibus multae utilitates impedirentur si omnia peccata distincte prohiberentur poenis adhibitis. Et ideo usuras lex humana concessit, non quasi existimans eas esse secundum iustitiam, sed ne impedirentur utilitates multorum.*

> Human laws allow some sins to go unpunished on account of the condition of imperfect men, wherefore much that is useful would be prevented should all sins be punished particularly by specific penalties. Therefore human law tolerates some usuries, not because considering them to be in accordance with justice, but lest many people's useful activities be interfered with.[121]

Much later Capel and others said almost the same. To have held an inquest on every commercial or financial transaction would have enmeshed trade and industry in a net that caught both innocent and guilty alike.[122]

---

[118] Calvin, *Psalmorum*, p. 47.

[119] Luther, *An die Pfarrherrn*, fos 399ᵛ–400.

[120] Ibid., fo. 401.

[121] Aquinas, *Summa Theologica*, qu. 78, art. 1, concl. ad 3um dicendum (*Opera*, vol. xxii, p. 323).

[122] Capel, op. cit., 2nd pagination, p. 297; R. Williams, *The Bloudy Tenent of Persecution*, ed. E. B. Underhill, Hanserd Knollys Society, 1848, p. 139; T. Cooper, *The Worldlings Adventure*, 1619, pp. 63–4.

CHAPTER THREE

Usury and Interest in England

English divines generally followed the teachings of the Schoolmen on the subjects of usury and interest, as being the true expression of Christian belief and thinking. Indeed, among the ranks of the Schoolmen were numbered Middleton, Hales, Duns and Ockham, all men of English stock. The breach with Rome brought no break with Christian teachings on usury and interest. As we shall see, the beliefs and attitudes of early modern English bishops and clergymen remained what they had always been. Although some divines, like Jewel and Perkins, had leanings towards Calvinism, English Calvinists were always a small minority. And where the clergy led, the laity followed. Yet many people, clerical and lay, read Calvin's works with a degree of admiration, and those who had not studied Erasmus discovered in Calvin the revived classical terminology of usury in the broad sense and the phrase 'biting usury' for what been once been called ocker and was now generally known simply as 'usury'. This terminological change intrigued, bemused or confused many readers. Some tried to follow it and others to reconcile it with traditional forms of expression by combining pure classical Latin with the teachings of the Schoolmen, or by translating *foenus* as 'biting usury'. Yet the Christian teachings on usury and interest remained essentially unchanged.

By the early modern period English people had come more and more to replace the word 'ocker' by 'usury', but it was not until towards the end of this period that 'interest' widely acquired its modern unspecific meaning of a fluctuating combination of price rises and the cost of the loan. In early modern England 'interest' often comprehended not only usury but also the cost of legitimate loans. But 'interest' in the sense of what was allowed under Christian extrinsic titles, was rarely referred to as such, but as taking such and such a number of pounds in the hundred under a particular title.

As we have already had occasion to notice in passing, nearly all English Protestants, and Christians in general, conformed strictly to the ancient, but now recently re-explained, Christian teachings on usury. Almost without exception, they all condemned usury in the generally accepted meaning of the word. The only easily found exception was the fictitious lawyer in Wilson's *Discourse*. He said only uncharitable usury was to be condemned. But he was 'not muche better than a petye fogger in lawe ... beeinge yet never allowed in anye Inne of Courte or Chauncery for his learning.[1] As Schumpeter pointed out long ago, as far as usury and interest were concerned, 'Between scholastic and anti-scholastic writers ... in the sixteenth and seventeenth centuries ... there was no battle'.[2]

John Wycliffe followed the Schoolmen's way of concentrating on the denunciation and penalizing of usury, rather than on technical explanations of it. Usury was forbidden in the Old Testament and in the New. The usurer sells time, which is not his to sell. (Doc. 33) As far as is known, the only specific field for usury he mentions is chevisance or merchandising: 'Marchauntis bi usure under colour of threuthe that thei clepyn chevysaunce, to blynde with the puple, – for the devyl schameth to speke of this thefthe.'[3]

In England, as in the rest of Christendom, usurers were seen as 'gnawing the detters to the bones, ingendring money of mony, contrary to the disposition of nature, and holding an inordinate desire of wealth'. They were 'thieves, robbers, and spoilers of the commonweal' (Becon), worse than Jews, who only preyed on Gentiles, not on their own kind. The only good usurer was a dead one.[4] As Fulbecke put it, 'Usurie may well be called the divels charitie'. He who borrows at usury finds his debts growing bigger. 'The bee that had a flower in her mouth, had a sting in her tail.' In the reported words of Henry Rowlands, Bishop of Bangor, preaching at St Paul's on 25 March 1610, usury 'is an unkinde kindnesse and an undoing helpe ... yt is not meete the riche borow, for they have no neede, yt is not fyt the poore borow, for yt will make them poorer.' As Henry Smith put it, the usurer 'claspeth the borrower with such bonds, that ever after he

---

[1] T. Wilson, *A Discourse uppon Usurye by way of dialogue and oracions for the better varietye and more delite of all those that shall reade thys treatise* (1572), ed. R. H. Tawney, 1925, p. 193.

[2] J. Schumpeter, *History of Economic Analysis*, 1954, p. 106.

[3] J. Wycliffe, *Select English Works of John Wyclif*, ed. T. Arnold, 3 vols, Oxford, 1869–71, vol. iii, pp. 154–5; and for chevisance, see vol. iii, p. 88.

[4] H. C. White, *Social Criticism in Popular Religious Literature of the Sixteenth Century*, New York, 1965, pp. 198 seqq.; H. M. Robertson, *Aspects of the Rise of Economic Individualism: A Criticism of Max Weber and his School*, Cambridge, 1933, pp. 111 seqq., 124–5, 133 seqq.; T. Floyd, *The Picture of a Perfit Common Wealth*, 1600, pp. 276–7; H. Smith, *The Works of Henry Smith; including sermons, treatises, prayers and poems*, 2 vols, Edinburgh, 1866, vol. i, p. 91; T. White, *A Sermon preached at St Paules Cross the 17. of November Anno 1589*, 1589, p. 38; G. Estey, *Certaine Godly and Learned Expositions upon divers parts of Scripture*, 1603, p. 70; T. Wilcox (Wilcocks) *A Very Godly and Learned Exposition, upon the whole Booke of Psalms*, 1591, pp. 35–6; M. Sutcliffe, *An Answere to a certaine Libel supplicatorie, or rather Diffamatory*, 1592, p. 155; G. Malynes, *Consuetudo, vel Lex Marcatoria or the Ancient Law-Merchant*, 1622, pp. 325–6, 337–8; T. Becon, *The Catechism of Thomas Becon, S. T. P.*, ed. J. Ayre, Parker Society, 1844, p. 162; T. Timme, *A Discoverie of ten English Lepers verie noisome*, 1592, 8th leper; T. Rogers, *Seven Treatises, containing such Direction as is gathered out of the Holy Scriptures*, 1603, p. 106; J. Northbrooke, *The Poore Mans Garden*, 1573, fos 267ᵛ, 268ᵛ, 269ᵛ; F. Trigge, *A Godly and Fruitfull Sermon preached at Grantham, A. D. 1592*, Oxford, 1594, sig. D.5.

diminisheth as fast as the usurer increaseth.'[5] Francis Bacon said, 'Usury is gainst morality, namely, that money should beget money'.[6] This belief was well founded: money of itself cannot beget money; idle money is perfectly sterile; and even the mere passage of time cannot, of itself, either add or detract value to or from anything.[7]

Taking usury was held to be not only unnatural, immoral and wicked, but also an impediment to enterprise and material advance. It was 'the canker of the commonwealth'.[8] What Luther said in Germany, Capel said in England:

> Ay, but when both parties gain, who is bitten, (say they)? The common-wealth (say I). That it is hurtfull to the common-wealth which is a burden to the *most*, and those who have *most need*, are those who buy commodities to spend for their need and use, and these are bitten when traders take up commodities for day, or take up money upon use to buy their commodities; for such must need sell the dearer, sith they pay the dearer, so much as the use-money comes unto ... And thus a long running we see that the poorer sort who buy for need are they who upon the matter do pay use for (almost) all.[9]

Bacon said in the Commons:

> Usury ... is against policy, for the great merchants will not venter at sea, winde etc., neither will the witt of men labor upon drayning of marshes, or in any good or ingenious devise, but imploy their money to more certaine profitt at use; and so this sluggish trade of usury taketh away all invention, and trade. Whereas other waies where money is, there would be devises to imploy it.[10]

In his essay Francis Bacon wrote:

> The discommodities of usury are: first, that it makes fewer merchants. For were it not for this lazy trade of usury, money would not lie still, but would, in great part, be employed upon merchandising; which is the *vena porta* of wealth in a state. The second, that it makes poor merchants. For as a farmer cannot husband his ground so well if he sit at a great rent, so the merchant cannot drive his trade so well if he

---

5 W. Fulbecke, *A Parallele or Conference of the Civil Law, the Canon Law, and the Common Law of this Realme of England*, 1618, fo. 53; Hampshire RO, Jervoise of Herriard Park MSS: Papers of Sir Ric. Paulet, 44M69, box F6, Diary of Sir Ric. Paulet; and see Smith, *Works*, vol. i, p. 93.

6 D. H. Willson, *The Parliamentary Diary of Robert Bowyer, 1606–1607*, Minneapolis, MN, 1931, p. 151; and see Bacon, *Essays*, 'Of Usury'.

7 B. W. Dempsey, *Interest and Usury*, 1948, pp. 175–6, 181; L. von Mises, *The Theory of Money and Credit*, Indianapolis, IN, 1981, pp. 106–7.

8 J. Blaxton, *The English Usurer, or Usury condemned*, 1634, p. 11.

9 R. Capel, *Tentations: their nature, danger, cure; to which is added a Brief Dispute touching Restitution in the Case of Usury*, 5th edn, 1655, 2nd pagination, p. 289; and see Smith, *Works*, vol. i, p. 106.

10 Willson, op. cit., p. 151.

sit at great usury. The third is incident to the other two, and that is, the decay of customs of kings or states, which ebb or flow with merchandising. The fourth, that it bringeth the treasure of a realm or state into a few hands. For the usurer being at certainties, and others at uncertainties, at the end of the game most of the money will be in the box; and ever a state flourisheth when wealth is more equally spread.[11]

'Usury is directly against the law of God', says Coke, and 'the suppression of usury tendeth to the honour of God, and to the common profit of the people.'[12] 'By the ancient laws of this realme, usury was unlawfull, and punishable.'[13] Indeed, 'So detestable' was a usurer in the eyes of the common law, before anything was provided by Statute, that if one died in this sin, so that the power of the Church could extend no further, because he died out of the Church: yet then even the common law 'tooke vengeance upon him in his goods and posteritie'. Testate or intestate, all his chattels whatsoever and wheresoever were all forfeited to the king and his lands escheated to his lord. But for these penalties to be imposed, the usurer had to have been proved by inquest to have died in his sin. The position was the same in the ancient law of Scotland, and since this was a branch of Anglo-Saxon law, usury must always have been illegal among the English.[14]

English usurers, like others, sought to conceal their usury in one way and another. Usury was often called 'forbearance' even though payable at or before the due day, or when the 'forbearance' lasted only a quarter of an hour.[15] The purchase of an annuity or rent-charge, not in itself usury, was nevertheless usury if the seller originally came to borrow off the buyer and the purported rent-charge or annuity was really a camouflage for usury on a loan.[16] But the commonest camouflage for usury was pretended

---

[11] Bacon, *Essays*, 'Of Usury'; *idem*, *The Works of Francis Bacon*, eds J. Spedding, R. L. Ellis and D. D. Heath, 14 vols, 1862–83, vol. xiv, pp. 415–16.

[12] E. Coke, *The Institutes of the Lawes of England*, 4 pts (vols), 1628, 1629, 1642–44 and var. edns, pt iii, pp. 151–2.

[13] Ibid., p. 152; and see E. Kerridge, *Trade and Banking in Early Modern England*, Manchester, 1988, p. 34; Wilson, op. cit., pp. 183–4, 257, 375–7.

[14] Glanvill, *The Treatise on the Laws and Customs of the Realm of England commonly called Glanvill*, ed. G. D. G. Hall, 1965, p. 89; R. Fenton, *A Treatise of Usury*, 1611, pp. 71–2.

[15] F. Moore, *Cases Collect & Report per Sir Fra. Moore*, 1688 and var. edns, pp. 397–8; T. Siderfin, *Les Reports de divers Special Cases argue et adjudge en le Court del Bank le Roy, et auxy en le Comen Banc et l'Exchequer, en les primier dix ans apres le Restauration del Son Tres-Excellent Majesty le Roy Charles le II*, 2 pts, 1714 and var. edns, pt ii, p. 88; G. Croke, *Reports ... of such select Cases as were adjudged ... during the Reign of Queen Elizabeth*, 1790 and var. edns, pp. 19, 20, 588, 643; W. Noy, *Reports and Cases taken in the Time of Queen Elizabeth, King James and King Charles*, 1669 and var. edns, p. 171.

[16] Ibid., p. 151; Croke, *Elizabeth*, p. 27, 28; and see E. Bulstrode, *The Reports of Edward Bulstrode ... of divers Resolutions and Judgements given ... in the Court of King's Bench in the time of the Reign of King James I and King Charles I*, 1688 and var. edns, pp. 36–7.

interest. The law recognized true interest, even though not as such but only under one of the titles, and refused to allow usury to masquerade as interest. As Noy put it,

> *Interest in cest sence pur le money due pur loane de money n'est terme ne conus in nostre ley ... je ne unques avoy oye que interest fuit conus in nostre ley pur tiel money, que est d'estre pay sur loane de money.*

> Interest in this sense, for the money owing for the loan of money, is not a term known in our law ... I have never heard that interest was known in our law for such money, which is to be paid upon a loan of money.[17]

Instances are given of the ways of usurers. 'A poore man desireth a goldsmith to lend him such a summe, but he is not able to pay him interest. If such as I can spare (saith the goldsmith) will pleasure you, you shall have it for three or foure moneths.' But he lends 'light, clipt, crackt peeces' and is repaid in good coin, and so commits usury. If a man lend a flock of sheep and take payment for the mere loan, he commits usury, but can conceal it in the payment for the fold of the sheep, which cannot be precisely valued. Some refuse open usury, but take the use of land or livestock, plate or furniture, or buy at a low price and sell back at a higher, or exact unpaid labour.[18] 'I sell wares, I give three moneths day of payment, and for that I am to forbeare my money so long, I sell above mine ordinarie price, and above a reasonable gaine: herein (no question) I commit usurie.'[19] 'I do buy a mans bille of 100 pounds, due three monethes hence, and geve unto hym in present money 95*li*. Here, although a bargayne and sale seeme in shewe, yet it is a lending, and so the partie an usurer that payeth the mony.'[20] Genuine interest on such a transaction could never have amounted to 20 per cent in the 1560s or after. Dry and fictitious exchange was apparently another common cover for usury in early modern England.[21]

---

17 H. Rolle, *Les Reports de Henry Rolle ... de divers Cases en le Court del' Banke le Roy en le temps del' Reign de Roy Jacques*, 2 vols, 1675–76 and var. edns, vol. ii, p. 239.

18 Fenton, op. cit., pp. 19, 23; Smith, *Works*, pp. 94–5; idem, *The Examination of Usury in two Sermons*, 1591, pp. 17 seqq.

19 M. Mosse, *The Arraignment and Conviction of Usurie: that is the iniquitie and unlawfulness of usurie, displayed in sixe sermons preached at St Edmunds Burie in Suffolke, upon Proverb 28.8*, 1595, p. 62; Smith, *Works*, pp. 95–6.

20 Wilson, op. cit., p. 294; and see Dempsey, op. cit., pp. 142–3, 164–5. The reference is to a bill obligatory.

21 R. De Roover, *Gresham on Foreign Exchange*, Cambridge, MA, 1949, pp. 161 seqq.; idem, *Business, Banking and Economic Thought in Late Medieval and Early Modern Europe: selected studies of Raymond De Roover*, ed. J. Kirshner, Chicago and London, 1974, pp. 183 seqq., 197–9; *Money, Banking and Credit in Medieval Bruges*, Cambridge, MA, 1958, pp. 81–3; Wilson's Preacher agreed with pope (*Discourse*, 305–6); R. H. Tawney and E. Power, *Tudor Economic Documents, being Select Documents Illustrating the Economic and Social History of Tudor England*, 3 vols, 1937, vol. iii, pp. 359, 361–3.

As it was illegal and so often well cloaked, usury had to be defined as strictly and comprehensively as possible. English definitions differed not a jot from most continental ones. One good definition was, 'The contract of usury is nothing but illiberal mutuation ... Usury is mutuation or lending for gain'.[22] In liberal mutuation, by contrast, the borrower might, of his own free will, give the lender an unsolicited gift out of sheer gratitude for a free loan.[23] The essence of usury was that it was not merely gain, but certain and assured gain. The borrower bore all the risk and uncertainty, the usurer none.[24] Musculus had noted the usurer's familiar excuse, '*Ich müss mein Gelt wagen*' – 'I have to risk my money',[25] but in truth, in Mosse's words, 'The usurer never adventureth or hazardeth the losse of his principall: for he wil have all sufficient securitie for the repaiment and restoring of it backe againe to himselfe.'[26] A contract of usury stipulated the payment of usury from the first moment the loan was made, and the borrower gave his bond or other security for the repayment of the principal and the payment of usury.

A long, standing mortgage, where the mortgagor's payments did not go to reduce the debt, was perfect usury, and as such illegal.[27] A gagee who gave a free loan and refused usury, would often have had an ulterior motive. According to Bacon,

> As for mortgaging or pawning, for either men will not take pawns without use, or if they do, they will look precisely for the forfeiture. I remember a cruel moneyed man in the country that would say: 'The devil take this usury, it keeps us from forfeitures of mortgages and bonds.'[28]

Like the rest of Christendom, early modern England recognized and allowed true interest. Like Luther, Melanchthon and Zwingli, too, English Protestants were at pains to explain interest in order that people could more easily distinguish it from usury. Fenton, for example, writes,

> A man lendeth for a time freely; that time being expired, his money is retained longer against his will, for want whereof he is damnified. If the lender receive an overplus on this case above the principall, answerable to the damage which he hath suffered, this is no usurie, but due and just satisfaction. No usury, because increase is not taken for the loane. For loane is a voluntarie act: whereas this money was not willingly lent, but retained by force after the time it was due ...

22 Blaxton, op. cit., p. 1.

23 Ibid., p. 8; Mosse, op. cit., pp. 2, 16, 17, 23.

24 Blaxton, op. cit., pp. 2, 6; F. H. Knight, *Risk, Uncertainty and Profit*, 1933, pp. 43–4.

25 W. Musculus, *De Usuris ex Verbo Dei*, Tübingen, 1558, sig. D.5.

26 Mosse, op. cit., p. 53; and see p. 57.

27 Ibid.; A. P. Usher, *The Early History of Deposit Banking in Mediterranean Europe*, vol. i, Cambridge, MA, 1943, pp. 138–9; and see Chapter 1, note 24.

28 Bacon, *Essays*, 'Of Usury'.

But the time being come out, to receive overplus for his losse sustained, is no usurie, but a just recompence, which is properlie termed interest ... To receive interest, that is to say, recompence for forbearance of his money, is no usurie.[29]

Mosse, a zealous parson, explains this rather more clearly:

There are two manifest and essentiall differences between usurie and interest, which doe so distinguish the one from the other, as they cannot possibly be confounded. One difference is this: usurie is an overplus or gaine taken more then was lent; interest is never gaine or overplus above the principall, but a recompence demaunded and due for the damage that is taken, or the gaine that is hindered through lending. Another difference is this: usurie accreweth and groweth due by lending, from the day of borrowing unto the appointed time of payment; interest is never due but from the appointed day of payment forward, and for so long as I forbeare my goods after the day, in which I did covenant to receive them againe. So that, if once I have lent freely unto a certaine day, I shall not demaund interest for any dammage susteined, or gaine hindered during that tearme of time, for which I have lent unto another. But if at the covenanted time I receive not mine owne againe, then what harme soever do betide me after that day for the forbearing thereof, reason will that it be recompenced of the borrower.[30]

Fenton was at pains to explain how best to go about providing for the contingency of emergent loss by means of *poena conventionalis*:

If thou lend thy neighbour for his reliefe in this case, it may be thou shalt be damnified, for want of thy money, more then thy estate can well beare ... so let thy covenant be conditional: 'If thou be thus or thus damnified, that then such and such satisfaction be made. This is equall and just interest, but no usury.'[31]

He also explains that partnership created *periculum sortis*.[32] Rightly, then, preachers never tired of using their persuasions on widows and other moneyed persons not to lend upon usury, but to occupy, or be partner in, a farm or a trade, or take a part in a ship or shipping venture, or some business where they stood to gain or to lose their capital.[33]

Usury was always unlawful in England. After the departure of the Jews in 1290, some usurers were prosecuted, and usury was still complained of, but for long attracted little further attention in Parliament. In 1341 a

---

[29] Fenton, op. cit., p. 20.

[30] Mosse, op. cit., p. 27; for Mosse, see P. Collinson, *The Elizabethan Puritan Movement*, 1967, p. 436.

[31] Fenton, op. cit., p. 127.

[32] Ibid., p. 19.

[33] Wilson, op. cit., p. 262; Blaxton, op. cit., pp. 60–61; Fenton, op. cit., pp. 118–19; R. Bolton, *A Short and Private Discourse betweene Mr Bolton and one M. S. concerning Usury*, 1637, p. 50.

statute confirmed that the Church was to deal with live usurers and the Crown with dead ones. Otherwise, however, usury for long received little notice in Parliament or elsewhere.[34] Amongst the other possible causes of this relative silence may be mentioned the efficacy of the common law against usury, the contraction rather than the expansion of credit, and the generally downward trend of prices. During a period of falling prices, the lender who takes back never a penny more than he lent, will, as often as not, receive back greater value than he lent, for on return the same sum will buy more than it would have done when lent. A short-term loan might bring little or no gain from falling prices, and might even attract a loss, for prices, though on a downward trend, nevertheless fluctuated over short periods. But a long-term loan was likely to reap advantage from falling prices, and the lender, therefore, had no need to charge usury in order to take it; it was paid to him willingly and unwittingly, silently and unsolicited. A hypothetical case was put by the Doctor in the *Discourse*: 'I do feare the fall of mony, and therefore, doe deliver my mony to another man, to have asmuche at 6 monthes after according as the money was then currant when I payd it. It is usury, for that there is more to be payd then was receaved.'[35] In such a situation no sermon or law against usury was of much avail.

Conversely, when the trend had been reversed and a period of generally rising prices ensued in the latter part of the fifteenth century, there was a great upsurge of complaint, sermonizing and legislation against usury, for now, in order to receive back as much real value as he had advanced, a lender had often to get slightly more back in face value. Also interest rates were rising rather than falling, and usurers tended to demand usury at an enhanced rate. One result in England was a series of parliamentary statutes that finally succeeded in curbing usury. Maximum rates were established for interest in all transactions under those extrinsic titles that usurers were accustomed to employ as camouflage. Understandably, the statutory rate had to be altered from time to time to keep it in step with natural and market rates of interest; in the seventeenth and early eighteenth centuries it had to be lowered. We need to stress, however, that the statutes merely supplemented the common-law prohibition of usury and the ecclesiastical jurisdiction against usurers.

There was no change in Christian attitudes to usury in the usual and narrow sense of the word. Anglican ecclesiastical courts always reproved and punished usury. They went on punishing petty usurers with censure

---

[34] Stat. 15 Ed. 3 stat. 1 cap. 5; W. Hudson, *Leet Jurisdiction in the City of Norwich*, Selden Society, (1891) 1892, v, 35.

[35] Wilson, op. cit., p. 294; cf. J. Thirsk and J. P. Cooper, *Seventeenth-Century Economic Documents*, Oxford, 1972, pp. 102–3.

and compulsory contributions to the poor box, and gross and contumacious ones with lesser or greater excommunication.[36] By the 1640s correction was also being meted out by nonconformist elders and ministers, and it is noteworthy that in their courts even the Calvinists had to resort to the common and narrow sense of 'usury'. In 1647, for instance, the Second Classis of the Province of Lancaster, meeting in Preston, ruled, 'That usury is a scandalous sin, deserving suspension upon obstinacy'. It could hardly

---

36 Stats 13 E. 3 c. 5; 3 H. 7 c. 5(6); 11 H. 7 c. 8; 37 H. 8 c. 9; 5 and 6 E. 6 c. 20; 13 Eliz. c. 8; 21 Jas c. 17; D. Cressy and L. A. Ferrell; *Religion and Society in Early Modern England: A Source Book*, London and New York, 1996, p. 163; Fenton, op. cit., p. 71; Bolton, op. cit., p. 32; R. Burn, *Ecclesiastical Law*, 4 vols, 1797, vol. iv, pp. 39, 40; R. H. Tawney, *Religion and the Rise of Capitalism*, Harmondsworth, 1938, pp. 150–52; Wilson, op. cit., pp. 184, 322–4; K. Thomas, 'Cases of conscience in seventeenth-century England', in J. Morrill, P. Slack and D. Woolf, *Public Duty and Private Conscience in Seventeenth-Century England*, Oxford, 1993, p. 47; F. G. Emmison, *Elizabethan Life: Morals and the Church Courts*, Chelmsford, 1973, p. 73; W. P. M. Kennedy, *Elizabethan Episcopal Administration: An Essay in Sociology and Politics*, 3 vols, Alcuin Club, xxvi, 1924, vol. ii, pp. 14, 57, 61, 63–4, 98, 121, 131, 142, 180, 184, 231, 248, 293, 348–9; W. H. Frere, *Visitation Articles and Injunctions of the Period of the Reformation*, 3 vols, Alcuin Club, xiv, 1910, vol. ii, pp. 338, 348, 387, 398, 424; vol. iii, pp. 228, 276, 291–2, 381; D. Wilkins, *Concilia Magnae Britanniae et Hibernae a Synodo Verolamiensi A.D. CCCXLVI ad Londiniensem A.D. MDCCXVII*, 4 vols, 1737, vol. iv, 509; W. H. Hale, *A Series of Precedents and Proceedings in Criminal Causes extending from the year 1475 to 1640: extracted from Act-Books of Ecclesiastical Courts in the Diocese of London, illustrative of the Discipline of the Church of England*, 1847, pp. 43, 70 (nos 159, 238); C. I. A. Ritchie, *The Ecclesiastical Courts of York*, Arbroath, 1956, p. 225; J. A. Sharpe, *Crime in Seventeenth-Century England*, Cambridge, 1983, p. 46; L. Andrewes, *Two Answers to Cardinal Perron and other Miscellaneous Works*, Oxford, 1954, pp. 121, 137; R. E. Rodes, *Ecclesiastical Administration in Medieval England: The Anglo-Saxons to the Reformation*, Notre Dame and London, 1977, p. 130; J. S. Purvis, *Tudor Parish Documents of the Diocese of York: A Selection with Introduction and Notes*, Cambridge, 1948, pp. 12, 13, 182, 184, 200–201; R. A. Marchant, *The Church under the Law: Justice, Administration and Discipline in the Diocese of York 1500–1640*, Cambridge, 1969, pp. 141, 176, 218–19; E. Grindal, *The Remains of Archbishop Grindal*, ed. W. Nicholson, Parker Society 1843, p. 143; R. Houlbrooke, *Church Courts and the People during the English Reformation 1520–1570*, Oxford, 1979, p. 40; idem, 'The decline of ecclesiastical jurisdiction under the Tudors', in R. O'Day and F. Heal, *Continuity and Change: Personnel and Administration in the Church in England 1500–1640*, Leicester, 1976, pp. 250, 254–7; E. Cardwell, *Synodalia: a collection of articles of religion, canons, and proceedings of convocation in the province of Canterbury from the year 1547 to the year 1717*, 2 vols, 1842, vol. i, pp. 124, 155, 226, 308; vol. ii, p. 436; R. H. Helmholz, *Roman Canon Law in Reformation England*, Cambridge, 1990, pp. 116, 161; idem, 'Usury and the Medieval English Church Courts', *Speculum*, 1986, **61**, 365 seqq., esp. 379–80; Capel, op. cit., 1st pagination, pp. 263, 265–6; J. Duns Scotus, *Quaestiones in Quartum Librum Sententiarum*, dist. xv, qu. II (in J. Duns Scotus, *Opera Omnia*, 26 vols, Paris, 1891–95, vol. xviii, p. 328); Aquinas, as Chapter 1, note 40; Cheshire RO, Chester Diocesan Records, Consistory Court, Court Papers: 1608, no. 71; 1612, no. 13; 1627, no. 51; 1628, no. 65; 1638, no. 153; York, Borthwick Institute of Historical Research, Court of High Commission, Act Bk 11 fos 53, 72ᵛ, 80; Court of Dean and Chapter, presentments and office, 3 and 14 Sept. 1602.

have spoken otherwise, for even the English version of the Geneva Bible rendered the relevant part of Psalm 15 as 'He that giveth not his money to usury ... shall never be mooved'.[37]

There was no completely new attitude to usury in the narrow sense. There was no new, generally accepted continental definition of usury. What there was in a few writers who dealt with usury, often only in passing and in a cursory fashion, was a preference for the old Roman civil-law terminology, which distinguished between licit *usura* such as farm rents, and illicit *foenus*, which was what everyone else called 'usury'. Nearly everyone condemned usury or *foenus*, except, perhaps, under rare and exceptional circumstances. Usury, either so called or dubbed *foenus*, was generally condemned by English people, just as it always had been.

One exception to this general rule was an anonymous and unpublished piece surreptitiously passed from hand to hand about 1633. This seems not to have survived, but Capel reviews it for us. The author declared all usury unlawful, but denied all lending for gain was usurious; if we lent money for trade, we might take payment for the loan itself, irrespective of whether the borrower gained or lost by it.[38] (Doc. 34) One bizarre remark about usury was attributed, rightly or wrongly, to John Selden, in his table-talk, perhaps when in his cups:

> The Jews were forbidden to take use one of another, but they were not forbidden to take it of other nations. That being so, I see no reason why I may not as well take use for my money, as rent for my house. 'Tis a vain thing to say, Money begets not money, for that no doubt it does.[39]

John Milton made a random jotting in much the same sense, but opposed 'biting usury'.[40] As far as we know, opinions like Selden's and those reported by Capel were, and remained, most unusual. Anyway, those who wanted to trade had no need to borrow, still less to borrow at usury. They had only to buy on the usual quarterly credit terms and then had a good chance of avoiding even interest by way of 'forbearance'.

There were also a few attempts to marry the classical Latin terminology adopted by Calvin and others to traditional beliefs and ordinary English speech. One of the earliest English works consistently to follow Roman

---

37 Hale, op. cit., p. 166 (no. 504); W. A. Shaw, *Minutes of the Bury Presbyterian Classis, 1647–1657*, pt i, Chetham Society, new series, 1896, vol. xxxvi, pp. 32–3; cf. *Register of the Ministers, Elders and Deacons of the Christian Congregation of St Andrews, 1559–1600*, pt i, 1559–82, Scottish History Society, 1889, vol. iv, p. 309.

38 Capel, op. cit., 2nd pagination, pp. 293–4, 298.

39 J. Selden, *Seldeniana, or the Table-Talk of John Selden esq., being his sense of various matters of weight and high consequence relating especially to religion and state*, n.d., p. 127.

40 J. Milton, *Complete Prose Works of John Milton*, New Haven, CT, and London, 8 vols, 1953–82, vol. ii, pp. 322, 656; vol. vi, pp. 775–7.

civil-law terminology is *A Treatise on Usury*, an anonymous, unpaginated, unfoliated, and apparently unpublished essay dated 1605. It follows Bucer and others in defining usury as any gain taken above the principal, and then divides usury into two kinds, lawful and unlawful. Biting usury is against God's law and always punishable, not least by excommunication. The author then outlines various kinds of lawful usury, of which the chief were by title of *damnum emergens* or *lucrum cessans*, when a man lending 'to a sett daie' has been 'disapointed of his money'. Truly liberal or voluntary usury was no less lawful. As for usury by compact 'with the intent to doe his neighbour good', it was lawful in God's eyes, even when not in the Magistrate's. Allowance is made for usury in aid of persons mentally or physically incapable or rendered weak by their sex, as widows were. But always the lenders must 'be carefull to what persons they lend ther mony for increase, least they be thought to preferr ther owne commoditie before Gods glory'. A covenant to pay usury after a specified date will make the debtor more careful to pay back on time. Apparently alluding to the Act of 1571, the author remarks, 'This lawe of 10 in 100 is greatly mistaken and much abused by the usurers of this kingdome ... they thinck that this lawe doth aucthorise and commaund them to take 10 in 100', whereas it was really intended for the punishment of evildoers. Usury should be charged not from greed, but merely from the desire for moderate gain, and even then only, if 'this encrease cannot be taken but with the great hurt of his debtor, hee is willing (notwithstanding all covenants) to remytt this consideracion in whole or in parte'. A lender also avoids sin if 'yett in his soule hee is inwardly resolved to hazard his princypall', and if the borrower 'shall loose his principall, he is willing ... to beare this loss in parte or in whole'. The virtuous lender 'often lendeth freely, not looking for his owne againe'. He forgives a defaulting debtor if he be in need, and gives to all who stand in need. Finally, he takes no gain above the principal but that which may stand with the common good. In chapter 9 all this argument is summarized under the two headings of lawful and unlawful usury. (Doc. 35) Generally the author shows complete conformity with Calvin's view of these matters, and eventually he openly reveals his mentors, namely, Calvin, Bucer, Bullinger and, to a lesser extent, Perkins, and then adds, 'Among thes late writers Calvin worthely hath the first place, who for his true religion, exceeding learning and singular judgment in the Church of God, is highly esteemed concerning the lawfullnes of usury'. Our author was obviously one of that rare breed, the English Calvinists. Understandably, what we have once again is a set of circumlocutions to describe in a vague way what ordinary mortals knew as either lawful titles to interest or as unlawful usuries. Thus most usury, in the broad sense, including *damnum emergens, lucrum cessans, periculum sortis* and *poena conventionalis*, is justified, for it is by compact 'with the intent to doe his neighbour good', and allowance is made for liberal, voluntary usury and that taken on behalf of orphans and other helpless persons. What is not allowable is the taking of increase where it 'biteth and gnaweth the borrower', exceeds the statutory rate, or fails to 'stande with common good'. In other words, all usury in the broad sense is justified, excepting only usury in the narrow sense, which is wicked.[41]

A partial apology for usury, in the sense of fenory or ocker, came from the pen of Robert Filmer about 1624. Usury, he said, was not absolutely forbidden by God and not forbidden by Christ. Indeed, the very word 'usury' is not found in the New Testament. Usury was only forbidden on loans to the poor, not on those to the rich. Usury was no sin unless it hurt the borrower. When merchants borrowed on usury to trade, they made goods cheaper than they would have been, because they exchanged dear things for cheap. There was no difference in principle between lending money and letting land or hiring out goods. It was just that money was more durable. To live idly on usury was a sin, but, then, all idle living was sinful. Usurers were by no means all evil men. Many were well disposed to good works and gave much money to charitable uses. Conscience should be the guide. None of this was truly original and most of it had been refuted long before.[42] Its main argument had already been refuted by Thomas Adams in 1618: 'They ... reason thus: I must give to the poore, therefore I must take usury of the rich, an argument of Standgate-hole: I may robbe some so that I can give to others. But ... the law ... is, "Thou shalt not lend upon usury." Studie an answere to that question.'[43] Even earlier, in 1605, Henry Howard, Earl of Northampton, had declared, 'It is an absurd distinction between biting usury and gentle usury, for ... by the Scripture all manner of usury is prohibited'. Lord Chancellor Egerton agreed, saying it was a great 'mistakinge' that usury at ten in the hundred was allowed by law; it was not so, for by the Act of 13 Elizabeth caput 8 all manner of usury was prohibited. By God's law it was a detestable sin. This agreed exactly with the views of religious writers like Richard Bernard.[44]

A work that came out in 1679 argued that the distinction between usury in the narrow sense and interest was no more than a flimsy legal technicality.

---

[41] Bodleian Library, Western Manuscripts, MS. Rawl. D. 677. Cf. G. Abbot, *An Exposition upon the Prophet Jonah*, 1600, p. 92.

[42] R. Filmer, *Quaesto Quodlibetica or a Discourse whether it may be lawfull to take Use for Money*, 1653, pp. 15, 16, 19, 20, 22, 27, 44, 56, 59, 107–8, 113–14, 126–7, 129–30, 146, 148–9.

[43] T. Adams, *The Happines of the Church*, 2 vols, 1618, vol. i, pp. 117–18.

[44] W. P. Baildon, *Les Reportes del Cases in Camera Stellata, 1593–1609*, p.p., 1894, pp. 236–7; R. Bernard, *The Isle of Man: or the Legall Proceeding in Man-shire against Sinne*, 1627, pp. 31, 75, 209; idem, *The Ready Way to Good Works, or a Treatise of Charity*, 1635, pp. 361–3.

A loan could be made for a period as short as three days and then so-called interest claimed for delay in repayment was really usury. Such a transaction was lawful if the three days were mentioned in the contract, unlawful if not. Much of what went on was something that might justly be called 'inter-usury'. All loans were risky, as all business was risky, and even bottomry was not exceptionally hazardous. If cessant gain and emergent loss were legal substitutes for usury, why should not all usury be legal? There was no proof that all gains from usury were evil. The Bible only condemned griping usury, as practised on the poor. Money lent was consumed, but then so might be arrented houses and fields. There was no harm in lending on usury to the rich, and borrowing on usury enabled some men to preserve or improve their estates. Anyway, in practice, statute law tolerated moderate usury, and if usury damned the soul, the law tolerated moderate damnation of the soul. As long as interest was lawful, it was not easy to condemn usury. Also usury (the word now being employed in its broad sense, *recte* interest by *periculum sortis*) was allowed when the principal was at risk. Finally, however,

> It becomes every man to look to his conscience in such and the like dealings and contracts: that nothing be done to the prejudice of Christian charity, moderation, equity and prudence, but in all things to be careful to do to others, as in like circumstances they judge it reasonable others should do to them.[45]

Here Calvin's doctrine is stretched to, and somewhat beyond, its limits. The point about letting real estate was that if it were destroyed, the owner could not recover it from the lessee. To leave all to the Christian conscience, gratuitously assumes that everyone has one. The drawback to relying on people to do as they would be done by, as Richard Turnbull had pointed out years before, was that many a usurer would have said he was doing as he would be done by. It would have been better to have put forward the precept that people should do to others whatsoever *good* thing they would have done to them.[46]

Some of Calvin's utterances were built upon by Richard Baxter, who was much inclined towards presbyterianism and followed Calvin with a degree of slavishness. Not all usury was unlawful. God only forbade it against the poor. Moses had not forbidden usury in general, and, anyway, we were no longer bound by mosaic law. No positive forbiddance of usury was to be found in the New Testament. To give and take usury was

---

[45] P. T., *Usury Stated: being a reply to Mr Jelingers* Usurer Cast, 1679, pp. 3, 5–8, 10, 13, 14, 21, 23, 25, 29, 36, 49, 58–9, 81–2, 89, 93, 95–7, 101, 103, 108–9, 116, 256, 258–9.

[46] R. Turnbull, *An Exposition upon the XV. Psalm devided into foure sermons*, 1591, fo. 50ᵛ; cf. T. Lupton, *A Dream of the Devill and Dives*, 1615, sig. E.6.

allowable when a merchant borrowed to trade on the principal, provided
he had adequate reserves and was almost certain to succeed in his venture;
when the borrower gained more than the lender; and when a guardian
lent an orphan's money to a rich man who was certain to repay. But Baxter's
definition of usury was hazy; it was 'the receiving of any additional gain
as due from money lent'. Charity and conscience were to be the only
guides.[47]

One man who tried to bridge the gap between the two sets of terminology
was Jeremy Taylor, the high-church chaplain in ordinary to Charles I and
Bishop of Down and Connor. He said if a commonwealth permitted a
usurious contract, it was not unjust. 'But if usury be unlawful, because
it is uncharitable: when it becomes necessary it is also charitable
comparatively; and as to charity, no man by the laws of God is to be
compelled.' Yet,

> The permission of the prince is no absolution from the authority of
> the Church. Supposing usury to be unlawful, as it is certain many
> kinds and instances of it are highly criminal, yet the civil laws permit
> it, and the Church forbids it. In this case the canons are to be preferr'd.
> For though it is permitted, yet by the laws no man can be compell'd
> to be a usurer; and therefore he must pay that reverence and obedience
> which is otherwise due to them that have the rule over them and the
> conduct of their souls.[48]

A well-balanced view came from Robert Sanderson. He set out three
basic criteria by which usurers were to be judged: first, whether their acts
were lawful or not; second, whether usury were a true calling in life; third,
whether or not it were good for the commonwealth. He concluded that
usury was unlawful, no true calling and harmful to the commonwealth.
The usurer fleeced many and clothed none.[49] (Doc. 36) Another balanced
view came from Joseph Hall: a good rule for our actions is, 'To do nothing
doubtingly'. Following this precept leads him to condemn usury and give
simple and lucid justification to *damnum emergens* and *lucrum cessans*.[50]
(Doc. 37)

English terminology was originally akin to the German. As 'ocker' passed
out of use in polite society, 'usury' was occasionally used in its original

---

[47] R. Baxter, *A Christian Directory or a Summ of the Practical Theologie and Cases of
Conscience*, 4 pts, 1673, pt iv, 'Christian Politicks', pp. 124 seqq.

[48] J. Taylor, *Ductor Dubitantium, or the Rule of Conscience*, 3rd edn, 1676, pp. 285,
571.

[49] R. Sanderson, *XXV Sermons*, 1681, 1st pagination, 200 seqq.; *idem*, *XXXVI Sermons*,
introduced by Isaac Walton, 1689, pp. 219–20.

[50] J. Hall, *The Works of Joseph Hall, D.D., successively bishop of Exeter and Norwich*,
12 vols, Oxford, 1837–39, vol. vi, p. 35; vol. vii, pp. 372–4; and see, I. H. (J. Hall), *Resolutions
and Decisions of divers practicall Cases of Conscience in continuall Use amongst Men*,
1649, pp. 6, 9–11, 14.

broad sense, but here, too, it acquired a bad name and a narrow sense, for fenory was so wicked that it besmirched every name it assumed. Later, as in Germany, it became a practice to refer merely to rates of return, to giving or taking, say, five in the hundred, ten in the hundred, and so on, without any characterization of the legal status of the transaction. In England, too, the word 'interest' was introduced and is found being used both truthfully and euphemistically. When writing in Latin, Englishmen usually equated *usura* and *foenus*, just as Melanchthon did, or, later, in deference to civil-law terminology, specifically condemned *foenus*.[51] Jewel was one of those who followed this terminology, even when not accepting all Calvin's conclusions. In a discourse on usury, A.B. asks Jewel,

> *An quicquid ex pacto supra sortem accipitur ab eo qui mutuo dat pecuniam mercatori illicitum foenus sit, quamvis non quaerat lucrum nisi ex lucro, idque animo mercatoris.*

> Whether as a result of an agreement anything taken by him who gives money to a merchant on loan be illicit fenory, even though he demand no profit nor any reward by way of profit, and it is by the merchant's own will?

Jewel answers, '*Imo foenerator saepe etiam ex jactura lucrum quaerit, non tantum ex lucro*' – 'Oh yes, a usurer often seeks gain by voluntary offering, not so much as by gain'. Here *foenus* and *foenerator* are being used to make a distinction between *foenus* and *usura*. Faced with a further series of questions, Jewel answers in the negative Calvin's query as to whether it were lawful for a poor man to lend on usury to a rich one. Jewel concludes that '*omnis usura damnata est*' – 'all usury is damned', but that,

> *inter usuram et mutuum multum est discriminis. Deus enim mutuo dare jussit, foenerari prohibuit; et mutuum cum caritate conjunctum est, usura cum avaritia.*

> between usury and lending in general there is a very sharp distinction. Truly, God commanded us to give loans, but forbade *foenus*; and lending is joined to charity, usury to avarice.

Jewel's answers may be summed up by saying he takes 'usury' in the broad sense and then analyses it in such a way as to justify lawful interest and condemn usury in the narrow sense.[52] (Doc. 38)

William Perkins, the Cambridge don with Calvinistic leanings, writes in a rather a similar way. He starts off by citing the Eighth Commandment – 'Thou shalt not steal' – and adds that stealing here includes malicious

---

51 Wilkins, op. cit., vol. i, p. 313; Cardwell, *Synodalia*, vol. vi, p. 226; Frere, op. cit., vol. ii, p. 387.

52 J. Jewel, *The Works of John Jewel*, ed. J. Ayre, Parker Society, 4 vols, 1845–50, vol. iv, pp. 1293–5, 1297.

damage, unjust dealing, forgery, deceitful bargaining, using false measures and weights, concealing goodness when buying or faults when selling, engrossing, bankruptcy, delaying repayment of loans, and to stoop 'to practise usury'. He explains,

> Usurie is a gaine exacted by covenant, above the principall onely in lue and recompence of the lending of it. Usurie beeing considered as it is thus described, is quite contrarie to Gods word, and may very fitly be tearmed biting lucre ... And this usurie, positive laws doe not onely restraine, but not allow.
> Question: Is it not lawfull to take at some time above the principall?
> Answer: Yes, surely, with these conditions: I. If a man take heede that he exact nothing, but that which his debter can get by good and lawfull meanes. II. He may not take more than the gaine, nay not all the gaine, nor that part of the gaine which drinketh up the living of him that useth the money. III. He must sometimes be so farre from taking gaine, that he must not require the principall, if his debter be by inevitable and just casualties brought behind, and it be also plaine that he could not make, no, not by great diligence, any commoditie of the money borrowed.

He then lists three reasons why a man may take above the principal: the debtor parts with some of his gain; the debtor who gains by the loan should show gratitude; and the creditor may have stood to benefit from having the money in his own hands. A short exchange follows:

> Objection: Money is not fruitfull, therefore it is unlawfull to receive more then we lent out.
> Answer: Albeit money in it selfe be not fruitfull, yet it is made very fruitfull by the borrowers good use, as ground is, which is not fruitfull except it be tilled.[53]

Once again, interest is allowed and usury condemned.

Some other learned divines followed the etymological and related arguments spread by Calvin, and tried to reconcile them with traditional Christian beliefs and the generally accepted meanings of 'usury' and 'interest'. Amongst these men may be numbered Willet,[54] Powel[55] and Spottiswoode. John Spottiswoode, Archbishop of St Andrews, wrote with great clarity. As befitted a Scots divine, he embraced the broad, etymologically proper sense of the word 'usury', but went on to discuss usury in the common, narrow, improper sense, declaring, 'Usurie

---

[53] W. Perkins, *The Workes of that famous and worthie Minister of Christ, in the University of Cambridge, M. W. Perkins*, Cambridge, 1603, pp. 63–5.

[54] A. Willet, *Hexapta in Exodum: that is, a sixfold commentary upon the second booke of Moses called Exodus*, 1608, pp. 508 seqq.

[55] G. Powel, *Theological and Scholasticall Positions concerning Usurie*, Oxford, 1602, pp. 1, 9, 13, 15, 19; idem, *Theologicall Positions concerning the Lawfulnesse of Borrowing upon Usurie*, 1605, pp. 1–3, 10, 11, 23.

improperlie so called, is simplie unlawfull'. Furthermore, forbidding usury on the poor did not make it permissible on the rich; it was always wrong. But usury in the proper, broad sense, as in arrenting lands and taking genuine interest was perfectly allowable. Christian charity should be the guide and would lead to this conclusion.[56]

It was Martin Bucer, the moderate reformer who moved from Strasburg to take the chair of divinity in Cambridge in 1548, who caused the greatest stir in England with his introduction of Roman civil-law terminology. He was accused of having told undergraduates that Christians were permitted to practise usury. This inflamed a don by the name of John Young and led to a heated controversy between the two. What had happened was, Bucer had been inveighing against *'foenerationem iniquam'* and *'mordentes usuras'*, by which he intended the wicked taking of *foenus* or biting usuries as distinct from licit ones. This made some of the young students anxious, for they failed to fathom his terminology and could only be financed by means of what he called usury. Bucer was therefore moved by compassion to explain to them that many forms of usury were perfectly in accord with Christianity, by which he meant many forms of usury in the broad Roman civil-law sense, such as letting lands to farm. In order to explain his position and placate all those he had offended or dismayed, Bucer felt obliged to write a booklet entitled *De Usuris*. Here he pointed out, amongst other things, that *'Patres atque philosophi simpliciter omnem usuram non insectantur'* – 'The holy fathers and philosophers do not simply attack all usury'. A taker of usury (in this broad, uncommon sense) should share any loss with the payer who had not been able to profit from the transaction, while the borrower should share some of his gains with the lender. This was a vague and circumlocutory way of justifying interest on the grounds of *periculum sortis*. Then he goes on to emphasize that *'usura mordens, qua proximus afficitur damno, non invatur'* – 'biting usury, which is inherently harmful, is unpleasing' in God's eyes. Bucer says:

> *Item ex non vero intellectu dicti Dominii, 'Mutuam dantes, et nihilinde sperantes', dogmati inesse usuram a Christo prohibitum, pecuniam accipere pro pecuniae usu, quocunque modo accipiatur.*

> Likewise it is not based on a true understanding of God's word, 'Lend, expecting nothing', to hold to the doctrine of usury being prohibited by Christ, to take money for the use of money, irrespective of the way it is taken.

Interesse, by *cessans lucrum* or *emergens damnum*, he goes on, is, of course, perfectly permissible. He is thus compelled by circumstances to use what

---

56 J. Spottiswoode (Spotswoode), *The Execution of Neschech and the Confyning of his Kinsman Tarbith or a Short Discourse shewing the Difference betwixt damned Usurie and that which is Lawfull*, Norwich, 1616, pp. 12, 13, 15, 23–4, 27, 29, 33, 35, 37.

he was normally at pains to avoid, namely, the standard Latin terms for interest, cessant gain and emergent loss. But he greatly disliked having to do this, and tried as fast as he could to put his loss of countenance behind him by turning back upon Young in words cast in Roman civil-law terminology:

> *Cum itaque Iungus non posset illud usurae genus, quod ego admitto, peccate convincere, hortabatur me, ut cum rursus de hac re agerem, bene explicarem, eum qui pro usu pecuniae suae partem lucri accipiat, quod Dei beneficio innoxium obveniat, communicet etiam damno, si quod ille qui pecuniam utitur, contraxerit.*

> Since therefore Young was unable to demonstrate that the derivation of usury that I accept, was wrong, it encouraged me, so that I come back to the matter again; I explain clearly: he who takes part of the gain for the use of his money, when it comes to him innocently by the grace of God, should also share in the loss, if he who uses the money, be in straitened circumstances.[57]

The two men were saying the same thing in different terminologies and each accusing the other of error.

The civilians, or professors of Roman civil law, who were engaged in the courts of the Constable and Marshal, High Commission, Admiralty, Star Chamber and later even Requests and Chancery, tended to follow the Roman terminology of *usura* and *foenus*,[58] but they understood that these were special uses that had to be handled carefully, for, as Matthew Hutton, dean of York, once burst out, 'Many things are termed usury in the civil law, which are not usury in the word of God'.[59]

Most scholars with Calvinistic leanings were no different from traditional Anglicans in their attitude to usury in the narrow sense of ocker. They learned from Calvin and other Europeans, but never followed them slavishly. Sir John Davies was orthodox and thoroughly opposed to all ocker, but translated the relevant line in Psalm 15: 5 as 'Nor hath for bitinge use his monie lent.'[60] William Ames, the famous Independent divine and associate of Hugh Peter (the New Model Army chaplain), denied that all usury was absolutely unlawful. Money was not sterile, because it could be exchanged for opportunities for labour that brought gain. Nevertheless,

---

[57] C. Hopf, *Martin Bucer and the English Reformation*, Oxford, 1946, pp. 122 seqq.; M. Bucer, 'De Usuris', in M. Bucer, *Scripta Anglicana fere omnia*, Basle, 1577, pp. 789 seqq.

[58] T. F. T. Plucknett, *A Concise History of the Common Law*, 1956, pp. 43–4, 184, 205–6, 295–6, 298–9; Coke, op. cit., vol. i (Co. Litt.) fo. 11ᵛ; vol. iv, pp. 134–5; T. Smith, *De Republica Anglorum*, 1583, p. 116.

[59] I. P. Ellis, 'The archbishop and the usurers', *Journal of Ecclesiastical History*, 1970, 21, 37.

[60] J. Davies, *The Works of Sir John Davies*, ed. A. B. Grosart, p.p., 3 vols, 1869–76, vol. i, p. 379.

he recognized such entitlements to interest as emergent loss and cessant gain, condemned biting usury and exhorted that nothing be done against equity and charity.[61] Holmes countered this by saying all usury was biting and cuttingly remarked that Ames, who was in exile in Rotterdam, was living amongst usurers and durst not condemn usury outright.[62] Thomas Adams, who generally followed Roman terminology, none the less lumped together as 'pleasing gobbets of avarice ... usuries, oppressions, exactions, enclosings, rackings, rakings'. In a catalogue of the diseases of the soul, 'Next to the dropsie of covetice, I would place the immoderate hunger of usurie'. Some have likened it to the gout, 'by reason of that diseases incidence to usurers', gout and usury both being incurable. The usurer miscalls usury 'interest', but 'he drownes the noyse of the peoples curses with the musicke of his money ... He sels time to his customers, his food to his coffer, his body to languishment, his soule to the Divell'.[63] Ainsworth denounces biting usury, so called 'because it biteth and consumeth the borrower and his substance'.[64] William Whately (Wheatlie) exhorted men to lend gratis to the needy, but nothing to the unthrifty and prodigal, and not to exact gain unconditionally from men of sufficiency irrespective of whether the borrower gained or lost from what he invested the loan in, which suggests he preferred partnerships or conditional loans to usurious ones.[65]

Robert Bolton, the highly learned parson of Broughton in Northamptonshire, gives one of the best expositions of this robust good sense in a clear and unpedantic view of usury. Even the usurers themselves know usury to be evil, which is why they eschew the name.[66] What is generally understood as usury differs radically from other forms of what is called usury in the broad sense. Land bears fruit to answer the rent; even without man's help, meadows, pastures, woods and so on go on

61 W. Ames, *De Conscientia et eius Iure vel Casibus*, Amsterdam, 1631, pp. 382 seqq.; W. Ames (Medulla), *Theologica*, Amsterdam, 1648, lib. II, cap. XX, para. xxiii, sentence 3 (p. 339).

62 N. Holmes, *Usury is Injury, cleared in an examination of its best apologie alleaged by a countrey minister, out of Dr Ames, in his Cases of Conscience, as a party and patron of that apologie*, 1640, pp. 5, 13–15, 21, 24, 28.

63 T. Adams, *The Sermons of Thomas Adams: The Shakespeare of Puritan Theologians*, ed. J. Brown, Cambridge, 1909, p. 27; idem, *Happines of the Church*, vol. i, pp. 117–18; idem, *Diseases of the Soule: a discourse divine, morall, and physicall*, 1616, pp. 27 seqq.

64 H. Ainsworth, *Annotations upon the Booke of Psalmes*, 1617, Psalm 15, v. 5; idem, *Annotations upon the Third Booke of Moses, called Leviticus*, 1618, Leviticus xxv. 36–7; idem, *Annotations upon the Fifth Booke of Moses, called Deuteronomie*, 1619, Deuteronomy xv. 7–8; xxiii. 19, 20.

65 W. Wheatlie (Whately), *A Caveat for the Covetous, or a sermon preached at Paules Crosse upon the fourth of December, out of Luke 12.15*, 1609, p. 64.

66 Bolton, op. cit., p. 2.

growing. Both landlord and tenant bear the risk of fire, flood, invasion and other calamities. The same applies to all hirings; if what be hired perish through no fault of the hirer, both the owner and the hirer lose. Fanciful interpretations of *nesheck, tarbith* and *marbith* are mere quibbling. They all mean usury in the narrow sense. There is no such thing as 'biting' usury as distinct from other kinds: 'all usury biteth'.

> Divines pretended for usury, deale with it, as the apothecary doth with poyson, working and tempering it with so many cautions, and limitations, that in the end, they make it no usury at all ... After they have examined the point, and answered the reasons, as they think, which are usually brought against usury by the Schoole; yet in conclusion, put all their limitations together, they agree upon no usury at all, as it shall be defined by and by. Single out one from another, there is not any one of them, who dares defend any such ordinary usury, as is amongst us practised with the greatest moderation.[67]

If money be taken at usury for provisions, ruin follows when the principal is exhausted. If any gain be made from the investment of borrowed money, it comes not from the money, but from labour, skill and industry. If money be borrowed for the purpose of trade or industry, the borrower must make two livings, one for himself and one for the usurer, and must therefore seek to push prices up.[68] Usury is not forbidden in the New Testament, but this proves nothing, for nor is polygamy. But usury is expressly forbidden in the Old Testament. Even if both sides gain from it, this makes usury no less evil. Often both sides gain from wicked deeds. Usury displaces free lending. It is a gainful form of idleness.[69] Just because it is forbidden to rob the poor, it does not follow that one may rob the rich. Divine law applies to rich and poor alike. Usury ruins the rich man who pays it. It is worse than useless merely to exhort people to do as they would be done by. For this precept to be worth anything, it must be expounded according to the dictates of a good conscience, and not everyone is endowed with a good conscience.[70] This is why 'usury is branded, and censurable both by 1. The common law, 2. statute law, 3. ecclesiasticall law'. All these are needed to bridle usury, and even then it cannot be extirpated. But even if usury must be, woe to the usurers. (Bolton's use of this last sentence suggests he had studied Luther, and his reference to the apothecary that he had read Fenton.)[71] Liberal usury, when the borrower gives the lender a purely

---

[67] Ibid, pp. 12, 13, 52.

[68] Ibid., pp. 14–16, 26.

[69] Ibid., pp. 24, 34–5, 38, 43.

[70] Ibid., pp. 7, 8, 10, 22. Cf. C. Gibbon, *A Work worth the Reading*, 1591, pp. 34, 37, 41–2.

[71] Bolton, op. cit., pp. 29, 32; and see M. Luther, *An die Pfarrherrn wider den Wucher zu predigen Vermanung*, 1540, in M. Luther, *Alle Bücher und Schrifften*, 8 pts (vols) Jena, 1555–58, vol. vii, fo. 401; Fenton, op. cit., p. 61.

voluntary gift, is allowable. Otherwise payment was to be made only under an extrinsic title, *ex damno emergentis* and *ex lucro cessante*, and then only after delay, *tituli morae*, with the interest independently assessed. (He ignores exceptional cases where payment might, rarely, be claimed before delay.)[72]

Amongst a few laymen who adopted Roman terminology, we may mention a London barber by name of Thomas Rugg.[73] But most ordinary Englishmen, like Nehemiah Wallington, a truly pious London turner, took 'usury' in its ordinary narrow sense and lumped it together with bribery, using false weights and measures and other sinful practices.[74] Some well-educated laymen took an interest in the arid terminological disputes between divines and attained to some understanding of them. Some were persuaded to adopt Roman terminology; some of these in turn did so because they had read some Roman civil law; others because they sympathized with Calvin or favoured his system of ecclesiastical organization. Nevertheless, it was only a matter of terminology, not of any different attitude to usury in the commonly accepted meaning of the word, for in this there was next to no disagreement among English Christians.[75]

The Usury Acts all forbade usury. Where they placed limits on rates of interest in many types of transactions, this was in order to penalize usury cloaked as interest, for excessive 'interest' was usury. The 1545 and 1571 Acts mention 'shift of interest' along with other corrupt bargains. The 1552 Act includes 'interest' amongst other deceitful forms of usury. The 1571 Act declared 'All usurie' to have been 'forbydden by the lawe of God'. The preamble to the 1621 bill that eventually became the 1624 Act had these words, 'All usury is forbidden by the lawe of God'. That this declaration was dropped and failed to appear in the Act was due to objections from some members who preferred the broad meaning of 'usury'. Rather than allow these objectors to disrupt proceedings and delay the passage of an Act so urgently needed, those who were steering the bill agreed to drop the declaration altogether. But at the end of the Act was added this proviso, 'That no wordes in this lawe contayned shalbe construed or expounded to allow the practise of usurie in point of religion

---

72 Bolton, op. cit., pp. 54–6.

73 J. T. Cliffe, *The Puritan Gentry: The Great Puritan Families of Early Stuart England*, 1984, pp. 60–61, 114–17; W. L. Sachse, *The Diurnal of Thomas Rugg 1651–1661*, Royal Historical Society, Camden 3rd series, 1961, xci, 107; cf. Anon., *The Death of Usury*, 1–3.

74 P. S. Seaver, *Wallington's World: A Puritan Artisan in Seventeenth-Century London*, 1985, p. 130.

75 T. E. Hartley, *Proceedings in the Parliaments of Elizabeth*, vol. i, 1559–81, Leicester, 1981, pp. 231 seqq.; Collinson, *The Elizabethan Puritan Movement*, p. 206; Wilson, op. cit., pp. 315–16, 351–2, 355–6.

or conscience'. This made due allowance for both terminologies and forbade usury to conformist and nonconformist alike. From 1660 onwards the statutes made no clear distinction between interest and shift of interest; but these measures, like those of 1624 and 1651, were framed with the sole purpose of lowering the legal maximum rate of interest to conform with lowered market rates. In all other respects, the 1571 Act remained in force until 1854, so usury remained a statutory offence.[76]

The espousal of Roman terminology gave rise to much confusion and misunderstanding, but did far less harm than did the usurers' deliberate corruption of language. Usurers liked to cloak their usury under the name of 'interest'. Properly speaking 'interest' was simply a generic name for what could be lawfully claimed under one or other of the extrinsic titles. No one could claim interest as such, but only under one of the titles. English law allowed no claim for interest unless under a title, so anyone who claimed interest simply so called, could be presumed to be claiming usury. When exactly 'interest' started to be used in England as an euphemism for usury is not known, but apparently it was no later than about 1540. In 1550 Crowley refers to 'interest' that seems to have been usury really. In 1595, Mosse tells his readers to,

> Note by the way for the better discoverie of the usurers evill dealing, that howsoever hee, to glose with the world, is wont to confound the names of interest and usurie – and men are woont to say, that they take interest, and lend upon interest, when indeed they take usurie and lend upon usurie.[77]

But even the best of men occasionally give way to deceitful usages constantly dinned in their ears, as nowadays with the word 'inflation'. In 1595 Fulbecke allowed himself to say, 'When the usurer letteth forth his money to interest ... yet shall he forfeit the full value of the interest'.[78] The Preacher in the *Discourse* makes the same kind of slip.[79] In excuse, it must be said it was difficult to find a form of words to cover open usury, usury masquerading as interest, and payments made up partly of one and partly of the other. 'Usurious interest' was a phrase sometimes used to cover such transactions. Little significance attaches to the employment by some

---

[76] Stats 37 H. 8 c. 9; 5 and 6 E. 6. c. 20; 13 Eliz. c. 8; 21 Jas c. 17; 12 Chas 2 c. 13; 13 Anne c. 15 (12 Anne stat. 2 c. 16); C. H. Firth and R. S. Rait, *Acts and Ordinances of the Interregnum*, 3 vols, 1911, vol. ii, pp. 548–50; *Journals of the House of Commons*, vol. i, pp. 679, 691, 694, 744, 747–8, 771, 775, 779; *Journals of the House of Lords*, vol. iii, pp. 322–3, 352, 327, 405; W. Notestein, F. H. Relf and H. Simpson, *Commons Debates 1621*, 7 vols, New Haven, CT, 1935, vol. iii, p. 184; vol. v, pp. 147–8; vol. vii, p. 209.

[77] R. Crowley, *One and Thyrtye Epigrammes*, n.d., in *The Select Works of Robert Crowley*, ed. J. M. Cowper, EETS, extra series, vol. xv, 1872, p. 50; Mosse, op. cit., p. 27.

[78] Fulbecke, op. cit., fo. 53ᵛ.

[79] Wilson, op. cit., p. 356.

accountants of the words 'use', 'interest' and 'consideration' (but not 'usury') as though they all meant the same.[80] But some terminological confusion was probably inevitable. What the usurers said, others were inclined to imitate. Thus the alleged victim of a Marlborough usurer artlessly describes him as one 'who did usually lend mony for interest'.[81] The euphemism had long been gaining ground. Even Francis Bacon had fallen into using it.[82] By 1668 Sir Thomas Culpeper the younger showed himself in two minds whether to keep to the 'usury' of his father's book title or to substitute 'interest'. Both father and son had the same sole end in view – the lowering of the statutory maximum rate, but perhaps there was some element of terminological confusion.[83] William Petty used first one word and then the other, as though he were uncertain of the difference in meaning.[84] Adam Smith was so befogged as to let slip the assertion that in olden times, 'To lend money at interest ... was considered as usury and prohibited by law', and that 'In the reign of Edward VI religious zeal prohibited all interest'.[85] It is no wonder that by the early nineteenth century it was being left to a few discerning men like Gurney the banker to distinguish usury from interest.[86]

Understandably, the corruption of language has succeeded in confusing many people.[87] Not long ago an excellent author was misled into the belief that English Protestants showed contradictory strains of thought and mixtures of 'medieval' and 'modern' ideas, and that consequently their trumpets sounded an uncertain note, when really they were all making the same valid and important distinction between usury and interest.[88]

---

[80] Huntington Library, Hastings MSS, HAF box 6, folder 3, payment entries for 6, 7, 9, 12, 13 Feb. 1605; 15, 16, 19, 21 Nov. 1606; 15 Feb. 1606; 6 Nov. 1607; 10 June 1608, et passim; J. Harland, The House and Farm Accounts of the Shuttleworths of Gawthorpe Hall, Chetham Society, xxxv, xli, xliii, xlvi, 1856–58, pp. 183, 186, 195, 204, 206, 210, 215–16, 218, 225–6 etc., but esp. 246, 249.

[81] PRO, Req. Proc. 29/8.

[82] Bacon, Essays, 'Of Usury'; and idem, Works, vol. xi, p. 325; vol. xiv, p. 416.

[83] T. Culpeper, A Tract against Usurie, presented to the High Court of Parliament, 1621; idem, A Tract against the High Rate of Usurie, presented to Parliament 1623, 1641; idem, A Tract against the High Rate of Interest, presented to the High Court of Parliament A.D. 1623, with preface by T. Culpeper jun., 1668; idem, A Tract against Usury, presented to the High Court of Parliament A.D. 1623, with preface by T. Culpeper jun., 1668.

[84] W. Petty, The Petty Papers, ed. Marquis of Lansdowne, 2 vols, 1927, vol. i, pp. 211, 246–7.

[85] A. Smith, The Wealth of Nations, ed. E. Cannan, 2 vols, 1962, vol. i, p. 99; vol. ii, p. 442; but see also vol. i, pp. 378–9.

[86] W. H. Bidwell, Annals of an East Anglian Bank, Norwich, 1900, p. 159.

[87] Tawney in Introduction to Wilson, op. cit., passim, and see e.g. pp. 165–6; C. F. Taeusch, 'The concept of "usury"', Journal of History of Ideas, 3, 1942.

[88] M. M. Knappen, Tudor Puritanism: A Chapter in the History of Idealism, Chicago and London, 1970, pp. 418–21.

Even Raymond De Roover fell into a similar trap.[89] But these errors, and others too many to list, preceded A. P. Usher's sapient observation that, 'Usury was a somewhat technical offence; a real distinction was made between lawful interest and usury. In much modern writing these distinctions are often ignored or treated as consciously sophisticated'.[90] Since Usher wrote, however, such errors have become inexcusable, and it is sad to see how they vitiate and render largely unintelligible what might otherwise have been good works of scholarship. When, in a book on the usury laws, the author, in his introduction, writes, in all seriousness, 'Throughout, for the sake of clarity, I have used the term "interest" in the modern sense, not in the way medieval lawyers understood it', one is left lost for words.[91]

Yet even the gravest matters of scholarship are as nothing compared to the transcendental importance of acquitting Christians of the charge of having countenanced usury and usurers.

---

89 De Roover, *Business, Banking and Economic Thought*, p. 185.

90 Usher, op. cit., p. 78.

91 The same fatal error has been repeated nowadays, e.g. A. A. Chafuen, *Christians for Freedom: Late Scholastic Economics*, San Francisco, 1986, pp. 139–41; S. Stein, 'The laws of interest in the Old Testament', *Journal of Theological Studies*, new series, 1953, 4, 161 seqq.; B. N. Nelson, *The Idea of Usury from Tribal Brotherhood to Universal Otherhood*, Princeton, NJ, 1949, *passim*; N. Jones, *God and the Moneylenders: Usury and Law in Early Modern England*, Oxford, 1989, p. 5 *et passim*; idem, 'Religion in Parliament', in D. M. Dean and N. L. Jones, *The Parliaments of Elizabethan England*, Oxford, 1990, pp. 131–3.

PART TWO
Select Documents

1

From J. Calvin, *Commentarii in Libros Mosis necum in Librum Josue,* Amsterdam, 1567, p. 527

Nec vero alium finem respexit Deus quam ut mutuo vigeret fraterna dilectio apud Israelitas. Hanc quidem politiae Judaicae fuisse partem liquet, quia permittitur Gentibus foenerari; quod discrimen lex spiritualis non admittit ... Porro quia diruta est maceria qua olim discernebantur Judaei a Gentibus, ratio nostra hodie diversa est: ideoque tam in foenore quam in aliis expilationibus parcendum est omnibus sine exceptione, et erga extraneos quoque servanda aequitas ... Quod autem ad jus forense spectat, nihil mirum si populo suo permiserit Deus foenus ab extraneis exigere: quia alioqui servata non fuisset mutua aequabilitas, sine qua alteram partem gravari necesse est. Mandat suis Deus ne foenerentur, ac proinde solos Judaeos hac lege, non exteras gentes, obstringit. Ergo ut vigeat ratio analogica, idem libertatis populo suo concedit quod Gentes sibi sumpturae erant: quia haec demum tolerabilis est mediocritas, ubi par est atque aequalis utriusque partis conditio.

Nor truly had God any other end in view save that mutual fraternal affection should prevail amongst the Israelites. It is evident this was part of Jewish polity, because it was lawful to lend to Gentiles on fenory: which distinction spiritual law allows not ... Next, since the wall that formerly separated Jews from Gentiles is smashed, our relation is nowadays different, and in consequence we must forego fenory as well as other plundering upon all without exception, and equity is to be observed towards strangers also ... However, looking at the political law, no wonder God permitted his people to exact fenory from foreigners: because otherwise mutual reciprocity would not have obtained, without which one side must needs be injured. God commands his people not to practise fenory, and therefore by this law lays the obligation on the Jews alone, not on foreign peoples. Therefore, in order that analogous conditions may prevail, he concedes the same liberty to his people that the Gentiles were arrogating to themselves, because precisely this moderation is tolerable, where the position of both parties is the same and equal.

2

From St Thomas Aquinas, *Summa Theologica*, in *Opera*, 28 vols, Venice, 1775–88, vol. xxii, pp. 332–3

Quod accipere usuram pro pecunia mutuata est secundum se iniustum: quia venditur id quod non est; per quod manifeste inaequalitas constituitur, quae iustitiae contrariatur.

Ad cuius evidentiam, sciendum est, quod quaedam res sunt quarum usus est ipsarum rerum consumptio; sicut vinum consumimus, eo utendo ad potum, et triticum consumimus, eo utendo ad cibum. Unde in talibus non debet seorsum computari usus rei a re ipsa; sed cuicumque conceditur usus, ex hoc ipso conceditur res; et propter hoc in talibus per mutuum transfertur dominium. Si quis ergo seorsum vellet vendere vinum et seorsum vellet vendere usum vini, venderet eandem rem bis, vel venderet id quod non est: unde manifeste per iniustitiam peccaret. Et simili ratione, iniustitiam committit qui mutuat vinum, aut triticum, petens sibi dari duas recompensationes, unam quidem restitutionem aequalis rei; aliam vero pretium usus, quod usura dicitur.

Quaedam vero sunt quorum usus non est ipsa rei consumptio; sicut usus domus est inhabitatio, non autem dissipatio. Et ideo in talibus seorsum potest utrumque concedi; puta cum aliquis tradit alteri dominium domus, reservato sibi usu ad aliquod tempus; vel e converso cum quis concedit alicui usum domus, reservato sibi eius dominio. Et propter hoc licite potest homo accipere pretium pro usu domus, et praeter hoc petere domum accommodatam, sicut patet in conductione, et locatione domus.

Pecunia autem, secundum Philosophum in V.Ethic.(cap.v. a med.) et I. Pol. (cap.v & vi) principaliter est inventa ad commutationes faciendas; et ita proprius, et principalis pecuniae usus est ipsius consumptio, sive distractio, secundum quod in commutationes expenditur. Et propter hoc secundum se est illicitum pro usu pecuniae mutuatae accipere pretium, quod dicitur usura: et sicut alia iniuste acquisita tenetur homo restituere, ita pecuniam quam per usuram accepit.

To take usury for the loan of money is in itself unjust; because it is selling what is not, by which an inequality is manifestly constituted, which is against justice. In evidence of which, it should be recognized that the use of some things is in their consumption: for instance, wine is consumed when used as a drink, and wheat when used for food. In such cases the use of a thing cannot be reckoned separately from the thing itself, so whenever a thing's use is granted to anyone, the thing itself is given at one and the same time. This is why in cases like this, ownership is made over by a loan. Were a man to sell both the wine and its use separately, he would be selling the same thing twice over, that is, would be selling what does not exist, and would clearly be sinning by an unjust action. And, by the same reasoning, he commits an injustice who demands two things in return for lending the wine or the wheat, to wit, the return of the same amount of the selfsame thing and, in addition, the price of its use, which is called usury. There are many other things whose use lies not in their consumption, as, for example, the use of a house, which lies in living in it, not destroying it. In such cases, the use of the thing and the thing itself can both be granted separately, as when, for instance, a man sells the ownership of a house to another, but reserves to himself the right to dwell in it for a time; or, again, when someone grants the occupation of a house to another, but keeps its ownership in his own hands. This is why it is allowed to a man to take a price for the use of a house, and also to sell the house itself, as may be seen clearly in the selling and leasing of houses.

Money, however, according to the Philosopher ... has been invented for the making of exchanges; and thus the proper and principal use of money lies in its consumption or in parting with it, according to its expenditure in exchanges. For which reason, then, it is unlawful to charge a price for the loan of a sum of money, which is called usury. And just as a man is bound to make restitution of other things he has acquired unjustly, so likewise what money he has got by usury.

3

From St Bernardine, *Quadraquesimale de Religione Christiana*, in *Sancti Bernardini Senensis Opera*, 5 vols, Venice, 1745, vol. i, cap. iii, art. i, sermo xxxiii, pp. 144–5

Usarii ... restituere obligantur quicquid ex impietate usuraria extorserunt. Sed nunquid tenentur restituere quicquid ex rebus usurariis, lucrati sunt? Ad hoc autem ... dicendum est quod res ab usurario pro usuris recepta, aut est de sui natura lucrosa, aut non est lucrosa. Primo, si res recepta est lucrosa, sicut domus sunt, vineae, agri, et consimilia, tunc non tantum res ipsae, sed etiam proventus restituendi sunt, secundum Scot.[us] in 4. et Richard [de Media Villa]. Ratio est, quia tales fructus sunt fructus rerum quarum alius dominus est: potest tamen inde deducere expensas, et forte etiam suas operas moderatas. Secundo autem, si res pro usuris soluta non est lucrosa, quia, scilicet, fuerunt denarii, frumentum, vinum, vel oleum, et similia, tunc sufficit restituere quod receptum est ... Si usurarius ex pecunia usuraria negotiatus est, et lucratus, vel inde praedia emit, et fructus percepit, non tenetur haec restituere; et hoc maxime propter tria. Prima, quia tale lucrum non est pecuniae fructus, sed humanae industriae actus; atque possessio de tali pecunia empta ementis est, et non ejus a quo usura accepta fuit, licet sit ei debite obligata. Secundum etiam quia quum jus pecuniae per usuras extortae, vel possessionis inde emptae semper de jure ad periculum usurarii currat, et inamissibile sit ei qui solvit usuram; hinc est quod lucrum quod ex tale inamissibili capitali procedit, et cui sublata pecunia fuit modo usurario proveniens est. Tertio, quia si usurarius cum denariis illis nihil fuisset lucratus, non tenetur nisi ad illud quod ex usuris pervenit ad eum, non autem amplius eo ... Damnum quod accidit injuriam passo dupliciter evenire potest. Primo per se et directe; secundo per accidens, et indirecte. Primo modo, quum per se et directe datur ab usurario damnum injurio passo, tunc usurarius satisfacere obligatur. Verbi gratia: Passus est aliquis damnum propter pecuniam per usuram sibi ablatam, quia ex ea volebat emere sibi necessaria pro sustentatione naturae, vel solvere debita, sive empta, et in expoliatione talis pecuniae incurrit damnum; quia necesse fuit sibi vendere possessiones, vel accipere ab alio pecuniam sub usuris; vel quia domum suam propter hoc vilius vendidit, aut aliam conduxit, et consimilia: tunc in tali casu usurarius hoc damnum restituere obligatur ... Ratio hujus est ... quia usurarius damno illius efficacem caussam praestat. Secundo modo dat usurarius damnum injuriam passo per accidens, et indirecte; scilicet, quia non consecutus est homo lucrum quod ex pecunia intendebat, vel consequi potuisset: et tale damnum restituere non tenetur, quia pecunia de sui natura non habet pactum. Quibusdam vero, non imprudenter, videtur aliter esse dicendum, ne facilis aditus praebeatur ad foenus. Nam, quum solutio pro usuris non fiat communiter, nisi de rebus infructuosis, sicut sunt denarii, vinum, frumentum, et similia; si lucrum proveniens usurario ex usurario lucro non sit restituendum, multi conabuntur lucrari per usurariam pravitatem. Quumque cumulaverint magnum lucrum, artem foenoris dimittentes, cum denariis ex foenore acquisitis conabuntur lucrari per licitas mercaturas, et artes, sperantes paulatim satisfacere usuraria lucra, et sic divites remanere, et animam suam salvere, vel potius multis deceptionibus, et periculis irretire. Constat enim, quantum fieri potest, esse periculis obviandum ... Propterea tutius dicendum est quod, si res pro usuris soluta non est lucrosa, et cum tali usurario lucro lucretur usurarius per alios contractus licitos, et honestos, de tali lucro tres debent fieri partes; quia prima remaneat apud usurarium, alia autem detur ei qui solvit usuras; tertia vero, tanquam incertum, pauperibus erogetur. Prima, inquam, pars usurario detur propter industriam et laborem suum secundum judicium boni viri, quemadmodum si lucratus fuisset cum pecunia aliena; dignus est enim mercenarius mercede sua. Secunda vero pars detur ei qui solvit usuras: et hoc ratione sui quodammodo interesse; quia res sua detenta est unde potuisset lucrari. Tertia vero tanquam incertum pauperibus dispensetur: cujus ratio est, quia apud usurarium remanere non debet propter rationem ostensam; nec ei qui solvit usuras restitui debet, quum ei quasi modo usurario proveniret. Restat ergo quod sit pauperibus dispensanda; quum regulare sit quod, quandocunque restitutio fieri debet, nec reperitur cui debeat fieri, habet pauperibus dispensari.

Usurers ... are obliged to give back whatever they have extorted by impious usury. But are they thereby bound to restore whatever they have gained by usurious dealings? To this ... it must be said that the thing received by the usurer for usuries is either by its nature profitable or unprofitable. First, if what is received is profitable, as for instance are houses, vineyards, fields and such like, then it is not enough that the thing itself be given back, but also the increase, according to Scotus in 4. and Richard [Middleton]. The reason is, such yields are the fruits of another man's domains: the usurer, however, is entitled to deduct for his expenses, and perhaps also for his labour. Secondly, moreover, if what was paid by way of usuries be unprofitable, for that, for instance, it was in coins, wine or oil and such like, then it is enough to give back what was received ... It follows, that if the usurer has traded with the usurious money and made a profit with it, or perhaps has bought landed estates with it and gathered the harvest, he is not bound to restore these; and this primarily on account of three things. First, because such profit is not the fruit of money, but of the exertion of human industry; and such money as he thereby acquires is by means of buying and selling and not by having taken what was taken in usury, even were it given him in gage. Secondly, also, because the right to money extorted through usuries, or to what was acquired with it by purchases, will always run into peril of the law against usury and not be open to be released to the man who paid the usury; hence profit accrues from such unreleasable capital, and so he to whom the money has been assigned is now profiting out of usury. Thirdly, because if the usurer made no profit from that money, he is bound and liable for nothing beyond what came to him by the payment of usuries … The damage that befalls can result in injury doubly suffered, first by itself and directly, secondly by mischance and indirectly. First, in one way, when, by itself and directly, damage is inflicted by the usury, then the usurer is obliged to make satisfaction. For example, someone has suffered from money being taken from him by usury, for he had intended to buy the necessities of life with it, or to pay debts or make purchases, and incurs damage through being despoiled of so much money; because he was thereby constrained to sell possessions or to borrow money at usury from someone else, or because on this account he has sold his house for less than it was worth, or has rented another, and such like: then in such a case the usurer is bound to make restitution for the damage … The reason for this is, that the usurer is to blame for the effectual cause of this damage. Usury causes damage in a second way, where the injury is inflicted by misfortune and indirectly, to wit, that the man cannot reap the gain he was aiming at with his money, or rather, what he could have reaped: and such damage the usurer is not bound to make restitution for, because money is of its nature a thing of uncertainty. Truly, in a few cases, it is not imprudent, but generally, it seems meet to be said, ocker should not be entered into lightly. However, since usury is not commonly paid except for the sake of unfruitful things, as, for instance, money, wine, corn and such like, if the gain arising from usury be not restored out of usurious profit, many people will try to gain through depraved usury. Some of those who by these means have amassed great gains, forsake the trade of usury and try to use the money acquired from ocker to profit from licit commerce and trades, hoping gradually to make amends for their usurious gains, and then stay rich and save their souls, or rather, perhaps, try to ensnare others in deceptions and lawsuits. Indeed, it is well known how much can be made by drawing on lawsuits … Therefore it is safe and meet to say, that if the thing bought by means of paying usury be unprofitable, and if with his usurious gains the usurer profits from other licit and honest deals, such gain ought to be divided into three parts, because one part should be left with the usurer, another go to him who paid the usuries and truly the third, being of unknown ownership, should be bestowed upon the poor. The first part, I maintain, should be given to the usurer for his industry and labour, according to a good man's judgement, just as if the profit had been made with any other money, for the servant is worthy of his hire. Truly the second part should be given to the man who paid the usuries, and this by reason of being by way of interest, because his property, from which he might have profited, was detained from him. The third part, being of unknown ownership should be dispensed to the poor, because, for obvious reasons, it should not be left to the usurer, and neither is it owed to the man who paid the usuries, seeing that it would accrue to him by way of usury. Therefore it remains that it should be dispensed to the poor, for it is taken as a standing rule that whenever restitution is due and it cannot be discovered to whom it ought to go, that it shall be dispensed to the poor.

4

From J. Calvin, *Praelectiones in Libris Prophetiarum Jeremiae et Lamentationes necnon in Ezechielis Propheta viginti capita priora*, Amsterdam, 1567, p. 170

Nomen usurae apud Latinos vitio caret et probo, est per se honestum: nomen foenoris odiosum est. Qui factum est, ut probum illud occultaretur? Finxerunt se abhorrere a foenoribus; interea nomen usurae sub se continuit omnia foenora, nec ullum fuit tam crudele, tam iniquum, tam barbarum, quod non obtegeretur colore illo. Jam, quia nomen foenoris Gallis fuit incognitum, nomen usurae etiam detestabile fuit. Galli ergo excogitarunt novam astutiam, quasi possent Deum fallere. Nam quia nemo poterat ferre usurae nomen, posuerunt Interesse: jam quid significat Interesse, vel id quod interest? Nempne significat omne genus foenoris. Nullum unquam fuit genus foenoris apud veteres, quod hodie non comprehendatur sub voce illa.

The word *usura*, among the Latins, is in itself honourable and no disgrace attaches to it, but the name of *foenus* is hateful. What has happened, that honesty be thus covered over? They fancied they shrank away from acts of fenory, nevertheless the name *usura* subsumes all forms of fenory, and there was nothing so cruel, so unjust, and so barbarous, that was not concealed under its colour. Now, since the noun *foenus* was unknown to the French, the name of usury has also become detestable. Therefore the French contrived a new piece of craftiness, as if they could deceive God. For, because no one could bear the name 'usury', they used 'interest' instead: but what means 'interest' save that that interests, and, of course, it signifies all kinds of fenory. There was no kind of fenory even among the ancients not today comprehended under that name.

5

From H. Bullinger, *Sermonum Decades quinque, de potissimis Christianae Religionis captibus, in tres tomes digestae*, Zurich, 1557, fos 93ᵛ–4

Usura est cum alteri concedis usum tui peculii, utpote agri, vel domus, vel pecuniae, vel alterius alicuis rei, unde in annum percipis fructum aliquem. Habes enim villam, praedium, agros, prata, pascua, vineas, aedes, pecunias, quas elocas alteri, sub certa pactione foenoris ad te redeuntis. Hic contractus, haec pactio per se non est illicita aut scripturis sanctis damnata. Et usurae vocabulum inhonestum non est, abusus reddidit inhonestum, ut non immerito hodie omnibus sit abominandum. Damnatur enim usura in scripturis, quatenus coniungitur cum iniquitate et pernicie proximi.

Usury is, when thou grantest to another the use of thy goods, as of land, houses, money or anything else, whereof thou receivest some yearly commodity. For thou hast a manor, a farm, lands, meadows, pastures, vineyards, houses, and moneys thou dost let out to hire unto another man upon a certain covenant of gain to return to thee. This bargain, this covenant, is not of itself unlawful, nor yet condemned in holy scriptures. And the very name of usury is not unhonest of itself: the abuse thereof hath made it unhonest, so that, not without cause, it is at this day detested of all men. For usury is in scriptures condemned, so far as it is joined with iniquity and the destruction of our brother or neighbour.

6

From M. Bucer, *Enarrationum in Evangelia Matthaei, Marci et Lucae*, Strasburg, 1527, fos 181ᵛ–2

Porro si frater non ita egeat, quin possit et creditum, et crediti foenus aliquod, cum suo commodo reddere, quis quaeso prohibebit illum gratum esse benefactori, aut hunc oblatam citra fratris incommodum, gratiam recipere? Denique ut recipere eam licebit, ita et stipulari non erit iniquum, modo nullam proximo fraudem meditetur, neque usuram inique exigat, imo ne recipiat quidem, si iacturam faciat dando debitor, hoc tantum accipiat et exigat, quod bona fide, et cum aequitate, vellet a se accipi vel exigi ... Non enim accipere usuram ut dictum, sed cum damno fratris accipere, dilectioni pugnat ... Iterum dico, ijs contractus iustus erit, qui non pugnarit cum hac lege, pro ult vultis ut vobis homines faciant ... Haec civilis lex, si ea debitor non gravetur, servari et a Christianis poterit. Non enim accipere usuram ut dictum, sed cum damno fratris accipere, dilectioni pugnat. Si tu igitur pecunia frater lucretur aliquid, partemque tibi lucri decidat, Domini benedictionem percipis, non alienam ... Iterum dico, ijs contractus iustus erit, qui non pugnarit cum hac lege, pro ut vultis ut vobis homines faciant.

Moreover, if thy brother be not thus in need, and, on the contrary, is well able to repay the loan, and, out of his gain, some usury on the loan, who, I ask, will deny his benefactor that reward, or forbid him to accept a reward offered, when not to his brother's loss? In short, considering it is permissible to receive it, then he will not be unjust in demanding it, provided nothing approaching fraud is practised, and he exact no usury unjustly, nay, rather, will not actually take anything if the debtor would suffer a loss by giving it, and provided he take and demand only as much as in good faith, and in fair dealing, he would be willing to have taken and demanded from himself. If thou shall have been a Christian and loving to thy neighbour, he will readily recognize that God's spirit moves thee not to exceed the bounds of love and affection in these matters ... Provided the debtor be not overburdened, this civil law will be fit to be observed, and by Christians. However, not to take usury in the way described, but to take it to thy brother's harm, that is wholly against love and affection. If, then, thou profit thy brother with the money and he bestow part of it on thee, thou art receiving God's blessing, nothing else ... I say again, justice will reside in those contracts that conflict not with this law: do as you would be done by.

7

From J. Calvin, *Epistolae et Responsa*, Geneva, 1575, pp. 355–7

Nondum ipse quidem tentari quid apposite responderi possit ad quaestionem propositam: sed aliorum exemplo didici, quanto res ex cum periculo coniuncta sit. Si enim omnino usuras damnamus, induimus strictiorem laqueum conscientijs, quam Dominus ipse voluerit. Si vel minimum concedimus, statim sub illo pretextu plurimi effrenem licentiam arripient, quae nulla deinde moderatione vel exceptione coerceri possit ...

Ac primum nullo testimonio Scripturae mihi constat usuras omnino damnatas esse. Illa enim Christi sententia quae maxime obvia et aperta haberi solet mutuum date nihil inde sperantes, male huc detorta est ... Nondum igitur constat usuram omnem esse prohibitatam ... Optandum quidem esset omnes usuras, ipsumque adeo nomen a mundo pridem exulare ... Sed quando vocabulum Hebraeum significat in genere fraudes, non ita stricte accipi hic quidem posse videretur. Sed ut concedamus agere illic Propheta de usuris nominatim, mirum non est quod inter ingentia quae grassantur mala, usuras quoque attigerit. Fere enim ubi ad usuram pecuniae elocantur, comites individuae accedunt crudelitas atque innumerae aliae fraudes et circumventiones ... Ratio Ambrosij quam etiam assert Chrysostomus non est magni momenti. Pecunia non parit pecuniam. Quidmaro? Quid domus ex cuius locatione pensionem percipio, an ex tectis et paretibus argentum proprie nascitur? Sed et terra producit, an mari advehitur quod pecuniam deinde producat, et habitationis commoditas cum certa pecunia parari commutarive solet. Quid si igitur plus ex negotiatione lucri percipi possit, quam ex fundi cuiusvis proventu, an feretur qui fundum sterilem sortasse colono locaverit ex quo mercedam vel proventum recipiat sibi, qui ex pecunia fructum aliquem perceperit, non feretur? Et qui pecunia fundum acquirit, anno pecunia illa generat alteram annuam pecuniam? Unde vero mercatoris lucrum: ex ipsius inquies diligentia atque industria ... Primum igitur illud esto, me, cum usuras in genere non damno, non omnes etiam promiscue probare posse, neque etiam mihi probari si quis usurariam quasi arte aliam quaesturiam factitet. Postremo sub istis semper exceptionibus usuram pecuniae legitime praecipi posse tantum, non secus.

Prima est, ne exigatur usura ab egentibus hominibus, neque ullum qui necessitate aut alia calamitate premature, ad pensionem usurae cogi fas esse.

Secunda, ut qui mutuum dat, non ita addictus sit lucro et commodo suo, ut interea omittat quod ex mera necessitate tenetur procurare; nempe ne dum cautum vult pecuniae suae, pauperum fratrum nullam rationem in ea apud illos etiam collocanda habeat.

Tertia est, ne quid in mutuo illo inseratur, quod non conveniat cum aequitate naturali, si expendatur ad illud Christi mandatum: quidquid vultis facere homines vestri causa, vos quoque perinde illorum causa facite.

Quarta, ut qui mutuo accipit, lucretur tantundem aut plus etiam ex ea pecunia, quam qui illi mutuo dat, sive industriam sive operam conferat.

Quinta, ne ex eo quod in usu est, quidvis et aequum sit aestimemus, neque aequum ipsum ex hominum iniquitate, sed ex Dei verbo metiamur.

Sexta, ne tantum rationem habeamus commodi unius illius cuicum res nobis erit, sed etiam attendamus quid expediat Reipublicae. Usura enim quam pendunt mercatores, est publicum vectigal. Videndum igitur ut contractus etiam magis sit ad utilitatem Reipublicae quam ad illius detrimentum.

Septima est, ne excedatur certus modus constitutus in quavis regione vel republica et si neque eo usque exigere etiam semper oportuerit. Saepe enim permittitur quod non potest corrigi vel coerceri edicto civili.

I have not hitherto myself attempted the resolution of this question: yet I perceive by what other men have done, that it is a perilous piece of work: for if we condemn usuries altogether, then do we lay a heavier burden upon men's consciences than God himself doth in His word. And if we but yield never so little, presently, under colour of it, a great many will take so much liberty, that no exception or caveat can bridle or restrain them ...

And first of all: I cannot see usuries altogether condemned by any testimony of Scripture. For the words of Christ so commonly alleged: Lend, expecting nothing, are but wrested and misapplied to this purpose ... But the Hebrew word in that place intimating any kind of deceit, it seemeth it should not be taken in so strict a sense: yet, granting it were so, that the Prophet there speaketh particularly of usuries, it is no wonder that taking other evils that abounded, he toucheth upon this with the rest. For where money is lent out to usury, individual operators practise cruelty, and also numberless and sundry kinds of guile and deceit ... Ambrose's reason, which Chrysostomos also puts forward, has no great force, to wit, that money begetteth not money. I pray you, what doth the sea? What doth a house, by the letting whereof I receive a yearly rent? Is money engendered by the roof and walls? But we see what the earth bringeth forth, and there is also brought in by the sea, that which bringeth money in its turn, and the commodity of a dwelling-house is wont to be purchased for money or exchanged for money. Now if there be greater gain made by trade than by the yield of any ground, shall it be suffered to that man that perhap hath let unto a husbandman a barren ground from which he raiseth yield or rent, shall it not be allowed to a man to receive profit of his money? And when a man purchaseth a piece of ground with money, doth not that money yearly beget further money? Also whence cometh a merchant's gain? Thou mayest reply, it cometh by his own diligence and industry ... First of all let it be uttered, that I condemn not all usuries of all kinds, just as I cannot indiscriminately approve all of them, yet neither do I allow those who make usury their trade, as though it were a lawful living and calling. Lastly, I think usury may be lawfully taken for the use of money, with these following caveats, but otherwise it cannot be lawful.

The first is, that usury never be demanded of poor and needy men, nor any taken from him who by necessity or overwhelming catastrophe has been forced to resort to borrowing on usury.

Second, that he who lendeth be not so addicted to his gain and profit that meantime he neglect what he is necessarily bound to heed, namely, that in taking security for his money, he hath proper regard for his poor brethren even when lending to them.

The third is, that there be no condition inserted or put into the covenant of loan other than is agreeable with Christ's commandment: do as ye would be done by.

Fourth, that he who borroweth, whether he trade with the money or be a workman, may gain as much or more by the money than he who lendeth.

Fifth, that we think not anything to be good and right because it is accustomably used to be done, nor measure equity itself by the iniquity of the race of mankind, but by God's word alone.

Sixth, that we pay heed not only to the good of that private man with whom we deal, but also have regard to the well-being of the commonwealth. As for the usury that merchants pay, it is a tribute that falls on the public at large. Care must therefore be taken that the covenants drawn up stand rather to the good than to the harm of the commonwealth.

The seventh is, that we exceed not the maximum rate or limit laid down in any country or commonwealth. Nor is it fitting that we should always exact just as much as this limit permits; for this is often allowed to run on because it cannot be corrected or reduced by a civil ordinance.

8

From M. Luther, *An die Pfarrherrn wider den Wucher zu predigen Vermanung*, 1540, in *Alle Bücher und Schrifften*, 8 pts (vols), Jena, 1555–58, vol. vii, fos 397–9

Wo man Geld leihet und dafür mehr oder bessers foddert oder nimpt, das ist Wucher in allen Rechten verdampt. Darumb alle die jenen so Fünffe, Sechs oder mehr auffs Hundert nemen vom gelihen Gelde, die sind Wucherer ... Also eben so man von Korn, Gersten und ander mehr Wahr auch sagen, das wo man mehr oder bessers dafür foddert, das ist Wucher, gestolen und geraubt Gut.

Denn Leihen heisst, das, wenn ich jemand mein Geld, Gut oder Gerete thu, das ers brauche wie langer jm not ist, oder ich kan und wil, und er mir dasselbe zu seiner zeit, weder gebe, so gut als ichs habe im gelihen. Wie ein Nachbar dem andern leihet schüssel, kannen, bette, kleider, also auch gelt oder gelds werd. Dafür ich nichts nemen sol. Wir reden dis mal nichts von geben or schencken, auch nicht von keuffen oder verkeuffen, noch vom widerkeufflichem Zinse, sondern von dem Leihen darin der Wucher fast alle seine geschefft jtzt treibet, sonderlich im Geld leihen ... Wer etwas leihet und nimpt dafür etwas drüber oder (das gleich so viel ist) etwas bessers, das ist Wucher ... Wer leihet und dafür etwas nimpt, der ist ein Wucherer ... Das Leihen und drüber nemen, sey Wucher ... Das Leihen sol nicht drüber nemen, oder ist Wucher und nicht leihen.

Where one lends money and demands or takes therefore more or better, that is usury, condemned by all laws. Therefore all those who take five, six or more in the hundred from the loan of money, they are usurers ... So in just the same way, too, shall one speak of corn, barley and other things, that where one demands therefore more or better, that is usury, stolen and plundered wealth. For to lend means that if I commit to anyone my money, my good or my implement, which he makes use of as long as he needs, or as long as I am willing and able, and he gives me the same back, in due time, as good as I have lent it him, as when one neighbour lends another dishes, pots, beds or clothes, so too money or something as good as money. For that I should take nothing. We are now not speaking at all about giving or making presents, nor about buying or selling, nor about redeemable rents, but only about lending, which nowadays is what usury conducts nearly all its business in, and particularly in the loan of money ... Whoever lends something and takes back for it over and above or (what amounts to the same) something better, that is usury ... Whoever lends and takes back something for the lending, he is a usurer ... Lending and taking over and above is usury ... Lending should not draw back over and above, or it is usury and not lending.

9

From P. Melanchthon (Melanthon), *Conciones Explicantes Integrum Evangelium: S. Matthaei (Breves Commentarii in Matthaeum)*, in *Operum Reverendi Viri Philippi Melanthonis*, 4 pts (vols), Wittemberg, 1562–67, vol. iii, pp. 312–13

Scias et hanc esse divinam ordinationem, quam utrinque et a creditore et a debitore vult fideliter servari Deus, ut nec dans mutuo petat accessionem usurariam propter officium mutuationis, et sumens mutuo, bona fide tantundem pecuniae reddat. Si igitur Deus ordinavit contractum mutuationis, utrique contrahentium quasi metis circumdatis.

Creditor, qui dat mutuo, non debet exercere quaestum pactione usurarum, nec aliquid ultra sortem postulare, nec ex alieno lucrari ... Atque ea demum re ipsa est et proprie dicitur usura, cum quis ab officioso debitore, que constituto die fideliter solvit, impudenter ultra sortem petit et flagitat lucrum, ut propter mutuationem plus recipiat quam dedit ... ut Magistratus sit vigilans custos et executor legum Decalogi, easque poenarum severitate tueatur, afficiat homicidas et adulteros capitali suplicio, coerceat item et puniat fures, praedones, grassatores et usurarios. Sed in conspectu est, proh dolor, affectata Magistratuum segnities et negligentia. Adultaria raro, usurae prorsus non puniuntur.

And thou shouldst know the divine ordinance in this case to be, God wants it to be observed faithfully by the creditor and by the debtor, that in giving a loan he seek not a usurious increase, and in taking up a loan, he with all good faith repay just as much money. If therefore, God has ordained the contract of mutuation, both contracting parties are, as it were, confined within limits. The creditor, who gives by way of a loan, is bound not to engage in collusion to practise moneymaking, nor to claim anything above the principal, nor to make gain from the other ... And, furthermore, precisely the selfsame thing is, and is properly called, usury, when anyone shamefully demands and importunes an increase above the principal from a debtor who pays faithfully on the appointed day, so that he receive on account of the mutuation more than he gave. As the Magistrate should be the vigilant guard and executor of the laws of the Decalogue, and is to be looked to to defend these by strictness in punishment, he should do justice upon murderers and adulterers by capital punishment, and likewise repress and punish thieves, robbers, footpads and usurers. But what is to be seen, woe and alas, is the affected sloth and negligence of Magistrates. Adultery is seldom punished, usury never.

10

From P. Melanchthon, *Enarratio Psalmi Dixit Dominus, et aliquot sequentium scripta Anno MDXLII et sequenti*, in *Operum*, vol. ii, pp. 772–3

Est enim mutuatio, cum non emitur aliqua merx, sed pecunia sine merce transfertur, ut tantundem pecuniae recipiatur. Hic contractus debet esse gratuitus, redditur enim tantundem. Quare si amplius daretur, iam fuerit inaequalitas, et lucraretur dans mutuo, cum alter nihil reciperet. Tale lucrum in mutuo, quod petitur propter ipsam mutuationem supra sortem, est proprie usura. Ideoque usura exhaurit facultates alienas, quia is qui solvit usuram, nihil recipit. Non potest autem esse perpetua communicatio, ubi est inaequalitas, sed necesse est alteram partem exhauriri. Prohibet igitur Deus usuram, sicut furta aut rapinas, quia sicut haec continent inaequalitatem et exhauriunt alienas facultates, sic usura continet inaequalitatem, et est hirudo multo perniciosior privatarum, et publicarum facultatum, quam caetera furta. Haec de usuris breviter adieci, ut studioso admoniti uno atque altero exemplo eruditius discernere possint contractus, et sciant vere damnandas esse usuras, et prohibendam rapacitatem foeneratorum, quae hoc tempore crescit, et grassatur turpius et atrocius, quam apud ethnicos.

There is, indeed, mutuation, when no ware of any kind is sold, but money is transferred without any transfer of wares, though just as much money is repaid. This contract should by rights be gratuitous, assuming just as much is returned. And, therefore, if more were given back, then inequality would result, and gain made from giving a loan when the other man received nothing. In making loans, such gain demanded over and above the principal, merely on account of the lending itself, is really and truly usury. And it follows that usury exhausts the other man's resources, because he who pays usury receives nothing. Where there is inequality, continuous reciprocity is impossible and inevitably the one party is exhausted by the other. Therefore God prohibits usury, just as he does thefts and pillages, because just as these contain inequality within themselves, and exhaust the other man's resources, so usury contains inequality within itself, and is a great leech, more ruinous to private and public resources than other thefts. I have here adverted briefly to usury, so that informed students may be able to distinguish it from a more sophisticated contract, and may know in all truth how damnable are usuries and how meet to be prohibited is the rapacity of usurers, which at this time is growing, and is prowling about more wickedly and more hideously than among the heathens.

11

From P. Melanchthon, *Definitiones Appellationum in Doctrina Ecclesiae usitatarum*, in *Operum*, vol. i, fo. 356

Usura est lucrum, quod propter mutuationem petitur. Expresse autem prohibita est usurae petitio Levit. 35. et Deut. 23. Et in Evangelio dicitur: Mutuum date nihil inde sperantes. Et pugnant usurae cum aequalitate. Nemo debet lucrari ex alieno. Accipiens usuras lucratur de alieno. Quia mutuatio transtulit dominium, et quidem rei non sua natura fructificantis. Non est igitur iustum lucrum. Ac res ostendit, propter hanc inaequalitatem exhauriri magnam partem hominum, eamque ob causam saepe seditiones in imperiis ortas esse.

Usury is gain demanded on account of the loan itself. But to claim usury is expressly forbidden. Lev. 35 and Deut. 23. And in the Gospel it is said: Lend, expecting nothing again. And usuries are repugnant to equality. No one ought to gain at another's expense. Taking usuries is gaining at another's expense. Because the loan has transferred outright ownership, and in fact the thing is not by nature productive. Therefore the gain is not fair. And moreover, this state of things is apparent; due to this inequality most men are like to be bled white, and so this is often the cause of the insurrections stirred up in empires.

12

From P. Melanchthon, *Catechesis Puerilis*, in *Operum*, vol. i, fo. 18^v

De Usuris. Licetne usuras accipere? Non licet, Quia Christus inquit: Mutuum date, et nihil inde sperantes. Et Lex prohibet Deuteronom. 23. Fratri tuo absque usura mutuabis id quod indiget. Et Psalmo 14, Qui pecunias suas ad usuram non dedit. Et Ezech. 18. Sunt autem usurae, quando in mutuatione paciscimur ut aliquid supra sortem nobis propter ipsam mutuationem detur. Ideo autem sunt iniustae usurae, quia exigitur non debitum. Solvens enim mutuum, nihil amplius debet, et tamen amplius exigitur pro nulla re. Ergo non servatur aequalitas. Et haec causa est, cur usurae exhauriant civitates, quia foeneratores auferunt plurimum, pro quo nihil recipit solvens. Non potest igitur talis communicatio esse perpetua, cum non sit mutua compensatio.

Of usuries. Is it not permissible to take usuries? It is not permissible, because Christ enjoins: Give loan, and expect therefrom nothing. And the Law prohibits. Deut. 23. Lend to thy brother who is in need without usury. And Psalm 14, He that putteth not out his money to usury. And Ezek. 18. There are, indeed, usuries, should we stipulate in a loan that anything over and above the principal should be given on account of the loan itself. This is why usuries are unjust, because what is not owed is demanded. And this is the reason why usuries ruin cities, for that the usurers steal the most part, for which payment nothing is received back. It is therefore impossible for such a set of transactions to be perpetuated when there be no reciprocal compensation.

13

From H. Zwingli, *Von göttlicher und menschlicher Gerechtigkeit wie die zemmen und standind: ein predge Huldrych Zwinglis an S. Johannes toufers tag gethon MDXXIII*, in *Huldreich Zwingli's Werke*, ed. M. Schuler and J. Schulthess, 7 vols, Zurich, 1828–42, vol. i, pp. 438–9

Gott heisst uns unser hab den dürftigen geben one widergelten. So wir aber ie das nit thünd, so heisst er uns one wücher lyhen, Exod. xxii. 25 und Levit. xxv. 36. So wir das nit thünd, ist der Schülmeister hie, und leert uns wücher geben und nemen. Und ob die straf des wüchrers glych nit ist usdruckt, is sy doch an den richteren gestanden, die darum gesetzt warend, dass sy die ynfallenden missbrüch und spän zertrügind, Exod. xviii. Welcher nun nit wücher trybt, ist deshalb vor den menschen fromm: denn der gwalt mag jm um den wücher nit zu; aber vor gott ist er dennoch nit fromm, er verkoufe denn all sin hab, und geb sy den armen Luc. xii. 33. Thüt das gheiner, so ist ouch gheiner nach der göttlichen grechtigheit fromm. Also wellend wir doch von dir für güt han, dass du dich einen sünder erkennist … Darum, all die wyl ein oberkeit Juden oder andre wüchrer duldet, so bist du ein dieb oder röuber.

God bids us give our worldly goods to the poor and needy without return. Do we not that, then he bids us lend without usury, Exod. xxii. 25 and Levit. xxv. 36. Do we not that, the 'Schoolmaster' is at hand and teaches us to give and take usury. And if the usurer's punishment be not pronounced at once, it be then passed to the judges in whose care is the law thereof, that they discover the incidence and minor details of the misdeed. Exod. xviii. Now the man that plies no usury is on this account righteous in the sight of men: for force may not drive him to usury; but in the sight of God he is still not righteous, for he should sell all his goods and give them to the poor, Luke xii. 33. As no one does that, so then is no one righteous according to divine rectitude. So we yet desire from thee that thou act for good, that thou acknowledgest thyself a sinner … For this reason, everyone who as much as tolerates a licensed Jew or other usurer, so art thou a thief or robber.

14

From J. Calvin, *Commentarii in Librum Psalmorum*, Amsterdam, 1567, p. 47

Iam quod ad foenus spectat, vix fieri potest ut inveniatur in mundo foenerator, qui non idem sit rapax et iniquo turpique quaestui deditus. Itaque non immerito olim Cato in eodem fere gradu posuit foenerari et hominem occidere: quia huic hominem generi propositum est, alienum sanguinem exugere. Et etiam valde indignum, dum singuli laboriose victum sibi acquirunt, dum se agricolae quotidianis operis fatigant, opifices multum sudando aliis serviunt, mercatores non modo se exercent laboribus, sed multa quoque incommoda et pericula subeunt, solos trapezitas sedendo vectigal ex omnium labore colligere. Ad haec scimus, ut plurimum non eos qui divites sunt, foenore exhauriri; sed tenues homines, qui potius levandi erant. Quare non abs re Deus foenerari vetuit, rationem hanc addens, Si attenuatus fuerit populus meus non gravabis eum usura.

Now, as to what concerns fenory, it is scarcely possible to happen, that in the whole world an ockerer be found who is not also grasping and devoted to unjust and sordid moneymaking. Accordingly, Cato of yore not unjustly put in the same category of crime the practice of fenory and murdering a man: because the purpose of this class of men is to suck the blood out of others. And also it is truly shameful that, while other men gain their own livelihood painfully, while husbandmen weary themselves with daily labours, craftsmen serve others with long and hard work, merchants not only busy themselves in ventures, but also undergo many discomforts and dangers, moneylenders, merely by sitting on their bottoms, exact tribute from everyone else's labours. Besides, we know it is not usually the rich who are ruined by fenory, but poor men, who should rather be relieved. Wherefore God has providentially forbidden fenory, adding this reason: If any of my people shall wax poor, thou shalt not burden him with usury.

15

From J. Calvin, *Praelectiones in Libris Prophetiarum Jeremiae et Lamentationes necnon in Ezechielis Propheta viginti capita priora*, Amsterdam, 1567, p. 170

In republica bene constituta nemo foenerator tolerabilis est: etiam hoc viderunt profani homines. Quisquis ergo ex professo foeneratur, ille omnino debet ab hominum consortio rejici. Nam si quaedam artes illiberales invidia onerant eos qui ipsis utuntur, foenerari certe est quaestus et illiberalis, et indignus homine tam pio, quam honesto ... Et certe foenerator semper erit latro, hoc est, qui quaestum faciet ex foenore, ille praedo erit, et grassabitur eius iniquitas perinde acsi nullae essent leges, nulla aequitas, nullus denique mutuus amor inter homines ... Foenerator, ut dixi, locum habere non debet, neque ferri in Ecclesia Dei.

In a well-ordered state no ockerer is to be tolerated: even profane men recognize this. Therefore whoever practises fenory as an occupation ought to be banished from all human fellowship. For if there be any mean tricks that earn ill will for the users of them, to be an ockerer is beyond doubt mean and money-grubbing, and unworthy of any upright or honourable man ... And certainly an ockerer will always be a brigand, that is, whoever makes a living out of fenory will be a robber and in his wickedness will go on the prowl, just as if there were no laws, no fairness, in short, no brotherly love among men ... As I have said, the ockerer should have no place in, nor be brought into, the Church of God.

16

From M. Luther, *An die Christlichen Adel Deudscher Nation*, in *Alle Bücher und Schrifften*, vol. i, fo. 314

Aber das grössest unglück Deudscher Nation ist gewislich der Zinskauff. Wo der nicht were müsst mancher sein Seiden, Sammet, Güldenstück, Specerey, und allerley prangen wol ungekaufft lassen. Er ist nicht viel uber hundert Jar gestanden, und hat schon fast alle Fürsten, Stifftt, Stedte, Adel, und Erben in armut jamer und verderben bracht. Solt er noch hundert Jar stehen, so were es nicht müglich das Deudschland ein pfennig behielte. Wir müssten uns gewislich unternander fressen. Der Teufel hat in erdacht und der Bapst wehe gethan mit seinem bestettigen aller Welt.

Darumb bitte ich und ruffe hie, Sehe ein jglicher sein eigen, seiner Kinder und Erben verderben an. Das jm nicht für der thür, sondern schon im Hause rumort. Und thü dazu Keiser, Fürsten, Herren und Stedte, das der Kauff nur auffs schierst werde verdampt und hinfurt erwehret. Unangesehen ob der Bapst und all sein Recht oder Unrecht dawider sey. Es seien Lehen oder Stifft darauff gegründet. Es ist besser ein Lehen in einer Stad mit redlichen Erbgütern oder Zins gestifft denn hundert auff den Zinskauff. Ja, ein Lehen auff dem Zinskauff erger und schwerer ist denn zwentzig auff Erbgütern. Fürwar es mus der Zinskauff ein Figur und anzeigen sein. Das die Welt mit schweren Sünden den Teufel verkaufft sey. Das zugleich zeitlich und geistlich Gut uns mus gebrechen. Noch mercken wirs nicht.

But the German nation's greatest misfortune is certainly the trade in rent-charges. Were there no such thing, many a man would indeed have to leave his silk cloths, velvets, golden ornaments and all manner of trinkets unbought. It has not been established much over a hundred years and already has brought well nigh all princes, endowed foundations, cities, nobles and heirs to poverty, misery and ruin. Should it go on for another hundred years, Germany could not possibly have two halfpennies to rub together. We would surely be forced to gobble up each other. The Devil thought it up and the Pope did the whole world a grievous mischief by authorizing it.

Therefore I here beseech you and call upon you, one and all, to recognize the portending ruin of his own self, his children and heirs, which is not just outside the door, but already creating an uproar in the house. And let the Emperor, princes, lords and cities see to it that this sort of dealing be clean condemned and forbidden in future. Regardless of whether the Pope with all his justice or injustice be opposed. There be trusts and charitable institutions founded upon it. Better one single, solitary foundation in a city endowed with an honest landed estate or on land-rents than a hundred based on rent-charges. Yea, one foundation based on boughten rent-charges is wickeder and more burdensome than twenty based on landed estates. Truly, this traffic in rent-charges must be a presentment and signal that the world be sold to the Devil with grievous sins, that at one and the same time both worldly and spiritual goods must fail us. Yet we regard it not.

17

From M. Luther, *Kleiner Sermon vom Wucher*, in *Alle Bücher und Schrifften*, vol. i, fo. 200ᵛ

Das Keuffer und Verkeuffer beider teil des jren bedörffen. Derhalben noch leihen noch geben vermügen, sondern sich mit des Kauffswechsel behelfen müssen. Wenn nu das geschicht on ubertrettung des geistlichen Gesetzs, das man auffs Hundert 4, 5, 6 Gülden gibt, lessts sich tragen. Doch sol allzeit die Gottes furcht sorgfeltig sein. Das sie mehr fürchte sie neme zu viel denn zu wenig. Das der Geitz nicht neben der Sicherheit des zimlichen Kauffs einreisse. Je weniger auffs hundert je Göttlicher und Christlicher der Kauff ist.

Es ist aber meines Wercks nicht anzuzeigen, wo man fünff, vier oder sechs auffs Hundert geben sol. Ich las es bleiben bey dem Urteil der Rechten. Wo der Grund so gut und reich ist, das man da sechs nemen müge ... Nu findet man etliche die nicht allein in geringen Gütern, sondern auch zu viel nemen, sieben, acht, neun, zehen auffs Hundert ... Er reisse aber ein in die Groschen und Pfenning ... Reuber und Wucherer.

The buyer and the seller, both sides, have their own needs. Therefore they can neither lend nor give, but must help each other by sale and purchase. If it now comes about, without overstepping the spiritual code, that 4, 5, 6 guilders be given in the hundred, let it carry on. Yet at all times have a care for the fear of God, that you fear rather to take too much than too little, that greed do not jeopardize the seemliness of the purchase. The fewer in the hundred, so the more godly and Christian the purchase. But it is not my task to indicate where one should give five, four or six in the hundred. I leave that to legal judgements. Where the soil is good and rich, one may take six ... Now one finds some who not only deal in petty landholdings but also take too much, seven, eight, nine, ten in the hundred ... But he scratches and snatches at the groat and the penny ... Robber and usurer.

18

From M. Luther, Letter to the Chancellor of the Elector of Saxony, in
Alle Bücher und Schrifften, vol. ii, fos 275ᵛ–6

*Erstlich ists ja war das der Zinskauff, sonderlich wie er bisher im schwang
und ganghafftig gewest wucherisch ist. Auch nicht wol müglich weil die
gemeine Welt geitzig und das ire allzeit sucht das er solt imer wol verfasset
und in gutem Brauch gebracht werden. Das allein sein Abthun das einige
und beste mittel ist im zurahten und ein Christlich edel werck were, das
Fürsten und Herrn zusamen theten und in abschafften.*

*Aber Doctor Strauss thut darin zu wenig das er oben hinlaufft und das
Interesse welchs der einige Schmuck und behelff ist dieses Kauffs nicht
gnugsam handelt. Derhalb das Buch den Stich nicht halten würde, so er
solt von den Widersachern angefochten werden.*

*Wiewol er dem gemeinen Man der es nicht anfechten kan mit
hochfarenden Worten, ein gut Mundwerck macht. Meinet vieleicht alle
Welt seien Christen oder Christus wort sol je so ein gemein ding sein, das
er so bald leben müsse wenn ers geredt hat.*

*Das fehrlichst aber in diesem Büchlin ist das er leret das der Zinsman
sey dem Wucherer die schuld zu reichen nicht schuldig. Sonst würde er
dem Wucherer verwilligen und mit im sündigen. Das ist nicht recht. Denn
der Zinsman hat wol gethan und ist entschuldigt wenn er dem Zinsherrn
den wucher ansagt und das unrecht bekennet. Aber dennoch sol er sich
selbs nicht rechen, sondern verwilligen zugeben den unrechten Zins oder
wucher. Gleich wie ich sol verwilligen dem mörder zugeben Leib, ehre
und Gut. Matth. 6. Denn freilich kein Zinsman sich verbinden würde zins
zugeben wo jn die not nicht zwünge …*

*Wie aber die Fürsten thun sollen damit der Zinskauff abkeme ist jtzt zu
kurtz anzuzeigen. Denn der Zinskauff ist also verwirret in ein Fürstenthumb
vom andern das nicht so hinein zufaren ist. In des sind die Leute dahin zu
halten, das sie Christlich solchen schaden noch ein zeit leiden und den
Zins reichen bis es besser werd.*

*Oder so sie mit Recht sich desselben wehren wollen mag man sie zu
verhör und klage komen lassen und darnach richten und Urteil lassen
gehen, wie recht und dem Evangelio gemes. Sonst ein gemein Edict
auslassen uber solche Sachen weis ich nicht ob mans thun künde. Der
Teufel hats zu wunderlich geflochten. Das Evangelium mus bas dazu
helfften.*

First, it is certainly true that rent-charge, particularly as it has hitherto generally been practised, smacks of usury. Also it is not really practicable ever to have it properly constituted and brought to good usage as long as the common world is greedy and always self-seeking. His only advice is that the sole and best measure is to do away with it, and it were a noble and Christian deed should princes and lords put their heads together and remedy it.

But Dr Strauss does not go into this deeply enough and just skates over the surface; and does not deal enough with interest, which is the only cosmetic and prop of this trade. Therefore the book would be vulnerable should it come under hostile attack. Although, with his high-flown language, he bestows a right gift of the gab on the common man who cannot call it into question, he perhaps thinks all the world to be Christian or Christ's word to be so commonplace that it must suddenly spring to life as soon as he has uttered it.

But the most dangerous thing in this booklet is that he teaches that the payer of rent-charge should not proffer the debt to the usurer, lest he exonerate him and join him in sin. That is not just. For the payer of rent-charge has acted correctly and is fully excused if he give notice of usury to the taker of rent-charge and point out the injustice. But still he should not avenge himself but willingly yield the unjust rent or usury, the same as I should willingly yield to the murderer my life, honour and estate. *Matt. 6.* For, of course, no payer of rent-charge would bind himself to pay rent-charge if need did not drive him to it ...

But how the princes should set about cutting back *Zinskauf,* time is now too short to indicate. For *Zinskauf* is in such a tangle in one princedom and another, that it is not all plain sailing. In this are the people to hold firm, that they bear with this wrong in Christian fashion a while longer, until matters are improved.

Or should they choose to defend themselves at law, one may wish they let it come to suit and trial, and let it go according to direction and judgement as law and the Gospel decide. As for issuing a general edict about such matters, I know not whether one could do it. The Devil has so marvellously ravelled it all up, that the Gospel must come to our aid.

19

From P. Melanchthon, *Enarratio Psalmi Dixit Dominus, et aliquot sequentium scripta Anno MDXLII et sequenti*, in *Operum*, vol. ii, pp. 771–2

Saepe quaeri solet, an contractus redemtionis sit licitus. Sunt autem tres formae, Prima est cum emitur certus fundus, pro iusto et usitato precio, sed cum pacto de revendendo. Secunda forma est, cum emitur reditus in fundo certo, cum pacto de revendendo.

Hae duae formae sunt haud dubie legitimi contractus, et non sunt usurarij, quia sunt verae et legitimae ac non simulatae emtiones. Continent enim substantialia emtionum, Mercem, precium iustum, et consensum. Nam merx est in priore casu ipse fundus, in posteriore casu merx est, ius illud in fundo constitutum, ut quotannis inde certi reditus solvantur. Id ius emi potest, ut si quis servitutem, actum, aut iter in alieno fundo sibi emeret.

Nec pactum de revendendo tollit naturam emtionis, quare et veteres leges approbant talem contractum, ut testatur Lex, si fundum, in codice, de pactis inter emtorem et venditorem. Debent autem Christiani, ut antea dictum est, legum iudiciis adsentiri de natura contractuum, praesertim cum doctorum bonorum et prudentum iudicia congruunt.

Debet autem accedere haec aequalitas, ut in aliis servitutibus, si periret fundus, periisset etiam iter in fundo: Sic reditus periisse existimandus est, cum fundus periit. Et quamvis accedit oppignoratio aliorum bonorum, seu hypotheca, tamen non propterea viciatur emtio. Quia oppignoratio non adversatur naturae emtionis. Ac de his duabus formis contractus, quas recensui, minus ambigitur. Nam si quis dextre indicabit, agnoscet vere esse emtiones.

De tertia forma plus est disputationum. Cum emitur reditus non in fundo certo, sed in omnibus bonis alicuius, ut si quis emat reditum ab aliqua civitate, quare promittit se, non ex fundo certo, sed ex omnibus bonis reipublicae soluturam quotannis certam pecuniam, ut saepe reditus a civitatibus emuntur. Probatur ab eruditis et haec emtio. Nam hic quoque sunt substantialia emtionis. Merx scilicet ius illud annui reditus capiendi. Item precium et consensus. Cumque ius fundatum esse in aliquo corpore debeat, in hoc casu, ius fundatum est in universis bonis, ut si in agro alicuius emta esset servitus iter aut actus.

Est igitur et in hoc casu vera emtio, sed illud videndum est, ut vere referatur contractus ad bona ipsa, non ad personas, hoc est, ut bona possint sustinere id onus, et cum attenuata sustinere non poterunt, pro proportione de reditu partem remittas.

Quod autem hic tertius casus sit emtio, confirmat haec ratio. Maxime proprium est emtioni, emtorem non habere ius repetendi precii. In hoc casu emtor prorsus amittit ius repetendi precii. Necesse est igitur vicissim aliquod ius tanquam Mercem in eum translatum esse. Nec potest hic contractus esse mutuatio, quia dans mutuo retinet ius repetendi mutui.

Hi contractus, quos iam recensui, sunt admodum usitati. Quare prodest eos, qui in Ecclesiis docent, admoneri quae formae probandae sint. Et haec exempla discrimen ostendunt inter emtiones, et mutuationes.

It is very usual to ask whether the contract of redemption is really lawful. But there are three forms. The first is when a specific landed property is bought, for a just and recognized price, but with a covenant for repurchase. The second form is when rent is bought in a specific landed property, with a covenant for repurchase.

These two forms are without doubt licit contracts and are not usurious, because they are genuine and legitimate and not simulated sales. They truly contain the substantial things pertaining to sales: saleable things, just price, and agreement. Now, the saleable thing is, in the former case, the land itself, in the latter, that right established in the land, that every year fixed rents should be paid. This right can be bought, as if anyone were to buy himself a due, a right of passage for beasts or a right of way in another man's land.

Nor does the covenant for repurchase take away the nature of a sale, whereby the ancient laws approve such a contract, as the Law bears witness, if for real estate, in a writing, involving covenants between buyer and seller. Moreover, as has been said before, Christians are bound to assent to judgements in law on the nature of contracts, especially when they agree with the opinions of good and wise doctors.

As in other obligations, however, one is bound to agree with this piece of evenhandedness: if the landed estate were wasted, then a right of way in the estate would likewise be wasted. Thus the rent is to be deemed extinguished whenever the estate shall have been wasted. And however much the pledge of the other man's goods, or the collateral security, nevertheless the purchase is not on that account to be cancelled, because the pledge is not repugnant to the nature of the purchase. And concerning these two forms of contract I have reviewed, there is little to wrangle over. Now, if anyone shall rightly examine it, he will acknowledge these truly to be purchases.

About the third form, there is more argument. When a rent is bought, not in a specific landed estate, but in all the goods and possessions of somebody or other, as if anyone were to buy rent from some city that binds itself to the annual payment of a fixed sum of money, not out of a specific estate, but out of all the municipality's goods and possessions, as rents are often bought from cities; and this purchase is approved by men learned in the law. Now, in this, too, are the substantial things pertaining to a purchase: the thing in sale is obviously that right to the taking of an annual rent; likewise the price and the agreement. And since the right is necessarily established in some substance, in this case the right is established in all the goods and possessions lumped together, as if an obligation were being bought in some land, right of way or passage for cattle.

And therefore in this case there is a true purchase, but what is meet to be observed is that the contract is really touching the goods and possessions themselves, not any person, that is, granted that at the outset the goods and possessions can bear the charge, and if then diminished, are unable to bear it, a proportionate part of the rent is to be remitted.

That this third case is indeed a purchase, this reasoning confirms: the precise and peculiar characteristic of a purchase is, the purchaser is to have no right to have his purchase money paid back to him. In this case the purchaser absolutely surrenders the right to repayment of his purchase money. Therefore it is in turn inescapable that all and any right in the goods is to be tranferred to him. Nor can this contract possibly be one of mutuation, because in giving a loan, the right to repayment of the loan is retained.

These contracts, which I have now reviewed, are widely used, wherefore it would be good for those who teach in the churches, to give warnings as to which contracts are fit for approval. And these examples reveal the distinction between alienations and mutuations.

20

From P. Melanchthon, *Catechesis Puerilis*, in *Operum*, vol. i, fos 18ᵛ–19

Estne usura, Reditus habere emptos in aliquo certo fundo fructificante, ut supra dictum est? Respondeo: Non est usura, quia ille contractus non est mutuatio, sed vera emptio. Concurrunt enim ibi substantialia emptionis, merx, precium et consensus. Merx est ius seu servitus in illo fundo fructificante. Atque hinc facile potest iudicari, quando sit vera emptio, scilicet, cum subest merci aliquod corpus, quo corpore pereunte, reditus periret. Item, in mutuatione is qui dedit mutuo, retinet ius repetendae sortis. Sed is qui emit reditum in alienis bonis, non habet ius repetendae pecuniae. Ergo ille contractus non est mutuatio.

Is it not usury, to have bought rents in some certain productive landed estate, as is said above? I respond: It is not usury, because that contract is not a loan, but a true sale. In fact, the substantial features of a sale are all present there together, goods, price and agreement. The goods are a right or liability in that productive landed estate. Also this can easily be shown when there be a true sale, of course, when some body gives rise to the goods, when the body be perished, the rent shall perish. Note, in a loan, he who gives the loan retains the right to demand the principal back. But he who buys rent in another's estate, has no right to demand his money back. Therefore this contract is not a loan.

21

From H. Zwingli, *Von göttlicher und menschlicher Gerechtigheit wie die zemmen und standind: ein predge Huldrych Zwingls an S. Johannes toufers tag gethon MDXXIII*, in *Huldreich Zwingli's Werke*, ed. M. Schuler and J. Schulthess, 7 vols, Zurich, 1828–42, vol. i, pp. 453–5

Zins ist man auch schuldig ze bezalen by dem gebot gottes: Ir söllend allen menschen geben, das jr jnen schuldig sind … Zum andren sind die zins nit göttlich, dass uns gott heisst lyhen oder wechsel geben und nüts darvon hoffen Luc. vi. 35. Exod. xxii. 25. So nun die menschen die ding, die sy eigen habend gemacht, dem dürftigen nit hand one nutz oder widergelten wellen fürsetzen; da dannen ist kummen, dass die arm menschlich gerechtigheit nachgelassen hat, dass er entlyhend dem lehner ab dem, daruf er jm glihen hat, nach anzal der summ frücht liesse werden, ouch nach anzal der gewachsnen früchten. Also: Ist das güt 100 guldin wert, und der entlehner nimmt 50 daruf, so ist er schuldig halbe frücht dem lehner ze lassen; hat er 25 daruf entlehnet, so ist er den vierteil früchten schuldig etc. Also müssend es die juristen verston, wenn sy den zins beschirmen wellend, er syg ein früchtkouf. Und wärind warlich nach menschlicher gerechtigheit die zins nit ein grosse beschwerd, so sy dergestalt gebrucht wurdind; wiewol sy vor gott nüt dess minder ungerecht sind, wie vor gseit ist. Aber dass einer ab eim güt oder acker oder wyngarten zins geben müss, den jr juristen ein früchtkouf oder bruch nennend, gott geb jm werdind frücht oder nit, das ist doch gar ze vil. Und nimmt mich wunder, dass, die das concilium ze Costenz oder Basel besessen habend, joch nach menschlicher gerechtigheit so unbesinnet sind gesyn, dass sy so ein unbillich ding habend nachgelassen, das unglöubigen fürsten warlich ze vil wäre unter jrem volk nachzelassen … Noch, so die gemein verhellung den zinskouf halt und bestät mit briefen und siglen der oberkeit, so soll ein ieder zins geben von dem houptgüt, das er wolbedacht an sin eigenthum darum genommen hat; oder aber er betrübte den menschlichen friden. Und das red ich allein von denen zinsen, die nach dem ynsatz der menschlichen gerechtigheit (die aber hie gar nach anderst möchte genämt werden: denn, die den zinskouf habend angesehen, hand das wort gottes nit angesehen noch das gesatz der natur) erkouft sind von 20 eins. Er sündete ouch wider gott, der heisst eim ieden geben, das man im schuldig sye … Jr söllend lyhen und nüts darvon hoffen. Aber hie so ich ie sich, dass wir an die vollkummenheit der göttlichen gerechtigheit nit schmecken

wellend, so rat ich: dass alle, die zins habend, die summ des gütes, daruf
sy es habend, liessind schätzen, und nemind demnach järlich nach der
anzal des gelihnen geltes ein teil der früchten ... Aber die zins, die nit nach
der oberkeit bestimmung erkouft werdend, die soll man nit geben anderst
nach anzal der summ. Verstands also: Man findt gytwürm, die von
fünfzechnen als vil erfordrend als von zwänzigen. Und findt darnebend
obren, die bestätend sölichen zinskouf mit brief und siglen.

Rent one is bound to pay by God's command: You shall give to all men
what you owe them ... On the other hand, rents are not godly, for God
means us to lend or to make an exchange and expect nothing in return
Luke vi. 35. Exod. xxii. 25. So now people will not have a mind to hand
over to the needy anything they themselves have made without requiring
use or repayment; thence it has then come about that the poor have
disregarded human justice, that the borrower will deprive the lender of
what he has lent him, according to the total sum of the principal lent,
according as well to the increase on the principal. Thus: Is the land worth
100 guilders and the borrower takes thereof 50, he is so liable to leave
half the increase to the lender; has he borrowed 25 thereon, he is so liable
for a quarter of the increase etc. This is how the lawyers must understand
it, if they want to defend the rent, that it is tantamount to a purchase of
the increase. And while, truly, according to human justice, rent is no great
vexation, so they would have used it in such a way as to make it one,
although before God they are no less unjust about it, as we have seen
before. But that someone should give, from an estate or a field or a vineyard,
a rent, that their lawyers call increase-buying or use, irrespective of whether
or not God give him an increase, that is, however, entirely too much. And
it makes me wonder what possessed the council at Konstanz or Basel, that
they have been so rash and thoughtless of human justice, that they have
let such an unjust thing pass, that verily infidel potentates would find too
much to allow among their peoples ... Yet be the ordinary agreement to
the *Zinskauf* confirmed and established with deeds and seals of authority,
everyone should give rent for the principal loaned, which he has, with
good consideration, taken on his property; otherwise he troubles the peace.
And this I pronounce only of those rents that are bought at one in 20,
after the manner of settlement of human justice (which, however, might
here quite be called something very different, for those who have
entertained the idea of *Zinskauf* have respected neither God's word nor
the law of nature). He also sins against God who intends to give to anyone
in order to put him in debt to him ... You shall lend, expecting nothing.
But I know as well as you do, that we shall not get a taste of the full
advent of God's justice, so my advice is, that all those who own rent should
have a valuation made of the sum total of the estate they have it on, and

thereafter take by the year, according to the amount of money lent, a set proportion of the increase ... But as for rent not bought after the authorized, settled procedure, here one should not give over and above the total amount of the principal lent. This is the way to understand it: one finds gutworms who demand fully as much from fifteen as from twenty, and one finds side by side in addition, those who confirm such *Zinskauf* with writing and seal.

22

From H. Bullinger, *Sermonum Decades quinque, de potissimis Christianae Religionis captibus, in tres tomes digestae*, Zurich, 1577, fo. 94

Et iurisperiti de his ita constituunt, non esse usuram, quando pacto de retrovendendo creditae pecuniae apponitur aliqua pensio extra sortem danda a debitore; quia mutuum esse definit, quod ita alterius usui subijcitur, ut debitore nolente, non liceat creditori illud repetere, donec ipse pensionem, ad quam se debitor astrinxit, solvat. Nam tale creditum transit in contractum emptionis ... Sed si quis alteri det pecuniam, qui praedium, aut villam, agros aut vineas ea pecunia sibi comparet, negotietur denique et lucretur, non video cur vir bonus non fructum aequum de pecunia elocata velut ex fundo accipere possit. Potuisset qui elocavit pecuniam, emere praedium, ex quo totus ad ipsum ementem redijsset fructus: iam vero alteri concedit pecuniae usum ad luculentam istius utilitatem. Paratis sibi accepta mutuo aut per contractum data pecunia peculium, ex cuius proventu totam suam alit familiam, portionem interim condictam ei pendit, a quo accepit pecuniam, quam cum restituit integram, ius proprietatis redemit, ac se a pensione annua liberavit.

The lawyers did discuss the matter thus: that it is no usury when, in recompense of the money advanced under contract of redemption, an annual instalment is taken of a debtor, for the thing doth cease to be lent that is subject to another man's use in such a way that, unless the debtor will it, the creditor has no right of reclaim so long as the debtor pay his annual instalment, for the assured payment whereof he hath entered into bonds. For such an advance is turned into a contract of sale ... If anyone put money out to another, wherewith he buyeth himself a farm, a manor, lands or vineyards for his own husbandry and gain, I see no reason why a good and honest man may not reap some lawful commodity of the advance of his money, just as of the letting and setting of a farm. It is within the power of him who so putteth forth his money, with that money to buy a landed property, and take the whole gain to himself, but now in fact he granteth to another man the use of his money, to this man's great advantage. This man, having accepted the money on loan or by contract, with the money doth acquire property in a living, with the yield thereof nourisheth all his family, payeth to him from whom he received the money, his agreed share, when he hath once repaid in full, redeemeth the title to the living, and acquitteth himself of the yearly instalment.

23

From M. Luther, *An die Pfarrherrn wider den Wucher zu predigen Vermanung*, in *Alle Bücher und Schrifften*, vol. viii, fo. 399

Ich Hans leihe dir Baltzer hundert Gülden, mit solcher masse, das ich sie muss auff Michaelis widerhaben zur notturffe oder werde (wo du seumest) drob zu schaden komen. Michaelis kompt, du gibst mir die hundert Gülden nicht wider. So nimpt mich der Richter bey dem halse oder setzt mich in thurn oder gehorsam oder kompt dergleichen ander Unrat daraus uber mich, bis ich bezale. Da sitze oder bleibe ich stecken verseume meine Narung und besserung mit grossem schaden, da bringestu mich zu mit deinem seumen, und lohnest mir so ubel für meine wolthat. Was sol ich hie thun? Mein Schade wacht weil du seumest und schleffest, und gehet teglich unkost oder schaden drauff, so lange du seumest und schleffest. Wer sol nu hie den Schaden tragen oder büssen? Denn der Schadewacht wird zu letzt ein unleidlicher Gast in meinem Hause sein bis ich zu grund verderbe.

Woran hie ist weltlich und Juristisch von der Sachen zu reden … So bistu Baltzer nur schuldig hin nach zu geben uber die hundert Gülden alles was der Schadewacht mit aller unkost drauff getrieben hat, Denn es ist dein schuld das du mich so gelassen hast. Und ist eben so viel als hettestu mirs genomen freuelich. Darumb ists billich auch der Vernunfft und natürlichem Recht nach, das du mir alles wider erstattest, beide die Heubtsumma mit dem schaden. Denn ich habe dir die hundert Gülden nicht geliehen das ich mich selbs oder du mich damit soltest verderben, sondern ich habe dir wöllen on meinen schaden helffen. Dis alles ist so klar und helle das wenn alle Jura und Juristenbücher verloren werden, so müsste es doch die Vernunfft noch setzen wie schwach sie were.

Solchen Schadewacht heissen der Juristen Bücher zu Latein Interesse, *Und solch leihen ist freilich kein Wucher … Aber diesen Schadewacht kan nu noch einer fürfallen und ist der wenn du Baltzer mir nicht wider gibest auff Michaelis die hundert Gülden, und stehet mir für ein Kauff, das ich köndte keuffen einen Garten, acker, haus oder was für ein Grund ist. Daran ich grossen nutz oder narung möcht haben für mich und meine Kinder. So mus ichs lassen faren und du thust mir den schaden und hindernis mit deinem seumen und schlaffen das ich nimermehr kan zu solchem Kauff komen. Hette ich nu meine hundert Gülden dir nicht geliehen, sondern daheim behalten, so köndte ich mit der helfft den Richter bezalen, mit der ander helfft den Garten keuffen. Nu ich dir sie geliehen habe machstu mir einen Zwilling aus dem Schadewacht, das ich hie nicht bezalen und dort nicht keuffen kan, und also zu beiden teilen mus schaden leiden. Das heisst man* duplex Interesse: damni emergentis et lucri cessantis, *so gut sie es haben können reden.*

Hie mus man nu den Juristen lassen die mancherley Disputation ob einerley hundert Gülden verseumet zu gleich beide Schaden oder den Zwilling bringen.

I, Hans, lend to thee Baltzer a hundred guilders, with the proviso, that I must have it back at Michaelmas for an urgent need or (if thou delayest) shall thereupon come to grief. Michaelmas comes, thou givest me not back the hundred guilders. So the judge takes me by the throat or sits me in the tower or puts me under constraint, or something or other rotten like that is brought upon me out of it, until I pay up. There I sit and stay, stuck fast, missing my food and betterment with the great damage thou bringst me to with thy delaying and repayest me for my kindness so evilly. What should I do here? My loss grows whilst thou delayest and sleepest, and day after day the loss or damage piles up, so long as thou delayest and sleepest. Who shall now bear or suffer the loss here? For the growing loss will in the end become an uninvited lodger in my house until I am brought to my knees a ruined man.

What is to be said about the matter in a worldly and legal way? ... So thou alone Baltzer art bound to give over and above the hundred guilders, all that the loss mounts up to, with all the expense incurred on that account. For it is thy fault that thou hast let me down so. And it is even just as though thou hadst, without further ado, simply taken it from me. That is why it is fair, both by reason and by natural justice, that thou shouldst reimburse me all of it, both the principal and the loss. For I have not lent thee the hundred guilders in order that I of myself or I through thee should ruin myself, but because I wanted to help thee without hurting myself. This is all so plain and clear, that even if all the law and the law books were to be lost, yet it would still only stand to reason, no matter how thickheaded you were.

A loss arising like this, the law-books call in Latin, *Interesse*. And, of course, to lend in this way is not usury ... But this arising of loss can now bring a further misfortune, and that is, if thou, Baltzer, givest me not back the hundred guilders at Michaelmas, and stopst me from making a purchase I could have made of a garden, a field, a house or whatever sort of real estate of which I might have made great use or gained sustenance for myself and my children, so I have to let it go, and thou dost me a loss and hindrance with thy delaying and sleeping, so that I can never more come to such a purchase again. Had I not lent thee my hundred guilders, but kept them at home, I would have been able to pay the judge with one half and buy the garden with the other. Now that I have lent thee them, thou makest me have a twin growth of loss, in that here I cannot pay and there I cannot buy, and so must bear the loss on both counts. This one calls *duplex Interesse* (double interest): of emergent loss and cessant gain, so well they can define it.

At this point we must leave to the lawyers the complicated disputation as to whether the selfsame hundred guilders defaulted brings about at the same time both losses or the one twin loss.

24

From P. Melanchthon, *Philosophiae Moralis Epitomes*, in *Opera quae supersunt Omnia*, 28 vols, Halle and Brunswick, 1834–60, vol. xvi, cols 138–40

Sed de damno emergente et lucro cessante ante moram in mutuo, iura quidem non dant actionem, nisi quis stipulatus sit, ut solvatur illud, quod interest. Itaque nunc usitata est haec stipulatio in mutuatione, et saepe praetextus est usurarum. Hoc igitur quaeritur, an liceat stipulari de eo, quod interest etiam ante moram. Respondeo: Licet stipulari de eo, quod interest etiam ante moram. Ratio: Iustam compensationem licet stipulari: solvere id, quod interest, est iusta compensatio: ergo licet eam stipulari. Minorem probo. Quia iura diserte discernunt inter usuras, et id quod interest.

Leges ipsae iudicant aequissimam et honestissimam esse compensationem eius, quod interest ... Commune et aequum interesse venit in omni contractu. Concludo igitur, quod liceat stipulari, quanti interest damni emergentis etiam ante moram, nec id valde obscurum est. Nam verum interesse solvere non est usura, et haec compensatio deberetur iudicio boni viri, etiamsi non intercessisset stipulatio, nemo enim debet alteri dare efficacem causam damni. Etsi autem obscurior est ratio de lucro cessante ante moram, tamen si sit probabilis ratio, etiam concedendum est, quod liceat stipulari, quanti interest ante moram lucri cessantis.

But of emergent loss and cessant gain before delay on the loan, the laws in fact give no action, unless it be stipulated in the contract what is to be paid by way of interest. And so it is now usual for such a stipulation to be made in the loan agreement, and it is often a pretext for usuries. Wherefore it is questioned whether it really be licit to make a stipulation about interest payable before delay. My answer is: It is licit to make a stipulation about interest payable before delay. The reason is: It is licit to stipulate just compensation: to pay interest is just compensation: therefore it is licit to stipulate it. I demonstrate no more, because the laws clearly distinguish between usury and interest.

The laws themselves decide the most equitable and honest compensation to him with an interest ... Common and just interest enters into all contracts. I therefore conclude, it is lawful to stipulate how much the interest is to be for emergent loss also before delay, nor is it much unknown. For to pay due interest is not usury, and this compensation is bound by the judgement of an honest man, even if the bargain had not been legally assured; no one, of course, ought to give another man effectual cause of loss. Even if, however, the reason for cessant gain before delay is less clear, nevertheless, if it be the probable reason, it should be conceded, for it is lawful to stipulate how much the interest shall be for cessant gain before delay.

25

From P. Melanchthon, *Definitiones Appellationum in Doctrina Ecclesiae usitarum*, in *Operum*, vol. i, fo. 357

Interesse est accidens aliorum contractuum, et est honestae rei appellatio ex naturali aequalitate sumta, de qua dicitur: Nemo locupletetur cum alterius iniuria. Est igitur Interesse debitum, quod debet iure naturae is qui efficacem causam damni alteri dedit, aut qui vere impedivit alterius iusta lucra: ut si quis in locato corrumpit aliquid, debet id quanti interest, id est, debet sarcire damnum, etiamsi nulla pactio de hac re praecessit. Quod aut vocabulum honestae rei Interesse praetexitur crudelibus usuris, perniciosa sophistica est.

Interest occurs in another sort of contract, and is the title taken by an honest transaction in accordance with natural equality, by which it is said: No one should be enriched by another's injury. Interest, then, is a debt owed by natural justice by him who gives effectual cause of loss to another man or who truly hinders another man's just gains: as anyone who should break some article held by contract, owes so much interest for it, i.e. is liable to repair the damage, even if there has been no prior covenant touching the matter. But this designation of an honest thing – interest– is, by pernicious sophistry, misappropriated as a disguise for cruel usuries.

26

From P. Melanchthon, *Catechesis Puerilis*, in *Operum*, vol. i, fo. 19

De eo quod interest, Estne usura, solvere id quod interest? – Respondeo:
Id quod interest, omnino differt ab usuris. Nam id quod interest, debetur
etiam sine pacto, et tunc habet locum, cum aliquis alteri dedit efficacem
causam damni, ut si quis promisisset se soluturum esse ad Calendas Maij,
et illo non solvente ego damno aliquo affectus essem, ob hanc ipsam
causam, quia illa pecunia caruissem, ille, quia dedit efficacem causam
damni, debet solvere id quod interest. Iusta est igitur ratio, et consentanea
naturae, cur solvendum sit id quod interest, quia nemo debet velle
locupletari cum damno alterius. Hoc exemplum aliquo modo indicat, quid
vocetur interesse, et ubi locum habeat. Non enim debet praetexi rapacitati
foeneratorum, qui mutuationem tantum in quaestum conferunt, nec petunt
id quod interest, quia mutuo accipiens dederit efficacem causam damni,
sed simpliciter petunt lucrum.

Is it not usury to pay that which is interest? – I respond: That which is
interest is wholly different from usuries. For that which is interest is also
owed in the absence of a covenant, and arises whenever anyone gives
effectual cause of damage, and if anyone should have promised he were
going to pay at the calends of May, and I were affected by any damage
from him not paying; if due to this selfsame cause, because I had lost that
money, because he gave effectual cause of the damage, he is liable to pay
that which is interest. There is just reason then, and agreeable to nature,
why that which is interest should be paid, because no man should want to
enrich himself by injuring another. This example shows, in some way,
what may be called interest, and where it may have its place. Of course, it
should not be a disguise for the rapacity of usurers, who bring lending so
much into disrepute, nor should those seek interest on the ground that
accepting a loan may give effectual cause of damage, but who are simply
seeking profit.

27

From J. Calvin, *Commentarii in Libros Mosis necum in Librum Josue*, Amsterdam, 1567, p. 528

Debitor si tergiversando tempus extraxerit cum dispendio et molestia creditoris, an consentaneum erit eum ex mala fide et frustratione lucrum capere? Nemo certe (ut arbitror) negabit usuras creditori solvendas esse praeter sortem, ut pensetur ejus jactura. Si quis locuples qui erit in suis nummis, fundum emere volens partem aliquam summae ab altero mutuetur: qui pecuniam numerat, annon poterit ex fundi reditu fructum aliquem percipere, donec sors repraesentata fuerit? Multa ejus generis quotidie accidunt, ubi, quod ad aequitatem spectat, usura nihilo deterior erit quam emtio. Nec vero arguta illa ratio Aristotelis consistit, foenus esse praeter naturam, quia pecunia sterilis est, nec pecuniam parit: poterit enim ille quem dixi frustrator, ex aliena pecunia quaestum uberem facere negotiando, fundi emptor metet ac vindemiabit.

If the debtor have shiftily defaulted at the due time, to the creditor's loss and injury, will it be reasonable that he should profit from his bad faith and deception? Surely no one, I think, will deny that usuries over and above the principal ought to be paid to the creditor to compensate his loss. Nor, indeed, will Aristotle's reasoning hold water, that *foenus* is against nature, because money is barren and money cannot beget money. If any substantial moneyed man, wanting to buy a landed estate, should take up some part of the sum from another, may not he who pays out this money receive some income from the rent of the land until the principal shall be repaid? Many cases of this kind occur daily, where, as far as equity is concerned, usury is no worse than purchase ... for such a defaulter as I have spoken of, might be able to make a tidy profit from trading with the other man's money, and the purchaser of the estate to cut and harvest the vintage.

28

From J. Jewel, 'A Paper on Usury found in Bishop Jewel's Study', in *The Works of John Jewel*, ed. J. Ayre, Parker Society, 4 vols, 1845–50, vol. ii, p. 858

A poor orphan left in his cradle hath a hundred pounds stock. This stock may be put out to usury, and the usury is allowed. This is a deed of charity; it is no usury, as shall appear. For, if the hundred pounds should lie still without increase and be bestowed from year to year to the use of the child, the whole stock would be spent before the child should come to years. But if the stock be put to occupying, and into an honest mans hands, something will grow to the relief of the orphan, and yet his stock remain whole. This is charity, to relieve the infant that cannot relieve himself. The like is in using the stock of a man that hath not his wits, and is not able to dispose of his goods. Or if a merchant, by sickness, or maim, or any other hindrance, be not able to follow his business, he desireth another to use and occupy for him, and to do with his stock as it were his own, only to maintain him with the increase thereof. This is not usury. Why? Because he that taketh the stock of the orphan, or of the madman, or of the diseased merchant, is not bound to answer all adventures and casualties that happen. As, if to like use, I take a stock in cattle, and they die without my default, or a stock in money or wares, and the wares be burnt by fire, or the money stolen, without my default, I am not bound to answer the principal: therefore it is no usury … He that occupieth the orphans money or stock is charged only to use it as his own, and no otherwise. If it perish or decay or miscarry without his default, he is not bound to answer it. Therefore, as I said, it is no usury.

29

From M. Luther, *Grosser Sermon vom Wucher*, in *Alle Bücher und Schrifften*, vol. i, fos 195–7

Interesse. Das edle, thewre, zarte Wörtlin laut auff Deudsch so viel: Wenn ich hundert Gülden habe, damit ich möcht im Handel durch meine Mühe und Sorge ein Jar lang fünff, sechs oder mehr Gülden erwerben, die thue ich von mir zu einem andern auff ein fruchtbar Gut, das nicht ich, sondern er mag damit handeln auff demselben; Darumb nim ich von im fünff Gülden, die ich hette möcht erwerben, und also verkeufft er mir die Zinse, fünff Gülden für hundert, und ich bin Keuffer und er Verkeuffer.

Hie spricht man nu: der Zinskauff sey billich, dieweil ich hette vieleicht mehr möcht gewinnen jerlich mit denselben Gülden, und das Interesse sey recht und gnugsam. Das alles hat so ein hübschen Schein, das es auff keinen Ort jemand taddeln mag. Aber das ist auch war, das ein solch Interesse nicht müglich auff Erden zu haben, darumb das ein ander Interesse ist gegen das, welchs ist also gethan: Wenn ich hundert Gülden habe und damit gewerben sol, mag mir hunderterley Fahr begegen, das ich nichts gewinne, ja noch viermal so viel verliere dazu, eben umb desselben Gelts willen; oder für Kranckheit nicht werben mag, oder keine Wahr noch Gut fürhanden ist, und der Felle unzelig viel; wie wir sehen, das des Verderbens, Verlust, Schadens mehr ist, denn des Gewins. Also ist das Interesse des Verlieren wol so gros oder grösser, denn das Interesse des Gewinsts ...

Wo nun der Zins würde kaufft auff das erste Interesse allein, damit solche Fahr und Mühe ausbleiben, und nimer mehr komen mag, das er mehr verliere denn er anlegt, und also das Gelt, gerad als möcht es alles und allzeit on das ander Interesse sein angelegt. So ists klar, das der Kauff auff nichts gegründet ist. Dieweil ein solchs Interesse nicht mag sein noch erfunden werden. Denn in solchem Kauff findet er allzeit Wahr fürhanden, und mag handeln stillsitzend, Kranck, Kind, Weib, oder wie untüchtig er sey, der keins nicht sein mag im Handel und Gewerben mit blossem Gelt. Derhalben, die auff solch Interesse allein sehen und handeln, sind erger denn Wucherer, ja sie kauffen das erst Interesse durch das ander Interesse, und gewinnen eben damit, da ander Leut mit verlieren ...

Darumb ist nicht Wunder, das die Zinsjunckern so schwind für andern Leuten reich werden. Denn dieweil die andern mit jrem Gelt im Handel bleiben, sind sie beiden Interessen unterworffen. Aber die Zinsjunckern mit solchem Fündle heben sie sich aus dem andern Interesse, und komen in das erst, und da mus jnen viel Fahr abgehen und Sicherheit zugehen.

Darumb solt nicht gestattet werden, das man Zinse keufft mit blossem Gelt, unangezeigt und unbestimpt den Grund der Zinse in sonderheit, wie jtzt der Brauch ist unter den grossen Kauffleuten und faren dahin legen das Gelt auff einen Grund, in gemein und unernant ... das man in einer gemein hin sagt: Ich möcht so viel Zinse dafür keuffen auff einem Grunde und das sol Interesse heissen.

Ja, lieber, mein Gelt möcht meinem Nachbarn sein Haus abkeuffen; so es aber jm nicht feil ist, gilt das mügen meines Gelt mit seinem Interesse nichts. Also ist nicht alles Gelts Glück, das es Zinse kauffe auff einem Grund, und wollen doch auff alles was gemüntzet mag werden, Zinse keuffen, das sind Wucherer, Diebe und Reuber, denn sie verkeuffen des Gelts Glück, das nicht ir ist, noch in irer Gewalt ... Weiter sage ich, Ist nicht gnug das der Grund bar da sey und ernennet werde, sondern sol klerlich stück bey stück angezeigt, und das Gelt und Zinse drauff geweiset werden, als nemlich das Haus, der Garte, die Wiese, der Teich, das Viehe, und das alles noch frey unverkaufft und unbeschweret und nicht blinde Küe spielen ... Und dis ist die einige enthaltung dieses Kauffs, das er nicht ein Wucher sey und mehr thut denn alle Interesse, das der Zinsjuncker sein Zins habe in alle Fahr und jr ungewis sey, als aller andern seiner Gütern. Denn der Zinsman mit seinem Gut ist unterworffen Gottes gewalt, dem Sterben, Krancken, Wasser, Fewer, Lufft, Hagel, Donner, Regen, Wolffen, Thieren und böser Menschen manifeltig beschedigung. Diese Fahr allesampt sollen den Zinsherrn betreffen, denn auff solchem und nicht auff andern Grund stehen seine Zinse ... Also, wo ich Zinse auff einem benanten Grund kauff, so keuff ich nicht den Grund, sondern die Arbeit und Mühe des Zinsmans auff dem Grund, damit er mir meinen Zinse bringe ... Denn wiltu ein Interesse mit haben zu gewinnen, musstu auch ein Interesse mit haben zu verlieren ... Im Zinskauff wird nur sicherheit, Geitz und Wucher gesucht ... Denn wo die Fahr nicht ist im Zinskauff, da ist kurtzumb eitel Wucher ... Nu findet man etlich, die nicht allein in geringen Güten, sondern auch zu viel nemen, sieben, acht, neun, zehen auffs Hundert ... Reuber und Wucherer.

Interest – That grand, precious, delicate little word runs in German much as this: If I have a hundred guilders with which I might earn with my toil and trouble in trade, in a whole year, five, six or more guilders, I put it out to someone, on a productive landed property, so that not I but he may trade with it on his own account, and for this I take from him five guilders, which I might have earned, and so he sells me the rent, five guilders in the hundred, and I am buyer and he seller.

Here one now says: the rent-charge be just, I might perhaps have made more by the year with these same guilders, and the interest be fair enough. All this has such a handsome appearance that no one can find fault with it on any point. But it is also true that such an interest is not to be had anywhere on earth, for that another interest is against it, which goes like this: If I have a hundred guilders and would earn on them, I am faced with one hundred and one kinds of risk that I shall gain nothing at all, yea, that I lose four times as much again on it, even up to as much as the money itself; or cannot earn for illness, or for that no commodity or land comes to hand, and numberless pitfalls. So we see there is more of ruin, loss and disadvantage than of profit. Thus the interest of losing is just as big or bigger than the interest of gaining ...

Now, where rent would be bought on the first interest alone, whereby such risk and trouble stay out of it and can never come again, that he lose more than he lay out, and invests the money as though all of it were exempt from the other interest, it is thus clear that the purchase is based on nothing, for such interest cannot be nor will ever be discovered. For in such buying, he always finds merchandise just at hand, and he can do business sitting still, if ill or a child or a woman, or however incapable he be; he can do nothing in trade and industry with bare money alone. For these reasons, those who fix their gaze and trade on such interest alone, are worse than usurers, yea, they buy the first interest by means of the second interest, and gain by it exactly what other people lose by it.

It is no wonder, then, that the rent-lords wax so rich at other people's expense. For all the while the others keep their money in trade, they are subject to both interests, but the rent-lords have with such trickery got themselves out of the other interest and come into the first, and there they shrug off great risk and get security. Therefore it should not be permitted one to buy rents with bare money alone, undeclared and undetermined as to the particular piece of land they relate to, as is at present the usage among the great merchants, and to proceed to put money on an undesignated and unnamed piece of land ... that one commonly says: I would buy so much rent for so much on a piece of land and that shall be called interest.

Yea, my dear people, my money might buy my neighbour's house off him, but if it is not for sale, the power of my money with its interest is as nothing. So it is not all money's good hap, that it buys rents on a piece of land, and yet those who want to buy rents on everything that can be used, those are usurers, thieves and robbers, for they sell the luck of money, which is neither theirs nor within their control ... Further say I, it is not enough that the land just be there and be named, but it should be clearly indicated parcel by parcel, and the money and rents thereon assigned, as, to wit, the house, the garden, the meadow, the ground, the livestock, and all that is still free and unsold and unburdened, and not to play blind man's bluff ... The only way to defend this business against the charge of usury – and it would do more good than all the chatter about interest –

would be for the rent-buyer to bear the same risk and uncertainty about his gain that he has with his other possessions: death, sickness, flood, fire, wind, hail, thunder, rain, wolves, wild beasts and the manifold losses inflicted by wicked men. So, where I buy rents on a specified piece of land, I am thus buying not the land itself, but the labour and toil of the rent-payer on the ground with which he produces my rents ... For wilt thou gain a credit interest, must thou also have a debit interest ... in rent-charge is sought only security, greed and usury, for where risk be not in rent-charge, there is, in short, bare usury ... Now one finds some who not only take on petty pieces of land, but too much, seven, eight, nine, ten in the hundred ... Robbers and usurers.

30

From M. Luther, *An die Pfarrherrn wider den Wucher zu predigen Vermanung*, in *Alle Bücher und Schrifften*, vol. vii, fo. 400

Hat Baltzer die hundert gülden auff Michaelis nicht wider gegeben, und Hans hat darüber müssen bezalen und schaden gelidden, so sol jm Baltzer den Bezalschaden wider erstatten nach weltlichem Recht. Hat er dazu damit verhindert das Hans den Garten nicht hat können keuffen, wil Hans strenge faren, so mus Baltzer auch was nachgeben, oder las es (das ist besser) gute Freunde vertragen und schlichten, denn es ist schweer und ferlich denselben Kauffschaden eben gleich zu schetzen und treffen, weil der Kauff zuvor nie gemacht noch beschlossen wie thewer der Garten erkaufft were worden und vieleicht ein ander Garte dagegen, ja so gut köndte noch fürfallen. In dem andern Schaden der bezalung kan man die unkost leichtlich rechen ...

Darein sihe aber und mercke wol mein Pfarrherr, das solch leihen da Schadewacht oder Interesse innen regirt in den hendeln jtzt nicht geschiet, sondern ist alles eitel Wucher mit inen. Denn nach dem sie gehöret das Hans mit seinen verliehen hundert gülden hat schaden gelidden und billiche erstattung seines Schadens fordert faren sie plumps einhin und schlahen auff ein jglich hundert gülden, solche zween Schadewacht, nemlich des bezalens Unkost und des verseumeten Gartenkauffs. Gerade als weren den hundert Gülden natürlich solche zween Schadewacht angewachssen. Das wo hundert gülden vorhanden sind die thun sie aus und rechen drauff solche zween Schaden und nemen davon erstattung solcher schaden die sie doch nicht erlidden haben. Denn das du hundert gülden hast darumb bistu nicht schuldig das du auff Michaelis bezalen müssest und ist darumb kein Garten feil den du auff Michaelis keuffen köndtest. Noch rechenstu solche nichtige beide Schaden auff deine gewisse sichere hundert gülden und nimpst dafür fünff, sechs, zehen gülden jerlich gerade als werestu der Hans der von Baltzer verseumet und verhindert ist. Nein hörestu es du bist nicht der selbe Hans, denn ist kein Baltzer da der einen solchen Hansen mache. Du ertichtest dir selbs das du ein solcher Hans seiest on alle Baltzer. Darumb bistu ein Wucherer der du selbs deinen ertichten Schaden von deines Nehesten geld büssest den dir doch niemand gethan hat und kanst in auch nicht beweisen noch berechen. Solchen Schaden heissen die Juristen Non verum sed fantasticum Interesse. *Ein schaden den ein jglicher im selber ertrewmet.*

Ja, sprichtstu, Es ist müglich und könte gleich wol geschehen das meine hundert gülden solche zween schaden lidden der mal eins. Da bistu recht. Las uns nu gleich gegen ander handeln. Deine Hundert Gülden könten vieleicht der mal eins solche zween schaden leiden. So köndte ich der mal eins wol dir fünff, sechs gülden geben. Las gleich sein, und die gülden still ligen. So lange deine Hundert Gülden solche zween schaden nicht leiden, so lange wil ich dir nichts geben. So sind wir der sachen eins, und ist das leihen recht. Es gilt nicht also sagen. Es köndten die schaden geschehen das ich weder bezalen noch keuffen köndte, sondern, Es heisst, Es sind die schaden geschehen das ich nicht habe können bezalen noch keuffen. Sonst heissts Ex contingente necessarium. *Aus dem das nicht ist machen das sein musse. Aus dem das ungewis ist, eitel gewis ding machen. Solt solcher Wucher nicht die Welt auffressen in kurtzem jaren?*

Had Baltzer not paid back the hundred guilders at Michaelmas, and due to this Hans had been forced to pay and suffer damage, so, according to temporal law, should Baltzer reimburse him the money damages. Had he also thereby prevented Hans from being able to buy the garden, if Hans take strict action, so must Baltzer also surrender something or (which is better) leave it to good friends to reconcile and settle the dispute, for it is difficult and chancy to assess and estimate evenhandedly and agree this same damage *re* purchase when the aforesaid purchase has never been made nor any conclusion come to as to how much the garden would have been bought for, and perhaps whether another garden just as good could yet have become available. In other payment of damages, one can easily reckon the costs to be repaid.

Therein, however, see and mark well, my pastor, that such lending, in which emergent loss or interest operates, does not occur in business nowadays, but it is all naked usury with them, for after it is heard that Hans, with his loaned hundred guilders has suffered damage and demands just recompense for his damage, they go and plunge straight in and slap on another hundred guilders, as twin emergent loss, namely, the loss of the payment and the missed garden purchase. Fair as were the hundred guilders, such twin emergent loss accrues as of course. So that where a hundred guilders are to come, they improve on that and reckon thereon twin damages and take therefrom compensation for such damages, which they have not suffered, for that thou hast a hundred guilders, for which reason thou wert not due to pay at Michaelmas, because no garden is for sale that thou couldst have bought at Michaelmas. Nor dost thou weigh such bogus damages on thy conscience, thou securest the hundred guilders and takest for them five, six, ten guilders by the year, just as though thou wert the Hans who was delayed and prevented by Baltzer. Nor does it belong to thee; thou art not the same Hans, for there is no Baltzer there to make such a Hans. Thou wovest it up thyself that thou beest such a Hans, without any Baltzer. Therefore art thou a usurer who thyself makest up thy woven damages from the money of thy neighbour who, however, has done nothing to thee and against whom thou canst neither prove nor render account. Such damages the lawyers call 'Not real but fantastic interest', a loss that is one one dreams up all by oneself.

Yea, sayst thou, it is possible and could very well happen, that my hundred guilders would bear such twin damages the one time. There art thou right. Let us now deal equally with the other side. Thy hundred guilders could perhaps bear such twin damages the one time. So I could well give you five or six guilders the one time. Let the same be, and the guilders lie still. So long as thy hundred guilders do not bear twin damages, so long will I give thee nothing, so we are at one about the matter, and the loan is just. It is not to say so. Damages could be incurred, for that I could neither pay nor buy, but, they say, damages could have been incurred in that I would have been able neither to pay nor buy, which is otherwise called 'from contingent need'. Out of what is not, make something that must be. Out of what is uncertain, make something that is certain. Would not such usury gobble up all the world within a very few years?

31

From M. Luther, *An die Pfarrherrn wider den Wucher zu predigen Vermanung*, in *Alle Bücher und Schrifften*, vol. vii, fos 399ᵛ–400

Hie mus man nu den Juristen lassen die mancherley Disputation ob einerley hundert gülden verseumet zu gleich beide Schaden oder den Zwilling bringen, denn ist Hans hundert gülden schuldig, so ist allein der eine Schadewacht da. Ist er fünffzig schuldig, so mögen beide Schadewacht da sein. Denn es kan niemand zu gleich mit ein hundert gülden bezalen und zu gleich den Garten für hundert Gülden keuffen. So ists auch ein anders. Ob der Garte feil gewest oder keufflich mit einbedingt ist, da Hans die hundert Gülden von sich geliehen hat. Denn was noch nicht feil ist, wenn schon bar geld da ist, kan niemand keuffen. Item, das Hans die hundert gülden wol hette mögen verlieren durch Diebstal, reuber, fewer und dergleichen, damit er weder bezalen noch keuffen kundte, denn es ist geld ein ungewis wanckelbar ding darauff man kein gewisses kan handeln. Solche und derselben unzeligen umbstende oder zufelle gebürt den Juristen zu rechen und zu bewegen, damit der Schadewacht oder Interesse nicht ein Schalck und Wucherer werde. Und können hie wol weise Leute feilen. Auch wie kan man alles so rein machen in dem unreinen Recht so die Welt in diesem elenden Leben mus brauchen? Ist gnug das es grob, schlecht, einfeltig recht sey. Subtil und scharff kans nicht sein, oder kriegt solche Scharten das es auch nicht untter schneiden kan, da es wol solte blöche und klötze scheitern. Es ist ander ding mit Christo und seinem Evangelio.

At this point we must leave to the lawyers the multifarious disputation as to whether the selfsame hundred guilders default brings about both losses at once or the twin loss, for if Hans be liable for a hundred guilders, then there is only the one emergent loss there. If he be liable for fifty, then both emergent losses may be there. For no one can at one and the same time with the one hundred guilders both pay and buy the garden for a hundred guilders. Another point, too, that is, whether or not the garden had been for sale or was conditionally for sale when Hans lent out the hundred guilders. For what is not for sale, even if the ready money be already to hand, no one can buy. Likewise, Hans could have lost the hundred guilders through theft, robbery, fire and such like, with the result that he could have neither paid nor bought. For money is an uncertain and inconstant thing on which one can place no reliance. Such and similar circumstances or accidents, the lawyers have a duty to reckon with and therewith to raise the question whether the claimant of emergent loss or interest prove not a rogue and a usurer. And here even right wise people can err. Also, how can one make everything so clear in the unclear law that the world must employ in this miserable life? It is enough that it be gross wrong or simple right. Subtle and sharp it cannot be, or it begets such lumps that it then cannot cut up as though it were really splitting blocks and logs. It is quite other with Christ and his gospel.

32

From M. Luther, *An die Pfarrherrn wider den Wucher zu predigen Vermanung*, in *Alle Bücher und Schrifften*, vol. vii, fo. 401

Sie sagen, Die Welt könne nicht on Wucher sein. Das ist gewislich war, denn so steiff und statlich wird kein Regiment in der Welt werden, ist auch nicht gewest das allen Sünden köndte wehren. Und wenn ein Regiment koendte allen Sünden wehren, so wird dennoch die Erbsünde, die quelle aller Sünden sampt dem Teufel (davon die Jura nichts wissen) müssen bleiben, welchen man mus imer auffs new wehren so viel es müglich ist. Darumb kan die Welt nicht sein on Wucher, on Geitz, on Hohmut, on Hurerey, on Ehebruch, on Mord, on Stelen, on Gotteslesterung und allerley Sünden. Sonst were sie nicht Welt und müsse Welt on Welt, Teufel on Teufel sein. Aber ob sie damit entshuldiget sind das werden sie wol erfaren. Der Herr spricht Matth. 18. Es müssen Ergernis komen, aber wehe dem Menschen durch welchen Ergernis kompt. Wucher mus sein, aber wehe den Wucherern.

You say, The world cannot exist without usury. That is certainly true, for, no matter how strong and majestic shall become any government in the world, it still cannot be that all sins can be guarded against. And if a government could ward off all sins, then there will needs remain original sin, the wellspring of all sins, together with the Devil (of whom the law takes no note), which things one must always guard against anew as far as possible. For this reason, the world can never be without usury, without avarice, without pride, without whoredom, without adultery, without murder, without stealing, without blasphemy and all sorts of sins. Otherwise, if the world were not, there would be world without world, Devil without Devil. But if these things were to be thereby pardoned, they would spread. The Lord saith (Matt. 18), 'It must needs be that untoward occasions come, but woe to him through whom the occasion cometh'. Usury must be, but woe to the usurer.

33

From J. Wycliffe, *Select English Works of John Wyclif*, ed. T. Arnold, 3 vols, Oxford, 1869–71, vol. iii, pp. 154–5

Bot usure is a comyne synne that mony men usen; and this is forfendid in the olde lawe, and more in tho new lawe, when luf schulde be more. Lord, what charite is wit hym that leeves his neghtbore worldly godes for a tyme, and after askes the same, or thing als myche worth, and owver this, encrees. So that, when al thing is sought, he selles pure tyme; bot by propurte of God, He is lord of tyme, and so charite is a wey bothe to God and mon. He may not by covenaunt have so mykel encrees, bot if bytwene him and other be bying and selling. He wil be certeyn of that he byes, and sumwhat he selles, or ellis hym fayles right. He selles not that thing that he leeves in a maner, for he askes that hool in ende of a tyme; ne he selles not wynnyng that comes of this catel, for mon selles not a thing that nevere was his, ne thing that stondes in fortune; and oft there comes no wynnyng. And so, if al thinge be soght, he selles no thing, bot lenght of tyme by whiche he leeves this money. And so, sith lenght of tyme and tyme is al one, he selles tyme to his neytbore, and that he may not; for God onely is Lord of tyme, and wil that tyme be comyne to alle manner of creature that dwellis in the tyme. Ne chaffaryng of tyme profits not to mon, for as God ordaynes tyme to mon, so mot hit be. And blessed be this Lord, that okeris on this wyse. He leewes mon frely giftis of grace and giftis of kynde to have for a tyme, and efft, in ende of tyme, he askes acounte, what this mon haves profited wit godes of God ... Bot tho usurere wolde leeve to men these godes, bot if he hoped wynnyng, that he lufs more then charite. Many other synnes ben more then this usure, bot for this men cursen and haten hit more then other synne.

34

**From R. Capel, *Tentations: their nature, danger, cure; to which is
added a Brief Dispute touching Restitution in the Case of Usury*, 5th
edn, 1655, 2nd pagination, pp. 293–4**

There is an English *manuscript* carried about from hand to hand, said to
be written by a great man and a great clerk. He takes it for granted that all
usury is unlawful ... but denieth all lending for gaine to be usury, forbidden
so much, and so often in the Scripture ... Lending (saith he) for *meat* is
usury, and must be restored whatever advantage is made. But if we lend
for *trade* to such men as meane to make advantage of our money, this
(saith he) is not usury; and we may contract for gaine, and take gaine,
albeit the *borrower lose* by it, under correction of the rules of equity, as
we may call for the rent of a ground, albeit the hand of God be so on the
renter that he lose by it ... *Keckerman* in his *Oeconomicks* Chap. 7, having
first confessed that even all the Greek and Latine fathers, almost all our
reformed divines, and all of the Roman Church, do hold usury to be a sin;
at last he sits downe by this very distinction, fathering it chiefly on the
civill lawyers (and by name on Molinaeus) and falls to this, that usury
was forbidden only to the Jews ... And *Zepper* ... at last comes to salve all
with this very distinction, that if we lend money for *trade* we may *take
encrease* for the loane of our money of those who borrow our money to
make encrease of our money.

35

From Anon. 'A Treatise of Usury', Bodleian Library, Western Manuscripts, MS. Rawl. D. 677

Chapter 9. Nowe plainely sheweth what kinde of usurer is lawfull

That it may appeere what usurie or usurer I hould to bee lawfull because I would not bee mistaken, I will once againe discribe this usurer by these particulars following.

1. This usurer lendeth his money for encrease not for any [un]godly covetuous desyre of worldly riches but for an honest care to lyve and a moderate desyre of wealth for his better maintenance.

2. Allthough for good ca[u]ses he covenannt with his debtor for a certeyne gayne above the principall yett if it shall so fall out that this encrease cannot be taken but with the great hurt of his debtor hee is willing (notwithstanding all covenannts) to remytt this consideracion in whole or in parte for his abyllytie.

3. Although hee take bills or bonds or pawnes for reasons before alleaged, for the repaying of his principall and therfor sometymes doth not according to the outward meanes adventure the same yett in his soule hee is inwardly resolved to hazard his principall. That howsoever he hath assurance for the restoring therof yett if his debtor by unexpected casualtie shall loose this principall he is willing for his power and abillitie to beare this loss in parte or in whole.

4. Though the gaine be somtymes exceeding greate which ariseth by the blessing of God from his mony carefully used yet for causes before recyted he seldoom or never exceedeth the comom rate sett downe by the lawes of the kingdom where he lyveth.

5. He never taketh byting excessive or multiplying usurie of his neighboure whether he bee rich or poor.

6. He often lendeth freely not looking for his owne gaine.

7. He is not onely redy to forgeve his debtor if hee see him in povertie but also to geve to him or to any that shall stand in neede.

8. As he carrieth a mercyfull hart to all men, so a thankfull mynd to the knowing that whatsoever earthly blessing come to him they all flowe from the fatherly providence of God.

That it may appeare cleerly what this lawfull usurie is I will heare set him downe by his contrary.

Usurie

Unlawfull	Lawfull
This lendeth for a covetous desyre of worldy riches	This from a moderate and carefull desyr of his better maintenance
This resolveth before of a certaine for his mony lent and looketh not to the gaine of the borrower	This taketh encrease allwayes according to the gaine of the borrower
This looketh to his own proffitt and not to the proffitt of the borrower nor to the common wealth	This looketh that his gaine taken may stand not only with the proffitt of the borrower but also with the common wealth
This doth tye his creditor with bonds and pawnes as with chaines that let him wyn or loose he will have his owne	This though hee tye his debtor with bonds and pawnes yett hee will never gaine but with his neighbours good
This in the intent of his minde is never willing to adventure the principall	This in the intent of his mynde doth adventure the principall for otherwise he knowith that all assurances are unlawfull
This standeth upon his bargaine and covenant without regard of mercy	This prefereth the works of mercy before all covenants whatsoever
This in taking encrease biteth and gnaweth the borrower	This doth not so
This taketh excessive gaine and often usurie upon usurie	This doth not so
This doth to another that in a certified will hee	This in taking of gaine observeth this rule, Look

would not have done to himself	what yee worke that men should do unto you so do you to them
This seldom or never taketh under the custom of the kingdom as 10. in 100. but often by dyvers meanes seeketh to exceede the common limitation	This very often taketh under 10. in 100. and seldom or never exceedeth the comon rate for cause before alleaged
This is the bayne and ruyne of families and kingdoms	This is preserver of them both
This is condemned in the word of God as simplie unlawfull	This is nowhere condemned in the holye scriptures

From this which hath bynn declared concerning the lawfullnes of usurie we may gether a more specyall definition therof, namely, that lawfull usurye is a gaine or parte of a gaine arising from the profitt of mony lent which a man taketh without the loss of his neyghbour.

36

From R. Sanderson, *XXXV Sermons*, 1681, 1st pagination, pp. 203–4

If usury be simply unlawful (as most of the learned have concluded) then the first rule hath him ... Yet the texts of Scripture are so express, and the grounds of reason, brought by learned men, seem so strong against all usury; that I have much ado to find so much charitty in myself, as to absolve any kind of usury (properly so called) with what cautions or circumstances soever quallified, from being a sin. But I suspect mine own and the common judgment herein, and admit for this once (*dato non concesso,*) that usury be in some case lawful, and so our usurer escape the first rule; which yet cannot be, till his teeth be knocked out for biting: But you must knock out his brains too, before he escape our second rule. I dare say, the most learned usurer that liveth ... will never be able to prove, that usury if it be at all lawful, is so lawful, as to be made a calling ... There is yet a third rule, like the sword of Elisha, to strike him stone dead ... Let him show wherein his calling is profitable to humane society ... He fleeceth many; but cloatheth none. He biteth and devoureth; but eateth all his morsels alone. He giveth not so much as a crum, no not to his dearest broker or scrivener; only where he biteth, he alloweth them to scratch what they can for themselves.

37

From (successively) J. Hall, *Heaven upon Earth: or a true peace and tranquillity of mind* and *Resolutions and Decisions of divers practical Cases of Conscience, in continual use amongst men*, in *The Works of Joseph Hall, D.D., successively bishop of Exeter and Norwich*, 12 vols, Oxford, 1837–39, vol. vi, pp. 35–6; vol. vii, pp. 373–4

To do nothing doubtingly ... For instance: I see that usury, which was wont to be condemned for no better than legal theft, hath now obtained, with many, a reputation of an honest trade; and is both used by many, and by some defended ... I conclude to refer this case wholly to the sentence of my inward judge, the conscience: the advocates, Gain and Justice, plead on either part at this bar, with doubtful success. Gain informs the judge of a new and nice distinction; of toothless and biting interest: and brings precedents of particular cases of usury, so far from any breach of charity or justice, that both parts therein confess themselves advantaged. Justice pleads even the most toothless usury to have sharp gums; and finds, in the most harmless and profitable practice of it, an insensible wrong to the common body; besides the infinite wrecks of private estates. The weak judge suspends, in such probable allegations; and demurreth: as being overcome by both, and of neither part; and leaves me yet no whit more quiet; no whit less uncertain. I suspend my practice accordingly; being sure, it is not good to do, what I am not sure is good to be done ...

All usury, which is an absolute contract for the mere loan of money, is unlawful, both by law natural and positive, both divine and human ... It is unlawful to covenant for a certain profit for the mere loan of money ... Yet there may be and are circumstances appending to the loan, which may admit of some benefit to be lawfully made by the lender for the use of his money: and especially these two; the loss that he sustains, and the gain that he misses, by the want of the sum lent ... If, then, I shall incur a real loss or forfeiture, by the delayed payment of the sum lent, I may justly look for a satisfaction from the borrower: yea, if there be a true danger of loss to me imminent, when the transaction is made, nothing hinders but that I may by compact make sure such a sum, as may be sufficient for my indemnity. And, if I see an opportunity of an apparent profit, that I could make fairly by disbursing of such a sum *bona fide*; and another, that hath a more gainful bargain in chase, shall sue to me to borrow my money out of my hand for his own great advantage; there can be no reason, why, in such a case, I should have more respect to his profit, than my own; and why should I not, even upon pact, secure unto myself, such a moderate sum, as may be somewhat answerable to the gain which I do willingly forego, for his greater profit?

38

From J. Jewel, 'A Paper on Usury found in Bishop Jewel's Study', in *The Works of John Jewel*, ed. J. Ayre, Parker Society, 4 vols, 1845–50, vol. iv, pp. 1293–5

[A.B.] *Nam quae in verbo Dei dicuntur contra foeneratores, huc non pertinent. Foenus enim (quod ab Hebraeis* Nesek, *id est, morsus, dicitur, et verbo Dei damnatur) tum demum exercetur, cum pecunia datur alicui mutuo, ut et sortem et aliquid supra sortem quoque jure exigam. In ea vero specie quae nobis proposita est, non proprie datur pecunia mutuo, sed societas quaedam initur, in qua unus faciendae mercaturae pecuniam ad emendas merces, alter vero suam operam in commune lucrum confert.*

Now, what things are said in God's name against ockerers are not pertinent here. Of course, fenory (which is called by the Hebrews *Nesek*, i.e. bite, and is damned by God's word) is practised only when money is granted in some sort of loan, so that I may demand, wherever it is just, both the principal and something over and above the principal. In the form proposed to us here, one's own money is not lent, but a kind of society is founded in which one man is to use the money in trade in merchantable goods, the other really gathers his gain in the joint profit.

[J.J.] *Sunt hodie multi viri no mali, qui verbo Dei prorsus omne genus usurae damnari putant. Certe David ita praedicat virum bonum: 'Quia pecuniam suam', inquit, 'non dedit ad usuram': idque non tantum non pauperi, sed prorsus nulli.*

Nowadays there are many good men who hold all kinds of usury to be damned by God's word. Certainly David pronounced the man good, 'For that he gave not his money in usury'; and this not to the poor only, but to absolutely anyone ...

[J.J.] *Non licet usuras exigere a paupere; ergo licet exigere a divite? Nam eodem modo prorsus possis dicere: Non licet affligere pauperem in judicio; ergo licet affligere divitem: atque etiam pueri in scholis hoc sciunt, ex negativa non recte concludi afirmativam ... Mercator enim, qui pecunias accepit foenori, cogitur merces suas tanto pluris vendere; et populus cogitur eas pluris emere. Itaque Chrysostomos recte dixit, foeneratorem communem esse hostem omnium.*

It is not permitted to exact usuries from a poor man; therefore is it permitted to exact them of a rich one? For in the same way thou couldst say: in all justice it is not permitted to afflict a poor man; therefore it is permitted to afflict a rich one; and yet, as every schoolboy knows, out of a negative it is not correct to infer an affirmative ... In fact, a merchant who takes up moneys at fenory, plans to sell his wares so much the dearer; and people expect to buy his wares the dearer. Thus Chrysostomos rightly pronounced the ockerer to be everyone's common enemy.

Summary of Select Manuscript Sources

Public Record Office

Court of Chancery:
  Early Chancery Proceedings 64/291, 1298/4, 5.
  Proceedings, series i, Jas B6/62; B15/6.
Court of Requests:
  Proceedings, 29/8, i, ii, iii; 107/3.
Duchy of Lancaster:
  Court Rolls, bdl. 83 no 1137.
  Miscellaneous Book 117.
  Special Commission 1040.
State Papers, Domestic, Elizabeth, 99/26;
  Supplementary 87.

British Library:

Additional Charter 10229; Additional Manuscripts 18458, 18597, 23955,
  23956, 31885, 38487; Additional Rolls 9283, 26341.
Egerton Manuscripts 2646 no. 407; 2983.
Harleian Manuscripts 339, 2239, 4606, 6383.
Lansdowne Manuscripts 46, nos 66, 67; 50, no. 39; 89, 90, 91, 92, 93;
  108, no. 80; 825, no. 66.

Bedfordshire Record Office:

BS/319 Court Rolls of Woodmanley

Bodleian Library:

Western Manuscripts, Rawl. MSS. D. 677, D. 911.

Bristol University Library:

Hannington Court Book

Cheshire Record Office:

Chester Diocesan Records, Consistory Court, Court Papers: 1608, no.
  71; 1612, no. 13; 1627, no. 51; 1628, no. 65; 1638, no. 153.

Hampshire Record Office:

Jervoise of Herriard Park Manuscripts, Papers of Sir Richard Paulet, 44M69 box F.6.

Hertfordshire Record Office:

Ashridge Collection, nos 1436, 1441.

Huntington Library, San Marino, California:

Ellesmere Manuscript 2468.
Hastings MSS, HAF box 6, folder 3; box 8, folder 8.

Leicestershire Record Office:

4D/51/1 Court Book of Castle Donington

Middlesex Record Office:

Accession 446, M. 102, Court Rolls of Harmondsworth

Northamptonshire Record Office:

Miscellaneous Ledger 145.
Montagu Collection, Norfolk, box P, pt 1.
Finch-Hatton Collection, nos 50, 119, 562, 1352, 1353, 1359, 1361, 1363, 1365, 1368, 1371, 1372, 1374, 1376.
Westmoreland Collection, nos 2. ix. 4 (B7–B11), 5. v. 1.

Shakespeare's Birthplace Library, Stratford-on-Avon:

Manorial Documents: Copy Court Roll Atherstone 11 Oct. 1632; Rowington custumal.

Suffolk Record Office (Ipswich):

51/10.17.3 Court Book of Stradbroke and Stubcrofte; V.5/23/2.1.

Wilton House:

Court Rolls of Manors 1689–1754, box 1, vol. 3.

York, Borthwick Institute of Historical Research:

Court of High Commission, Act Book 11.
Court of the Dean and Chapter, Papers: presentments and office, Sept. 1602.

Select Bibliography

(Place of publication London unless otherwise stated.)

Anonymous and various:

Biblia, Dordrecht, 1729.
Biblia Sacra Utriusque Testament, Zurich, 1539.
Biblia Sacra Vulgate Editionis Sixti Quinti, Frankfurt on the Main, 1826.
Biblia Sacrosancta Testamenti Veteris et Novi, Zurich, 1543.
Biblia Utriusque Testamenti, sine loco, 1557.
Bibliorum Codex Sacer et Authenticus, Testamenti Utriusque Veteris et Novi, Zurich, 1564.
Cases Argued and Decreed in the High Court of Chancery from the 12th year of King Charles II to the 31st, 1697; and see Keck.
'Chancery Proceedings *temp.* Elizabeth', *Collections for the History of Staffordshire*, 3rd series (1926) 1928.
Dawn of Modern Banking, Center for Medieval and Renaissance Studies, New Haven, CT and London, 1979.
Die Bibel nach der Übersetzung Martin Luthers, Stuttgart, 1984.
Holy Bible: Authorized and Revised versions.
Holy Bible translated from the Latin Vulgate, Douai (1609), 4 vols, 1750.
'Mortgage of the Manor of Foxton, Co. York', *Yorkshire Archaeological Journal*, **24**, 1917.
Register of the Ministers, Elders and Deacons of the Christian Congregation of St Andrews 1559–1600, pt i, 1559–82, Scottish History Society, iv, 1889.
Testamenti Veteris Biblia Sacra, Geneva, 1630.
Testamenti Veteris Biblia Sacra sive Libri Canonici, Geneva, 1530.
Testamenti Veteris Biblia Sacra sive Libri Canonici, 1581.
The Bible (Breeches Bible), Geneva, 1560.
The Bible, Geneva, 1606.
The Case of Usury further debated, in a letter to the author of Usury Stated, 1684.
The Death of Usury, or the disgrace of usurers, Cambridge, 1594.
Usurie Arraigned and Condemned, 1625.

Abbot, G., *An Exposition upon the Prophet Jonah*, 1600.

Adams, T., *Diseases of the Soule: a discourse divine, morall and physicall*, 1616.

———— *The Happines of the Church*, 2 vols, 1618.

———— *The Sermons of Thomas Adams: The Shakespeare of Puritan Theologians*, ed. J. Brown, Cambridge, 1909.

Ainsworth, H., *Annotations upon the Booke of Psalmes*, 1617.

———— *Annotations upon the Fifth Booke of Moses, called Deuteronomie*, 1619.

———— *Annotations upon the Five Bookes of Moses and the Booke of Psalmes*, 1622.

———— *Annotations upon the Second Booke of Moses, called Exodus*, 1622.

———— *Annotations upon the Third Booke of Moses, called Leviticus*, 1618.

Ambrose, St, *Sancti Ambrosii Mediolanensis Episcopi Opera*, 8 vols, Venice, 1781, in which:

De Excessu Fratris Sui Satyri, vol. iv.

De Tobia, vol. i.

Enarrationes in XII Psalmos Davidicos, vol. ii.

Epistolarum Classis I, vol. iii.

Expositio Evangelii Secundum Lucam, vol. ii.

Ames, W. (alias Medulla), *De Conscientia et eius Iure vel Casibus*, Amsterdam, 1631.

———— *Theologica*, Amsterdam, 1648.

Anderson, B. L., 'Money and the structure of credit in the eighteenth century', *Business History*, **12**, 1970.

Andrewes, L., *Ninety-Six Sermons*, 5 vols, Oxford, 1841–43.

———— *Two Answers to Cardinal Perron and Other Miscellaneous Works*, Oxford, 1954.

Antonine, St, Sanctus Antoninus, *Chronicorum Opus*, 3 vols (pts), Leiden, 1586.

———— *Summa Major*, 4 vols (pts), Venice, 1503.

Appleby, J. O., *Economic Thought and Ideology in Seventeenth-Century England*, Princeton, NJ, 1978.

Aquinas, St T., *Opera*, 28 vols, Venice, 1775–88, in which:

De Excessu Fratris Sui Satyri, vol. iv.

Epistolarum Classis I, vol. iii.

Expositio Evangelii Secundum Lucam, vol. ii.

In Duo Praecepta Caritatis, et Decem Legis Praecepta expositio Psalm. XIV, vol. viii.

Questiones Disputatae de Malo, vol. xv.

Questiones Quodlibetales, vol. xvii.

Summa Theologica, vol. xxii.

Aristotle, *Politics*.

Bacon, F., *Essays*.

———— *The Works of Francis Bacon*, eds J. Spedding, R. L. Ellis and D. D. Heath, 14 vols, 1862–83.

Baildon, W. P., *Les Reportes del Cases in Camera Stellata, 1593–1609*, p.p., 1894.

Bankes, J. and Kerridge, E., *The Early Records of the Bankes Family at Winstanley*, Chetham Society, 3rd series, xxi, 1973.

B[arbon], N., *A Discourse of Trade*, 1690.

Batholomaeis, see Hostiensis.

Barton, J. L., 'The common law mortgage', *Law Quarterly Review*, 83, 1967.

Baxter, R., *A Christian Directory or a Summ of the Practical Theologie and Cases of Conscience*, 4 pts, 1673.

Becon, T., *The Catechism of Thomas Becon, S. T. P.*, ed. J. Ayre, Parker Society, 1844.

———— *The Early Works of Thomas Becon, S. T. P.*, ed. J. Ayre, Parker Society, 1843.

Beer, M., *Early British Economics from the XIIIth to the Middle of the XVIIIth Century*, 1938.

Bellarmine, R., *Explanatio in Psalmos*, Leiden, 1858.

Beloff, M., 'Humphrey Shalcrosse and the Great Civil War', *English Historical Review*, 54, 1939.

Bentham, J., *The Christian Conflict*, 1635.

Bergier, J. F., 'Les Taux de l'Interêt et Crédit à Court Terme à Genève dans la seconde moitié du XVIe siècle', in *Studi in Onore di Amintore Fanfani*, vol. iv, Milan, 1962.

Bernard, R., *The Isle of Man: or the Legall Proceeding in Man-shire against Sinne*, 1627.

———— *The Ready Way to Good Works, or a Treatise of Charity*, 1635.

Bernardine, St, of Siena, *Opera*, 5 vols, Venice, 1745, in which:
In Apocalypsim beati Joannis Commentarii, vol. v.
Duo Adventualia, vol. iii.
Quadragesimale de Evangelio Aeterno: Caritatis et ... de Usura, vol. ii.
Quadragesimale de Religione Christiana, vol. i.

Bernardinus a Piconio (Henri Bernardine de Picquigny), *Opera Omnia Bernardini a Piconio*, 3 vols, Paris, 1870–74.

Beza, T., *The Life of John Calvin*, in J. Calvin, *Tracts relating to the Reformation*, vol. i, ed. H. Beveridge, Edinburgh, 1844.

———— *Poemata: Psalmi Davidici XXX; Sylvae; Elegiae; Epigrammatica*, sine loco, 1576.

Bidwell, W. H., *Annals of an East Anglian Bank*, Norwich, 1900.

Biéler, A., *La Pensée Economique et Sociale de Calvin*, Geneva, 1959.

Blackstone, W., *Commentaries on the Laws of England*, 4 vols, Oxford, 1778.

Bland, A. E., Brown, P. A. and Tawney, R. H., *English Economic History: Select Documents*, 1914.

Blaxton, J., *The English Usurer, or Usury condemned*, 1634.

Bolton, R., *A Short and Private Discourse betweene Mr Bolton and one M. S. concerning Usury*, 1637.

Bowyer, R., see Willson, D. H.

Bracton, H. de, *De Legibus et Consuetudinibus Angliae*, ed. T. Twiss, Rolls Series, 6 vols, 1878–83.

Braudel, F., *Civilization and Capitalism 15th–18th Century*, 3 vols, 1984.

Brook, R., *Some New Cases of the years and time of King Henry VIII, King Edward VI and Queen Mary*, 1651 and various editions.

Brown, K. M., 'Noble indebtedness in Scotland between the Reformation and the Revolution', *Historical Research*, 62, 1989.

Bucer, M., *Enarrationum in Evangelia Matthaei, Marci et Lucae*, Strasburg, 1527.

———— *Scripta Anglicana fere omnia*, Basle, 1577.

Bullinger, H., *Sermonum Decades quinque, de potissimis Christianae Religionis captibus, in tres tomes digestae*, Zurich, 1557.

Bulstrode, E., *The Reports of Edward Bulstrode ... of divers Resolutions and Judgments given ... in the Court of King's Bench in the Time of the Reign of King James I and King Charles I*, 1688 and various editions.

Burn, R., *Ecclesiastical Law*, 4 vols, 1797.

Calvin, J., *Commentarii in Libros Mosis necum in Librum Josue*, Amsterdam, 1567.

———— *Commentarii in Librum Psalmorum*, Amsterdam, 1567.

———— *Commentarii in Quatuor Evangelistas necnon in Acta Apostolorum*, Amsterdam, 1567.

———— *Epistolae et Responsa*, Geneva, 1575.

———— *Homiliae Joannis Calvini in Primum Librum Samuelis*, Amsterdam, 1567.

———— *Letters of John Calvin*, ed. J. Bonnet, 4 vols, New York, 1972.

———— *Lettres de Jean Calvin*, ed. J. Bonnet, 2 vols, Paris, 1854.

———— *Opera Omnia*, 9 vols, Amsterdam, 1571.

———— *Praelectiones in Librum Prophetiarum Jeremiae et Lamentationes necnon in Ezechielis Propheta viginti capita priora*, Amsterdam, 1567.

Capel, R., *Tentations: their nature, danger, cure; to which is added a Brief Dispute touching Restitution in the Case of Usury*, 5th edn, 1655.

Cardwell, E., *The Reformation of the Ecclesiastical Laws as attempted in the Reigns of King Henry VIII, Edward VI and Queen Mary*, Oxford, 1850.

———— *Synodalia: a collection of articles of religion, canons, and proceedings of convocations in the province of Canterbury from the year 1547 to the year 1717*, 2 vols, 1842.

Chafuen, A. A., *Christians for Freedom: Late Scholastic Economics*, San Francisco, 1986.

Choisy, E., *L'Etat Chrétien Calviniste à Genève au temps de Théodore de Bèze*, Geneva, 1902.

—— *La Théocratie à Genève au temps de Calvin*, Geneva, n.d.

Cliffe, J. T., *The Puritan Gentry: The Great Puritan Families of Early Stuart England*, 1984.

Coke, E., *The Institutes of the Lawes of England*, 4 pts (vols), 1628, 1629, 1642–44 and various editions.

Collinson, P., *The Elizabethan Puritan Movement*, 1967.

—— 'The reformer and the archbishop: Martin Bucer and an English Bucerian', *Journal of Religious History*, 6, 1971.

Cooper, J. P., *Wentworth Papers 1597–1628*, Royal Historical Society, Camden 4th series, xii, 1973.

Cooper, T., *The Worldlings Adventure*, 1619.

Cope, E. S., *The Life of a Public Man: Edward, First Baron Montagu of Boughton, 1562–1644*, American Philosophical Society, Philadelphia, cxlii, 1981.

Croke, G., *Reports of Sir George Croke knt ... of such select cases as were adjudged ... during the reign of King James the First*, 1791 and various editions.

—— *Reports of Sir George Croke knt ... of such select cases as were adjudged ... during the reign of Queen Elizabeth*, 1790 and various editions.

Crowley, R., *One and Thyrtye Epigrammes*, n.d., in *The Select Works of Robert Crowley*, ed. J. M. Cowper, Early English Text Society (EETS), extra series, xv, 1872.

Culpeper, Sir T., sen., *A Tract against the High Rate of Interest presented to the High Court of Parliament A.D. 1623*, with preface by Sir Thomas Culpeper jun., 1668.

—— *A Tract against the High Rate of Usurie presented to Parliament 1623*, 1641.

—— *A Tract against Usurie presented to the High Court of Parliament*, 1621.

—— *A Tract against Usury, presented to the High Court of Parliament A.D. 1623*, with preface by Sir Thomas Culpeper jun., 1668.

Culpeper, Sir T., jun., *A Discourse shewing Advantages by Abatement of Usury*, 1668.

—— *The Necessity of Abating Usury re-asserted in reply to the discourse of Mr Thomas Manley*, 1670.

Davies, J., *The Works of Sir John Davies*, ed. A. B. Grosart, 3 vols, p.p.,

1869–76, consisting of *The Complete Poems*, 1869, and *The Complete Prose Works*, 2 vols, 1876.

Dean, D. M. and Jones, N. L., *The Parliaments of Elizabethan England*, Oxford, 1990.

Dempsey, B. W., *Interest and Usury*, 1948.

Dering, M., *Workes*, 1597.

De Roover, R., *Business, Banking and Economic Thought in Late Medieval and Early Modern Europe: Selected Studies of Raymond De Roover*, ed. J. Kirshner, Chicago and London, 1974.

———— *Gresham on Foreign Exchange*, Cambridge, MA, 1949.

———— *Money, Banking and Credit in Medieval Bruges*, Cambridge, MA, 1958.

———— *San Bernardino of Siena and Sant' Antonio of Florence: The Two Great Economic Thinkers of the Middle Ages*, Boston, MA, 1967.

Divine, T. F., *Interest: An Historical and Analytical Study in Economics and Modern Ethics*, Milwaukee, WI, 1959.

Dollfus-Zodel, E., *Bullingers Einfluss auf das zürcherische Staatswesen von 1531–1575*, Zurich, 1931.

Duns Scotus, J., *Opera Omnia*, 26 vols, Paris, 1891–95, in which: *Quaestiones in Quartum Librum Sententiarum*, vol. xviii.

Ellis, I. P., 'The archbishop and the usurers', *Journal of Ecclesiastical History*, 21, 1970.

Elman, P., 'The economic causes of the expulsion of the Jews in 1290', *Economic History Review*, 7, 1936–37.

Emmison, F. G., *Elizabethan Life: Morals and the Church Courts*, Chelmsford, 1973.

Erasmus, D., *Opera Omnia*, 10 vols, Leiden, 1706, in which: *Collectanea Adagiorum Veterum*, vol. ii. *De Puritate Tabernaculi sive Ecclesiae Christianae*, vol. v. *Ecclesiastes sive Concionatur Evangelicus sive De Ratione Concionandi*, vol. v.

Estey, G., *Certaine Godly and Learned Expositions upon divers parts of Scripture*, 1603.

Farmer, A., *Die Lehre von Kirche und Staat bei Zwingli*, Tübingen, 1910.

Fenton, R., *A Treatise of Usurie*, 1611.

Filmer, R., *Quaestio Quodlibetica or a Discourse whether it may be lawful to take Use for Money*, 1653.

Finch, M. E., *The Wealth of Five Northamptonshire Families 1540–1640*, Northamptonshire Record Society, xix, (1954–55) 1956.

Firth, C. H., and Rait, R. S., *Acts and Ordinances of the Interregnum*, 3 vols, 1911.

Fishwick, H., *Pleadings and Depositions in the Duchy Court of Lancaster at the Time of Henry VII and Henry VIII*, 2 vols, Record Society for Lancashire and Cheshire, xxii, xxv, 1896–97.

Floyd, T., *The Picture of a Perfit Commonwealth*, 1600.

Fortrey, S., *Englands Interest and Improvement*, Cambridge, 1663.

Frankel, S. H., *Money: Two Philosophies: The Conflict of Trust and Authority*, Oxford, 1977.

Frere, W. H., *Visitation Articles and Injunctions of the Period of the Reformation*, 3 vols, Alcuin Club, xiv, 1910.

Fulbecke, W., *A Parallele or Conference of the Civil Law, the Canon Law, and the Common Law of this Realme of England*, 1618.

Furnival, F. J., *Four Supplications 1529–1553*, Early English Text Society, (EETS) extra series, xiii, 1871.

George, C. H., 'English Calvinist opinion on usury, 1600–1640', *Journal of History of Ideas*, 18, 1957.

Gesenius, W., *Hebräisches und Aramäisches Handwörterbuch über das Alte Testament*, ed. F. Buhl, Leipzig, 1921.

Gibbon, C., *A Work worth the Reading*, 1591.

Glanvill, *The Treatise on the Laws and Customs of the Realm of England commonly called Glanvill*, ed. G. D. G. Hall, 1965.

Gordon, B., 'Lending at interest: some Jewish, Greek, and Christian approaches, 800 B.C. to A.D. 100', *History of Political Economy*, 14, 1982.

Gouge, W., *A Guide to goe to God, or an explanation of the perfect patterne of prayer*, 1636.

Grampp, W. D., 'The controversy over usury in the Seventeenth Century', *Journal of European Economic History*, 10, 1981.

Gras, N. S. B. and Gras, E. C., *Economic and Social History of an English Village*, Cambridge, MA, 1930.

Grassby, R., *The English Gentleman in Trade: The Life and Works of Sir Dudley North, 1641–1691*, Oxford, 1994.

Greaves, R. L., *Society and Religion in Elizabethan England*, Minneapolis, MN, 1981.

Grice-Hutchinson, M., *Early Economic Thought in Spain 1177–1740*, 1978.

Grindal, E., *The Remains of Archbishop Grindal*, ed. W. Nicholson, Parker Society, 1843.

H., I., see Hall, J. (Joseph).

Habakkuk, H. J., 'The long-term rate of interest and the price of land in the seventeenth century', *Economic History Review*, 2nd series, 5, 1952.

Hale, W. H., *A Series of Precedents and Proceedings in Criminal Causes extending from the year 1475 to 1640; extracted from Act-Books of Ecclesiastical Courts in the Diocese of London, illustrative of the Discipline of the Church of England*, 1847.

Hales, Alexander (of) Hales, *Summa Theologice*, Leiden, 1516.

Hall, J., *Resolutions and Decisions of divers practicall Cases of Conscience in continuall Use amongst Men*, 1649.

———— *The Works of Joseph Hall, D.D., successively bishop of Exeter and Norwich*, 12 vols, Oxford, 1837–39.

Harland, J., *The House and Farm Accounts of the Shuttleworths of Gawthorpe Hall*, Chetham Society, xxxv, xli, xliii, xlvi, 1856–58.

Hartley, T. E., *Proceedings in the Parliaments of Elizabeth*, vol i, 1559–81, Leicester, 1981.

Hauser, H., *Les Débuts de Capitalisme*, Paris, 1927.

Helmholz, R. H., *Roman Canon Law in Reformation England*, Cambridge, 1990.

———— 'Usury and the Medieval English Church Courts', *Speculum*, 61, 1986.

Henderson, E., 'Relief from bonds in the 16th century', *American Journal of Legal History*, 18, 1974.

Hessels, J. H., *Ecclesiae Londino-Batavae Archivum*, 3 vols in 4 pts, Cambridge, 1887–97.

Hill, R., *The Pathway to Prayer and Pietie*, 1615.

Holderness, B. A., 'The clergy as money-lenders in England, 1550–1700', in R. O'Day and F. Heal, *Princes and Paupers in the English Church 1500–1700*, Leicester, 1981.

Holdsworth, W. S., *A History of English Law*, several vols,1909 and after.

Holland, H., *The Historie of Adam, or the foure-fold state of Man, well-formed in his creation, deformed in his corruption*, 1606.

Holmes, N., *Usury is Injury, cleared in an examination of its best apologie alleaged by a countrey minister, out of Dr Ames, in his Cases of Conscience, as a party and patron of that apologie*, 1640.

Homer, S., *A History of Interest Rates*, Rutgers University Press, New Brunswick and New Jersey, 1963.

Hooper, J., *Early Writings*, ed. S. Carr, Parker Society, 1843.

Hopf, C., *Martin Bucer and the English Reformation*, Oxford, 1946.

Hoppit, J., 'Attitudes to credit in Britain, 1680–1790', *Historical Journal*, 33, 1990.

Hostiensis, H. (Bartholomaeis), *Summa Aurea*, Leiden, 1548.

———— *Summa Hostiensis*, Leiden, n.d.

Houlbrooke, R., *Church Courts and the People during the English Reformation 1520–1570*, Oxford, 1979.

———— 'The decline of ecclesiastical jurisdiction under the Tudors' in R. O'Day and F. Heal, *Continuity and Change: Personnel and Administration of the Church in England 1500–1640*, Leicester, 1976.

Hudson, W., *Leet Jurisdiction in the City of Norwich*, Selden Society, v, (1891) 1892.

Hutt, W. H., *Individual Freedom: selected works of William H. Hutt*, Westport, CT and London, 1975.

Jewel, J., *The Works of John Jewel*, ed. J. Ayre, Parker Society, 4 vols, 1845–50.

Jones, N.(L.), *God and the Moneylenders: usury and law in Early Modern England*, Oxford, 1989.

———— 'Religion in Parliament', in D. M. Dean and N. L. Jones, *The Parliaments of Elizabethan England*, Oxford, 1990.

Jordan, W. C., 'Women and credit in the Middle Ages: problems and directions', *Journal of European Economic History*, 17, 1988.

Justinian, Emperor, *Corpus Juris Civilis*, eds P. Krueger, R. Schoell and W. Kroll, 3 vols, Berlin, 1906–12.

Keble, J., *Reports in the Court of Kings-Bench at Westminster from the XIIth to the XXXth Year of the Reign of our late Sovereign Lord King Charles II*, 3 pts, 1685 and various editions.

[Keck, A.], *Cases Argued and Decreed in the High Court of Chancery from the 12th year of King Charles II to the 31st*, 1697 and various editions.

Kelly, J. B., *A Summary of the History and Law of Usury*, 1835.

Kennedy, W. P. M., *Elizabethan Episcopal Administration: An Essay in Sociology and Politics*, 3 vols, Alcuin Club, xxvi, 1924.

Kerridge, E., *The Agricultural Revolution*, 1967.

———— 'The movement of rent 1540–1640' in E. M. Carus-Wilson, *Essays in Economic History*, 3 vols, 1954–62, vol. ii.

———— *Trade and Banking in Early Modern England*, Manchester, 1988.

Kew, J. E., 'Mortgages in mid-Tudor Devonshire', *Devonshire Association, Report and Transactions*, xcix, 1967.

Knappen, M. M., *Tudor Puritanism: A Chapter in the History of Idealism*, Chicago and London, 1970.

Knewstub, J., *Lectures upon the twentieth chapter of Exodus*, 1577.

Knight, F. H., *Risk, Uncertainty and Profit*, 1933.

Larmimie, V., 'The Undergraduate Account Book of John and Richard Newdigate, 1618–1621', in Royal Historical Society, 4th series, xxxix, *Camden Miscellany*, xxx, 1990.

Latimer, H., *Sermons of Hugh Latimer, sometime bishop of Worcster, martyr, 1555*, ed. G. E. Corrie, 2 vols, (2nd vol. entitled *Sermons and Remains ...*), Parker Society, 1844–45.

Leconfield, Lord, *Sutton and Duncton Manors*, 1956.

Lee, W., *An Essay to ascertain the Value of Leases and Annuities for Years and Lives*, 1738.

Le Goff, J., 'The Usurers and Purgatory', in *Dawn of Modern Banking*, q.v.

———— *Your Money or Your Life: Economy and Religion in the Middle Ages*, New York, 1988.

Letwin, W., *The Origins of Scientific Economics*, 1963.

Lever, T., *Sermons* (1550) ed. E. Arber, 1870.

Liebermann, F., *Die Gesetze der Angelsachsen*, 3 vols, Halle,1903–16.

Locke, J., *The Works of John Locke*, 10 vols, 1823.

Lodge, T., 'An Alarum against Usurers, containing tryed experiences against worldly abuses', in T. Lodge, *A Defence of Poesie, Music and Stage Plays*, Shakespeare Society, 1853.

Lupton, T., *A Dream of the Devill and Dives*, 1615.

Luther, M., *Alle Bücher und Schrifften*, 8 pts (vols), Jena, 1555–58 (and 4th reprint, 1575), in which:

An den Christlichen Adel Deudscher Nation, 1520, 1. Teil.

An die Pfarrherrn wider den Wucher zu predigen Vermanung, 1540, 7. Teil.

'Bedencken vom Zinskauff, an Doc. Gregorium Brücken Curfürstlicher durchleuchtigkeit zu Sachsen Cantzler', Ander (2.) Teil.

'Dem erbarn fursichtigen Lazaro Spengler der Stad Nurmberg syndico', 5. Teil.

Grosser Sermon vom Wucher, 1519, 1. Teil.

Kleiner Sermon vom Wucher, 1519, 1. Teil.

'Ordnung eins gemeinen Kastens', 2. Teil.

Von Kauffshandlung, 1524, 2. Teil.

Werke: Briefwechsel (being vol. iii of *Luthers Werke: Kritische Gesamtausgabe*, 14 vols, Weimar, 1930–70).

Tischreden, in *Luthers Werke in Auswahl*, 8 vols, Berlin, 1930–35, vol. viii, ed. O. Clemen.

Maclure, M., *The Paul's Cross Sermons 1534–1642*, Toronto, 1958.

Malynes, G., *Consuetudo, vel Lex Marcatoria or the Ancient Law-Merchant*, 1622.

Marcham, W. M. and Marcham, F., *Court Rolls of the Bishop of London's Manor of Hornsey 1603–1701*, 1929.

Marchant, R. A., *The Church under the Law: justice, administration and discipline in the diocese of York 1500–1640*, Cambridge, 1969.

Marot, C. and Bèze, T. de, *Les Pseaumes de David*, Amsterdam, 1700.

———— *Les Pseaumes de David*, Hamburg, 1716.

McIntosh, M. K., 'Moneylenders on the periphery of London, 1300–1600', *Albion*, 20, 1988.

McLaughlin, T. P., 'The teaching of the canonists on usury', *Medieval Studies*, 1, 1939; 2, 1940.

Medulla, see Ames, W.

Melanchthon (Melanthon), P., *Opera quae supersunt Omnia*, 28 vols, Halle and Brunswick, 1834–60, in which:

Commentarii in aliquot Politicos Libros Aristotelis, vol. xvi.

Dissertatio de Contractibus, vol. xvi.

Ethicae Doctrinae Elementorum, vol. xvi.

Philosophiae Moralis Epitomes, vol. xvi.

Prolegomena in Officia Ciceronis, vol. xvi.

———— *Operum Reverendi Viri Philippi Melanthonis*, 4 pts (vols), Wittemberg, 1562-67, in which:

Catechesis Puerilis, vol. i.

Conciones Explicantes Integrum Evangelium: S. Matthaei (Breves Commentarii in Matthaeum), vol. iii.

Definitiones Appellationum in Doctrina Ecclesiae usitarum, vol. i.

Enarratio Psalmi Dixit Dominus, et aliquot Sequentium scripta Anno MDXLII et sequenti, vol ii.

Mellows, W. T. and King, P. I., *The Book of William Morton, almoner of Peterborough Monastery 1448–1467*, Northamptonshire Record Society, xvi (1951–53) 1954.

Melton, F. T., *Sir Robert Clayton and the Origins of English Deposit Banking 1658–1685*, Cambridge, 1986.

Middleton, R. (Ricardus de Media Villa), *Sententiarum Questiones Persubtilissime*, 4 bks, Venice, 1507–09.

Milton, J., *Complete Prose Works of John Milton*, 8 vols, New Haven, CT, and London, 1953–82.

Mises, L. von, *The Theory of Money and Credit*, Indianapolis, IN, 1981.

Moore, F., *Cases Collect & Report per Sir Fra. Moore*, 1688 and various editions.

Morrill, J., Slack, P. and Woolf, D., *Public Duty and Private Conscience in Seventeenth-Century England*, Oxford, 1993.

Mosse, M., *The Arraignment and Conviction of Usurie: that is the iniquitie and unlawfulnes of usurie, displayed in sixe sermons preached at St Edmunds Burie in Suffolke, upon Proverb 28.8*, 1595.

Mundy, J., *Europe in the High Middle Ages, 1150–1309*, 1973.

Munro, J. H., 'Bullionism and the bill of exchange in England, 1272–1663', in *Dawn of Modern Banking*, q.v.

Münzer, T., *Thomas Müntzer: sein Leben und seine Schriften*, ed. O. H. Brandt, Jena, (1933).

Musculus, W., *De Usuris ex Verbo Dei*, Tübingen, 1558.

Nef, J. U., *The Conquest of the Material World*, Chicago and London, 1964.

———— *La Naissance de la Civilisation Industrielle et le Monde contemporain*, Paris, 1954.

Nelson, B. N., *The Idea of Usury from Tribal Brotherhood to universal Otherhood*, Princeton, NJ, 1949, 1969.

Noonan, J. T., *The Scholastic Analysis of Usury*, Cambridge, MA, 1957.

North, D., *Discourses upon Trade; principally directed to the cases of the interest, coynage, clipping, increase of money*, 1691.

Northbrooke, J., *The Poore Mans Garden*, 1573.

Notestein, W., Relf, F.H. and Simpson, H., *Commons Debates 1621*, 7 vols, New Haven, CT, 1935.

Noy, W., *Reports and Cases taken in the Time of Queen Elizabeth, King James and King Charles*, 1669 and various editions.

Ockham, W. (of), (de Ockham, Occam), *Opus Nonaginta Dierum*, in vol. i of G. de Ockham, *Opera Politica*, eds J. G. Sikes, B. L. Manning, H. S. Offler, R. F. Bennett and R. H. Snape, 3 vols, Manchester, 1940–56.

O'Day, R. and Heal, F., *Continuity and Change: Personnel and Administration of the Church in England 1500–1640*, Leicester, 1976.

Oecolampadius, J., *Commentarii Omnes in Libros Prophetarum*, 2 vols in 1, (Geneva) 1553–58, in which:
In Threnos et Orationem Jeremiae Enarrationes, vol. i.
In Ezechielem, vol. ii.

P., T., *Usury Stated: being a reply to Mr Jelinger's* Usurer Cast, 1679.

Pascal, R., *The Social Basis of the German Reformation: Martin Luther and his Times*, 1933.

Pauli, R., 'Drei Volkswirthschaftliche Denkschriften aus der Zeit Heinrichs VIII. von England', *Abhandlungen der Königlichen Gesellschaft der Wissenschaften zu Göttingen*, xxiii, 1878.

Pearson, A. F. S., *Thomas Cartwright and Elizabethan Puritanism 1535–1603*, Cambridge, 1925.

Perkins, W., *The Workes of that famous and worthie Minister of Christ, in the University of Cambridge, M. W. Perkins*, Cambridge, 1603.

Pettet, E. C., 'The Merchant of Venice and the problem of usury', in *Essays and Studies*, English Association, xxi, (1945) 1946.

Petty, W., *The Economic Writings of Sir William Petty*, ed. C. H. Hull, 2 vols, Cambridge, 1899.

———— *The Petty Papers*, ed. the Marquis of Lansdowne, 2 vols, 1927.

Pie, T., *Usuries Spright Coniured or a Scholasticall Determination of Usury*, 1604.

Pilkington, J., *The Works of James Pilkington, B.D.*, Parker Society, 1842.

Plucknett, T. F. T., *A Concise History of the Common Law*, 1956.

Porder, R., *A Sermon of Gods fearefull Threatninges for Idolatrye, mixing of Religion, retayning of Idolatrous Remnants, and other Wickednesse, with a Treatise against Usurie* (1570) n.d.

Potter, G. R., *Zwingli*, Cambridge, 1976.

Powel, G., *Theologicall and Scholasticall Positions concerning Usurie*, Oxford, 1602.

———— *Theologicall Positions concerning the Lawfulnesse of Borrowing upon Usurie*, 1605.

Purvis, J. S., *Tudor Parish Documents of the Diocese of York: A Selection with Introduction and Notes*, Cambridge, 1948.

Quick, J., *Synodicon in Gallia Reformata or the Acts, Decisions, Decrees and Canons of those famous National Councils of the Reformed Church in France*, 1692.

Raleigh, W., *Select Observations of the Incomparable Sir Walter Raleigh relating to Trade, Commerce and Coin, as it was presented to King James*, 1696.

Riemersma, J. C., 'Usury restrictions in a mercantile economy', *Canadian Journal of Economics and Political Science*, 18, 1952.

Ritchie, C. I. A., *The Ecclesiastical Courts of York*, Arbroath, 1956.

Ritchie, J., *Reports of Cases decided by Francis Bacon in the High Court of Chancery (1617–1621)*, 1932.

Robertson, H. M., *Aspects of the Rise of Economic Individualism: A Criticism of Max Weber and his School*, Cambridge, 1933.

Robinson, H., *Englands Safety in Trades Encrease*, 1641.

Rodes, R. E., *Ecclesiastical Administration in Medieval England: The Anglo-Saxons to the Reformation*, Notre Dame and London, 1977.

Rogers, T., *The English Creede, consenting with the true, auncient, catholique, and apostolique Church in al points and articles of religion*, 2 pts, 1585–87.

———— *The Faith, Doctrine and Religion professed and protected in the Realm of England*, Cambridge, 1691.

———— *Seven Treatises, containing such Direction as is gathered out of the Holy Scriptures*, 1603.

Rolle, H., *Les Reports de Henry Rolle ... de divers Cases en le Court del' Banke le Roy, en le Temps del' Reign de Roy Jacques*, 2 vols, 1675–76 and various editions.

Rosenmüller, E. F. C., *Scholia in Vestum Testamentum*, 24 vols, Leipzig, 1821–28.

Sachse, W. L., *The Diurnal of Thomas Rugg 1651–1661*, Royal Historical Society, Camden 3rd series, xci, 1961.

Sanderson, R., *XXXV Sermons*, 1681.

———— *XXXVI Sermons*, introduced by Isaac Walton, 1689.

Schmid, R., *Die Gesetze der Angelsachsen*, Leipzig, 1858.

Schumpeter, J. A., *Business Cycles: A Theoretical, Historical and Statistical Analysis of the Capitalist Process*, 2 vols, New York and London, 1939.

———— *History of Economic Analysis*, 1954.

Scotus, see Duns.

Seaver, P. S., *Wallington's World: A Puritan Artisan in Seventeenth-Century London*, 1985.

Selden, J., *Seldeniana, or the Table-Talk of John Selden esq., being his sense of various matters of weight and high consequence relating especially to religion and state*, n.d.

Sharpe, J. A., *Crime in Seventeenth-Century England*, Cambridge, 1983.

Shatzmiller, J., *Shylock Reconsidered: Jews, Moneylending and Medieval Society*, Berkeley and Los Angeles, CA, and London, 1990.

Shaw, W. A., *Minutes of the Bury Presbyterian Classis, 1647–1657*, pt i, Chetham Society, new series, xxxvi, 1896.

Siderfin, T., *Les Reports de divers Special Cases argue et adjudge en le Court del Bank le Roy, et auxy en le Comen Banc et l'Exchequer, en les primier dix ans apres le Restauration del Son Tres-Excellent Majesty le Roy Charles le II*, 2 pts, 1714 and various editions.

———— *La Second Part (mes le prima en temps) de les Reports du Thomas Siderfin ... esteant plusieurs Cases come ils estoyent argue et adjugees en le Court del Upper Banck, en les Ans 1657, 1658 et 1659*, 1714 and various editions.

Simpson, A. W. B., *A History of the Common Law of Contract: The Rise of the Action of Assumpsit*, Oxford, 1975.

Smith, A., *The Wealth of Nations*, ed. E. Cannan, 2 vols, 1962.

Smith, H., *The Examination of Usury in two Sermons*, 1591.

———— *The Works of Henry Smith; including sermons, treatises, prayers and poems*, 2 vols, Edinburgh, 1866.

Smith, T., *De Republica Anglorum*, 1583.

Spottiswoode, (Spotswoode) J., *The Execution of Neschech and the Confyning of his Kinsman Tarbith or a Short Discourse shewing the Difference betwixt damned Usurie and that which is Lawfull*, Norwich, 1616.

Stein, S., 'The law of interest in the Old Testament', *Journal of Theological Studies*, new series, 4, 1953.

Stenton, D. M., *English Society in the Early Middle Ages*, Harmondsworth, 1951.

Stockwood, J., *A verie Godly and profitable Sermon of the Necessitie, Properties, and Office of a good Magistrate*, 1584.

Stone, G. and Meston, D., *The Law Relating to Money-Lenders*, 1927.

Stone, L., *The Crisis of the Aristocracy 1558–1641*, Oxford, 1965.

Sutcliffe, M., *An Answere to a certaine Libel supplicatorie, or rather Diffamatory*, 1592.

Sutton, R. and Shannon, N. P., *Sutton and Shannon on Contracts*, ed. K. W. Wedderburn, 1956.

Taeusch, C. F., 'The concept of "Usury"', *Journal of History of Ideas*, 3, 1942.

Tawney, R. H., *Religion and the Rise of Capitalism*, Harmondsworth, 1938.

Tawney, R. H. and Power, E., *Tudor Economic Documents, being Select Documents Illustrating the Economic and Social History of Tudor England*, 3 vols, 1937.

Taylor, J., *Ductor Dubitantium, or the Rule of Conscience*, 1676.

Thirsk, J. and Cooper, J. P., *Seventeenth-Century Economic Documents*, Oxford, 1972.

Thomas, K., 'Cases of conscience in seventeenth-century England', in J. Morrill, P. Slack and D. Woolf, *Public Duty and Private Conscience in Seventeenth-Century England*, Oxford, 1993.

Timme, T., *Discoverie of ten English Lepers verie noisome*, 1592.

Tittler, R., 'Money-lending in the W. Midlands: activities of J. Jefferies, 1638–49', *Historical Research*, 67, 1994.

Trevithick, W., *Sermon preached at the Funeral of the Honorable Colonel Robert Rolle of Heaton Sachville in the County of Devon, Esq.*, 1661.

Trigge, F., *A Godly and fruitfull Sermon preached at Grantham, A. D. 1592*, Oxford, 1594.

———— *A Touchstone whereby may easilie be discerned, which is the true Catholike Faith*, 1599.

Turnbull, R., *An Exposition upon the XV. Psalm, devided into foure sermons*, 1591.

Turner, R., *The Usurers Plea Answered*, 1634.

Turner, R. W., *The Equity of Redemption: its nature, history, and connection with equitable estates generally*, Cambridge, 1931.

Usher, A. P., *The Early History of Deposit Banking in Mediterranean Europe*, vol. i, Cambridge, MA, 1943.

Viner, J., *Religious Thought and Economic Society: four chapters of an unfinished work*, ed. J. Melitz and D. Winch, Durham, NC, 1978.

Vinogradoff, P., *Roman Law in Medieval Europe*, 1909.

West, W., *The Second Part of Symboleography*, 1611.

Wheatlie (Whately), W., *A Caveat for the Covetous, or a sermon preached at Paules Crosse, upon the fourth of December, out of Luke 12.15*, 1609.

White, H. C., *Social Criticism in Popular Religious Literature of the Sixteenth Century*, New York, 1965.

White, T., *A Sermon preached at Pawles Crosse on Sunday the ninth of November, Anno 1589*, 1589.

Whitgift, J., *The Works of John Whitgift*, ed. J. Ayre, 3 vols, Parker Society, 1851–53.

Wilcox (Wilcocks), T., *A Short, yet sound Commentarie written on that woorthie Worke called, the Proverbes of Salomon*, 1589.

———— *A Very Godly and Learned Exposition, upon the whole Booke of Psalms*, 1591.

Wilkins, D., *Concilia Magnae Britanniae et Hiberniae a Synodo Verolamiensi A.D. CCCCXLVI ad Londinensem A.D. MDCCXVII*, 4 vols, 1737.

Willet, A., *Hexapla in Exodum: that is, a sixfold commentary upon the second booke of Moses called Exodus*, 1608.

Williams, R., *The Bloudy Tenent of Persecution*, ed. E. B. Underhill, Hanserd Knollys Society, 1848.

Willson, D. H., *The Parliamentary Diary of Robert Bowyer, 1606–1607*, Minneapolis, MN, 1931.

Wilmot, E. C., *A Succinct View of the Law of Mortgages*, 1819.

Wilson, T., *A Discourse uppon Usurye by way of dialogue and oracions, for the better varietye and more delite of all those that shall reade thys treatise* (1572), ed. R. H. Tawney, 1925.

Wycliffe, J., *Select English Works of John Wyclif*, ed. T. Arnold, 3 vols, Oxford, 1869–71.

Yale, D. E. C., *Lord Nottingham's Chancery Cases*, 2 vols, Selden Society, lxxiii, lxxix (1954–62), 1957–61.

———— *Lord Nottingham's 'Manual of Chancery Practice' and 'Prolegomena of Chancery and Equity'*, Cambridge, 1965.

Zwingli, H., *Huldreich Zwingli's Werke*, ed. M. Schuler and J. Schulthess, 7 vols, Zurich, 1828–42, vol. i, *Von göttlicher und menschlicher Gerechtigheit wie die zemmen und standind: ein predge Huldrych Zwinglis an S. Johannes toufers tag gethon MDXXIII*.

———— *Writings*, ed. E. J. Furcha and H. W. Pipkin, 2 vols, Allison Park, PA, 1984.

Index